DOUBLE-ACT

DOUBLE-ACT

The remarkable lives and careers of
Googie Withers and John McCallum

BRIAN MCFARLANE

MONASH University Publishing

Monash University Publishing
Matheson Library and Information Services Building
40 Exhibition Walk
Monash University
Clayton, Victoria, 3800, Australia

www.publishing.monash.edu

Monash University Publishing brings to the world publications which advance the best traditions of humane and enlightened thought.

Monash University Publishing titles pass through a rigorous process of independent peer review.

www.publishing.monash.edu/books/da-9781922235725.html

Design: Les Thomas

Cover Images

    Front cover: McCallum and Withers in *It Always Rains on Sunday* (1947). Image courtesy of Arts Centre Melbourne.

    Inside front: McCallum and Withers in *The Loves of Joanna Godden* (1947). Image courtesty of Arts Centre Melbourne.

    Back cover (l–r): Googie in the early 1940s; John and Googie at Bayview; John in the 2/5 Field Regiment of the Australian Imperial Force (AIF). Images courtesy of Arts Centre Melbourne.

    Inside back: Brian McFarlane (2014).

Creator:	McFarlane, Brian, author.
Title:	Double-Act : the remarkable lives and careers of Googie Withers and John McCallum / Brian McFarlane.
ISBN:	978-1-922235-72-5 (paperback)
Notes:	Includes bibliographical references, chapter notes and index.
Subjects:	Withers, Googie.
	McCallum, John.
	Actors--Australia--Biography.
	Actors--Britain--Biography.
	Entertainers--Australia--Biography.
	Entertainers--Britain--Biography.

Printed and bound by CPI Group (UK) Ltd, Croydon, CR0 4YY

FSC MIX Paper from responsible sources FSC® C013604 www.fsc.org

For Brenda Niall

ACKNOWLEDGMENTS

A great many people have contributed helpfully to this book, but my first thanks must be to the three children of Googie Withers and John McCallum: Joanna McCallum, Nicholas McCallum and Amanda McCallum Archibald. All were extremely generous with their time and recollections and their enthusiasm for the project was an ongoing encouragement. While I was in England, Joanna and her husband Roger Davenport were most hospitable on several occasions and Joanna gave me access to boxes of her parents' personal correspondence and other papers, including John's notes for his proposed, but unpublished second volume of memoirs. I also thank Joanna's daughter, Alex Davenport, and Amanda's children, Gus and Emma Archibald, for sharing their reminiscences of their grandparents. Other family members who provided valuable insights were Mrs Claire Baistow and Mrs Nan McCallum.

Among those who so willingly gave their time to recollections of the pair are: (in Australia) Phillip Austin, Elspeth Ballantyne, Peggy Carter, Simon Chilvers, Richard Cottrill, John Frost, Cheryl Gagliano, Liz Goodman, Nicholas Hammond, John Krummel, Sue Nattrass, George Ogilvie, Roland Rocchicioli, Geoffrey Rush, John Sumner, Doreen Telfer, John Turnbull, Frank Van Straten, and Helen Gilligan (New Zealand), Scott Hicks (Canada); (in Britain) Rona Anderson, Dame Eileen Atkins, Isla (Tait) Baring, Michael Blakemore, Tony Britton, Rosemary Caws, Robin Dalton, Diane Fletcher, Jean Fox, John Gale, Patricia Garwood, Julie Harris, Jean Kent, James Laurenson, Patricia Marmont, Muriel Pavlow, Vanessa Redgrave, Jeffrey Richards, The Hon Frances Russell, Mark Scrase-Dickins, Ann (Tait) Seddon, Sir Donald Sinden, David Yelland,.

I am very much indebted to Lucy Spencer of the Research Centre of the Performing Arts Collection, Melbourne, where an enormous collection of the Withers-McCallum papers are housed. Without the ready access to this resource, this present study could scarcely have been attempted. Also at the

Arts Centre, Margot Anderson was very helpful on a number of occasions, as were staff at the Australian Centre for the Moving Image, Mary Murphy, archivist at Her Majesty's Theatre Melbourne, British Film Institute staff including Jo Botting, Steve Tollervey and Ian O'Sullivan, and Ms Sue Snowden of Oatlands School, Harrogate.

There are also many others who shared informally their memories of the McCallums, whether professionally or personally, and I am grateful to all of them, as I am to those who read chapters and made helpful comments –Ian Britain, Andrew Spicer, Joyce Woolridge and Jonathan Croall, who also provided some useful contacts, as did Rosemary Campbell and Deidre Rubenstein – and to my daughters Susannah McFarlane, who suggested ways of presenting the material, and Sophie Scully, who typed some very long interviews into accessible form.

At Monash University Publishing, I have had assistance and advice from its Director, Nathan Hollier and his staff. Nathan's interest in the project from the first preliminary discussion to the eventual publication has been exemplary and I am most grateful.

Finally, this book is dedicated to long-time friend Brenda Niall, whose ongoing interest in and comments on the book's progress have been so valuable and whose own biographies have set such a challenging benchmark in Australian publishing.

Brian McFarlane, Melbourne 2015

CONTENTS

INTRODUCTION

Anyone who was going to the theatre in Australia from 1955 to the end of the century would have known a great deal about John McCallum and Googie Withers, whose instant success in *Simon and Laura* and *The Deep Blue Sea* ensured enduring popularity. In fact, they came to assume almost the status there of theatrical royalty. And though they would not have registered the producer's name, children who were allowed to watch television from the late 1960s, and, in several continents, sat glued to episodes of *Skippy*, might in middle age have wondered who was responsible for this bushland saga.

As well, they both had notable careers on the English stage and in the heyday of British cinema – that is, after the war in John's case, before, during and after in Googie's. She came to the fore in a couple of potent war films, then established herself as a formidable leading lady in a run of late 1940s films. In several of the latter, such as *It Always Rains on Sunday*, she was joined by John. Whereas Googie's career was always that of actor, John branched out as producer, director, writer and arts administrator.

In reviewing *Wilson*, a recent biography of Woodrow Wilson, Bob Carr wrote 'My interest is sparked and heightened, my appetite whetted, when a biographer dwells on flaws, darkness, colossal errors, criminality.' Well, there may be 'flaws' but perhaps not much in the way of 'darkness, colossal errors, [or] criminality' in the lives of the Withers-McCallum pair. As their younger daughter, Amanda, said: 'There was a lot of temptation in both their lives: I couldn't say whether they acted on it, but I don't think so... They were very happy together.'

It is thoughtless of them not to have provided the basis for one of those biographies usually described as 'unauthorised', in which no stone is left unturned in the search for scandal. Nor is this an 'authorised' one in which the over-all effect is apt to be sanitised. The family gave unstinted support to the project but made no conditions about how it was to be carried out. As for all those colleagues who worked with them over more than half a century, they were no help either in providing 'unauthorised' information. They simply, one after the other, reinforced the idea of a partnership, on and off stage, whom it was a pleasure to know and to be associated with in various ways.

What, then, particularly fascinated me was the idea of two people coming from widely different backgrounds, indeed from widely different parts of the world, initially brought together by contractual obligations and thereafter staying together for over sixty years. By staying together, I mean of course not merely professionally – their careers diverged and converged constantly during that time – but also personally in one of the longest-lasting marriages in show business.

What surprised me when I first had the idea of this book was that no one had written about them before. When you think of the comparatively minor figures who have been chronicled within an inch of their lives, as it were, it is hard to imagine why two people who made such an impact on the entertainment media on both sides of the world over several decades hadn't been 'done'.

The book's subtitle is 'The remarkable lives and careers of Googie Withers and John McCallum' because the aim is to give a full sense of what the careers were like, not just a chronological account of the 'lives'. If for instance you want to know what kind of actress Googie was, it will be necessary to have a clear sense of the sorts of roles she played on stage and on screens, large and small, or if you want to know how John helped bring Australian television to overseas awareness, you will need some idea of what those programmes were like. My own background as a critic no doubt influences me here. When I read biographies of film or theatre luminaries, I always hope for a clear account of the work that has made me interested enough to want to read about them in the first place. For these two, the personal lives and professional activities were inextricably intertwined and the potential pitfalls skilfully negotiated.

My own personal knowledge of them was spread over the last twenty years of their lives. It began with a couple of extended interviews with them for a critical book about British cinema which in turn gave rise to a further book collecting the interviews and for which Googie, assisted, as she said, by John, wrote the Foreword. Even at this earliest time of our acquaintance, they showed the sort of lively interplay of ideas and opinions that marked all my further meetings with them. There were further interviews when I was co-editing the *Oxford Companion to Australian Film*, during which Googie expressed some characteristically astringent views about Australian film and filmmakers (and Australian habits of speech) and John obliged with more measured but perceptive and often witty accounts of his dealings with the local industry. In 2003 they performed a very engaging double act when they launched my *Encyclopedia of British Film* in Sydney to an appreciative audience more likely drawn by their names than by the book in question. In becoming friends with the pair, it is now clear to me that the other testimonies to their partnership, on stage and screen and in life at large, seem rooted in the same sort of affectionate regard that I came to feel for them.

The biographer Lucy Hughes-Hallett has written recently that 'A "Life" can never be an exact representation of a life'. We can see, in her word, the 'outside' from other people's views of the biographed one, and may get glimpses of the 'inside' but about the latter there has always to be room for uncertainty. There are plenty of letters from Googie and John to friends and associates that can take us so far in the journey to the interior but our subjectivity will inevitably colour what we make of personal documents such as these, just as theirs dictated what they chose to reveal. What we can be sure about is that we are left with two lives that found impressive fulfilment on several levels.

A note on sources

Because I want *Double-Act* to read as a story of two crowded lives, I've chosen not to clutter the text with numbers referring to either footnotes or end notes. Instead, the source of all quoted materials is given under chapter headings and page numbers at the back; in other words, it's there if you want it, but you don't have to be distracted by it as you read. The comparatively rare use of 'I' or 'me' in the text signals information or opinions given to me directly.

Chapter 1

GOOGIE

What's in a name? Quite a lot as it happens. The name was always the starting-point for interviews with Googie Withers. In the days when she was getting her film career going in England or when, a decade or so later, she arrived in Australia, reporters invariably asked about its origins. She was born Georgette Lizette Withers on 12 March 1917, in Karachi, British India (now Pakistan), to Edgar Clement Withers, an English naval captain in the Royal Indian Marines, and his Dutch-French-German wife Lizette Catharina Willemina (Noëls Van Wageningen), who was called 'Wuz' in the family. There are varying accounts of how Georgette Lizette became 'Googie', a name to which early reviewers were apt to draw disbelieving attention, often giving it in inverted commas. One explanation is that the first language she spoke was Hindustani in which it meant 'crazy child'. By the time she was co-starring with comedian George Formby, it had become 'clown'. On another occasion, it was translated as 'a turn in the road' in Tamil. Elsewhere it's been seen as a variant on her childish 'googoo', amended by her Indian ayah or nanny to 'Googie', which was apparently Punjabi for 'dove'. And, by the way, the double 'o' was pronounced as in 'wood', not as in 'boo'!

It was amazing how long this matter seemed to fascinate writers of various levels of seriousness, to the point when it must have taxed Googie's patience. I suspect she rather enjoyed giving different explanations as the mood seized her. Before she first came to Australia, John warned – and teased – her that to the locals 'googie' was simply slang for 'egg'. I particularly liked the anecdote about the Romanian Marcel Hellman, who produced one of her 1930s films and who had no problem with 'Googie' as a name, in fact 'luffed it', then added in his heavily accented English, 'But who can pronounce "Vizzers"?'

When manager-producer 'Binkie' Beaumont suggested her for a role in J.B. Priestley's allegorical drama, *They Came to a City* in 1943, he tried to persuade her that 'Googie' wouldn't do for a serious actress. (You could argue that someone widely known as 'Binkie' wasn't in a strong position to quibble.) 'He insisted no one would be interested in someone called "Googie" playing Lady Macbeth or whatever, and I pointed out that someone called Ginger Rogers appeared to be doing rather well despite her name', she recalled having argued. A long article in a Sydney newspaper is entitled 'I'll not change my name for anyone', and that remark seems to resonate with the firmness of purpose that was part of the personal apparatus of this independently-minded woman.

As she pointed out her real name was more than a little cumbersome, perhaps the by-product of a mother called Catharina Willemina. Those parents help to account for certain key aspects of the girl who eventually became famous as Googie Withers. The naval-commander father, Edgar Withers, has been described as 'always on the bridge', and John suggested in interview that Googie had inherited his forcefulness. For all her liveliness and wit and charm, she was never going to be the docile idea of 'woman' that might have been favoured in her years of growing up. The maternal inheritance was also influential. When I first met her in 1990, I put it to her that she was like no other actress in British films in the 1940s, a decade marked in British cinema by high achievement all round but nowhere more so than in the line-up of attractive and gifted women stars. Think of Celia Johnson or Joan Greenwood or the ineffably ladylike Anna Neagle, and others, all of them making a real mark in the films of the day. But Googie was something else. There was nothing genteel or pliable about her; she was bold and brazen and sexy; and she put this down to the fact that she's not really, or at least not wholly, British, drawing attention to her mother's completely non-English background, though she would in later life speak as if her roots were essentially English.

Whatever the sources, she invariably looked like a woman who could proficiently seduce or murder or run a farm, as the screenplays of some of her best films required her to do. With some of those other actresses, you felt that if they were about to commit a crime they might have begun by saying, 'Do you mind frightfully if I murder you?' whereas Googie just got on with it as to the manner born.

I

Just as she attributed her sensuous – and sensual – screen persona to her genetic inheritance, she attributed the fact that she never looked stagey in films, as not a few English screen actors of the period did, to not having had any drama training. Writing about her 1937 film, *Accused*, a *Picturegoer* journalist said of her: 'We have a player uninfluenced by stage experience.' She had trained as a dancer, not as an actress, and, years later in an article attributed to her, she wrote: 'I think every girl who aspires to be an actress should first learn to dance. To be a good actress one must know how to walk across a stage gracefully. A dancer learns how to use the stage and gets that feeling, so necessary to an actress, that the stage belongs to her.' Crucial or not, it's how she began. And 'began' goes back to her Indian childhood when a doctor recommended dancing lessons as a way of straightening her bandy legs. She'd already endured a long time with her legs bound in iron splints at night without this having had the desired effect. The lessons, though, quite quickly revealed her as a very proficient dancer and this would influence the direction of her career.

Along with the dancing lessons, she remembered her earliest years in India with affection, but there was no shortage of drama in the lead-up to them. Googie's mother had come to England as a young girl to work as a governess, and she had changed her name slightly because her father had been involved in a disgrace that had led to prison. She cut off the 'Noëls', which would have identified who she was. She went to Dorset as a governess to a family called Outram. Young Mrs Outram's brother, Edgar Withers, who came to visit his sister, was captivated by this beautiful young Dutch-French woman called Lizette, with her hooded green eyes, strawberry-blonde hair and charming accent. Not too long after, they were married.

As a naval officer, he was posted to Mesopotamia, and their son, Harry, was born somewhere in Arabia. Googie once said that if ever she wrote her autobiography, she would begin with: 'I was conceived in the Garden of Eden,' the actual site, Bushire, legendarily where it was all meant to have begun for people. When Lizette was pregnant with Googie, it was decided that it was too dangerous for her to stay, as there was a price on her head for ransom, so Commander Withers arranged for someone to take her and Harry out, on the back of a camel, accompanied by a man with a knife, into the desert to join the Bedouins briefly. This doesn't really sound very safe, but it was away from the Turks, who constituted a greater danger. As her pregnancy advanced, it was decided she should be sent by boat to Karachi, then part of British India.

She was a brave woman. There she was in a hospital where she was the only European, with just her little boy of seven, whom she was looking after, standing there while she had a baby, and acting as intermediary between mother and nursing staff. At the end of the war, Edgar was sent to Chittagong, now in Bangladesh. They had a big house with servants, and Googie remembered their being visited one night by Gandhi, who came to ask her father to convey a message to the British Viceroy in Delhi. He arrived with a big entourage of people carrying lighted torches above their heads and the chanting went on all through the night. There were two enormous men with kukris drawn, guarding the door. Her mother was terrified that the mob might suddenly attack and burn down the house, and she communicated her fear to her small daughter. As it turned out, everything was peaceful. On a less potentially alarming note, the Withers family would spend the hottest months with Edgar's brother, a tea-planter in Assam, where Googie was given a baby elephant on whose back she would ride, while it held on to its mother's tail.

When Googie, aged seven, and her mother left India, they settled first in Paris (brother Harry, fourteen, was already at school in England). The idea was that Commander Withers would follow at some later stage when his duties permitted. However, his two sisters in England, rather Victorian in their views, felt it was unwise for him to leave his young and attractive wife at large in Paris, a city dangerously full of allurements. So Googie's father then moved them to Dorset. Googie, now eight, was sent to a boarding school at

Fredville Park, Nonington, Kent, which was run by two Irish sisters. They 'had no qualms about meting out punishment. "We got beatings on our bottoms, and quite frankly I think I deserved it"', Googie said years later. She later attended the Anglo-Catholic Convent of the Holy Family, a day school, in London. Her school reports while at Fredville Park tend to suggest that she wasn't stretching herself academically, with frequent suggestions that she 'could do much better work', was inclined to 'slack', even that she was 'far too careless' in Composition, and 'Does not concentrate enough' in History. However, in an Elocution Festival, she showed a 'Good sense of rhythm' and 'Very fair sense of imagination.' At the Holy Family, where she seems to have pulled up her scholastic socks a little, she was nevertheless described as 'inclined to leave things about and lose them'. This may well be the result, as she later suggested, of having, as a child in India, had servants to pick up anything she dropped, and she found it hard to do without such essential services.

Throughout these school years, she continued to take dancing classes, still supposedly to correct the bandy legs. A suggestion of bandiness remains in a publicity photo of her in shorts in 1936, but later on (as the shot of her snapping on suspenders in *The Lady Vanishes*, 1938, confirms) the classes seem to have had the desired effect. The unexpected but much-desired effect as far as Googie was concerned was that she was hooked on the idea of being a dancer. Her mother had favoured the idea of dancing school on the grounds that it would be good for deportment, would make her little girl graceful. She became, in her own words and without any false modesty, 'a very, very good dancer indeed, and won the All England Championships, and that sort of thing.' She had succeeded well beyond the expectations of her mother who had never intended her becoming a professional dancer, and her father 'could think of nothing worse than me being a little sort of dancer on the stage'.

She had her first professional engagement, aged twelve, in 1929, as a dancer in the chorus of *The Windmill Man*, a children's show at the Victoria Palace Theatre, London, in which she played a toy soldier and a rabbit and a fairy. All this whetted her appetite for the stage: she'd never enjoyed the

Christmas holidays so much in her life till then. When she moved on in the following year to the convent in London, she persuaded her parents, now back from India and living in London, to let her become enrolled in the Italia Conti School for young actors. For nearly two years, she went on to Italia Conti after her day at the convent. However, her parents, like so many others whose offspring have opted for precarious professions, insisted that she needed to finish her schooling, at least till she was sixteen. They knew she wasn't academically inclined, but felt they should let her do her little stage jobs as a means of 'getting it out of her system'.

When the family moved to Birmingham, where Captain Withers took a position with a steel factory, Googie enrolled in a dancing school run by one Helena Lehmiski, who recognised her talent and took a personal interest in her, beginning a friendship that lasted throughout Googie's career. Another graduate of this school recalled meeting Googie many years later in Australia, where this woman was performing *Snow White* in one of the theatres John McCallum was responsible for: 'Googie wanted to introduce herself and wish me well in the first performance to be held there. After the initial introductions, I tested her reaction to two words: "Madame Lehmiski!". She smiled. "Oh, Madame! Dear Madame!" she sighed. "What lovely days!"' In all her recollections, Googie speaks fondly of her dancing days.

The Birmingham position hadn't been rewarding for Googie's father and he had not found it easy to get a job in London, so he and his wife took the children to live a life of quiet retirement in a Dorset village. Googie and Harry enjoyed their lives there, but it must have been frustrating to their father, a man used to command, and one can't imagine Googie, who had inherited his forcefulness, settling for long in such a spot, however charming. When Googie died, her daughter Joanna brought a tiny amount of her ashes to plant them, in the garden of the aptly named 'Harry Warren', Studland, with a tree, as a memento of the time she had spent in a part of England she always loved. Harry went on to the Royal Military Service College at Woolwich, and, again possibly an aspect of his paternal inheritance, had subsequently a notable career in the Army. After this he retired with his second wife to the part of Dorset where he and Googie had spent some of the happy years of their childhood. He and Googie were always close, and a vivid recollection of Googie's daughter Joanna is of being in a train with her mother who was weeping at the news of the break-up of Harry's marriage, to his first wife Lola Anderson.

In May 1932, Googie (now having left Dorset) and another dancer called Vera Morris are depicted on the cover of *The Dancing Times*. They are described as two of 'Madame Helena Lehmiski's Young Ladies', from the Studio School of Dancing, Birmingham, performing in a dance group called 'The Super-Optimists', at a gala night at the Floral Pavilion, New Brighton, Liverpool. In the programmes associated with such early performances, she is listed as just another name in the chorus, but even in these first years of her career she seemed to understand the importance of publicity. She was already getting her picture in the papers, advertising a firm called 'Smart Bros' in the *Daily Mail*, 1933, and visiting 'The Cunarder No. 534' in Glasgow shipyards, 1934. She took the press in her stride, and it was happy to report on her progress. She always knew the value of publicity, and this is reinforced by the fact that she so scrupulously preserved all sorts of clippings and photos and other memorabilia from the earliest years of her career. It seems in hindsight less a matter of ego than of determination, of knowing where she was going and preserving anything that might prove useful along the way.

In considering Googie's 1930s career, I'm struck by how extraordinarily busy she managed to be in such an overcrowded profession. She was one of the 'Ballyhoo Girls' in the revue *Ballyhoo* in 1933, at the May Fair Hotel, Berkeley Square, London, and must have impressed someone there because she was subsequently billed as one of the 'May Fair Girls'. Later in the same year, she was one of 'a shapely chorus' in the musical comedy, *Nice Goings On*, at London's Strand Theatre, starring a big 'name' of the time, the comedian Leslie Henson. She is now billed as one of Buddy Bradley's 'Rhythm Girls'. Names such as Henson and choreographer Bradley may not be much remembered now but they were very well known then. Sixty-odd years later she recalled her training with Bradley, whose approach was considered avant-garde, partly because of his teaching of acrobatic dancing as well as ballet.

She had to give up this sort of dancing when she fell and damaged her left arm very severely.

It was in the following year that her breakthrough came when she was promoted from the 'small but lovely and efficient chorus' of *Happy Weekend* (at the Duke of York's theatre, London) to play her first speaking role. This came about when a girl with a small role broke her leg, and Googie, as understudy, received a phone call in the morning to tell her to take over that evening. She received quite a bit of publicity when the play was performed in Brighton and Hove. As it happened, in the audience that night was Sergei Nolbandov, casting director for Warner Bros' British operation, and he asked her if she would come to its Teddington studio to see if she were suitable for films. The result of this meeting would be another of those turning points that punctuated her career.

It probably seemed like a big opportunity when she was cast as Miss Worrall in J.B. Priestley's *Duet in Floodlight* at the Apollo Theatre in June 1935. There was some publicity about finding 'the right red-head in a young woman interestingly named Googie Withers', but the play, directed by actor Cedric Hardwicke, was generally held to be a disappointment in the light of Priestley's recent successes, *Dangerous Corner* (1932) and *Laburnum Grove* (1933). The *Times* reviewer thought it 'desperately thin' and felt that blonde film-star beauty Madeleine Carroll had chosen an unsuitable vehicle for her return to the stage. The play elicited a vitriolic response from the 'gallery first-nighters', who, Googie remembered, cruelly shouted out to Carroll at curtain call, 'Get back to your films', causing the star to collapse in tears. Despite this rugged reception for Carroll, and though Googie was only mentioned fleetingly in reviews, there were pictures of her in shorts (no sign of bandiness) with the play's male star, Anthony Ireland, in at least two papers.

There were few, if any, bigger names on the revue stage in the 1930s than that of ribald, outrageous Hermione Gingold, so that it can only have been a feather in Googie's cap (or hat – she was mad about hats, she said) to appear in a dozen numbers in the Gingold vehicle *This World of Ours*, which ran for several months over Christmas 1935. Googie was singled out for praise in the item named 'Literary Widows', a satirical tilt at a species of celebrity-seeking.

This revue was written by some of the most prestigious names of the decade and the genre, including the husband-and-wife team Robert MacDermott and Diana Morgan, so that Googie was in very good company this time. Her last stage performance of the 1930s brought her some serious notice. She played a neurotic 'deb' called Diana in *Ladies and Gentlemen*, a play by N.C. Hunter, who would have major popular success in the early '50s with *Waters of the Moon*. Unfortunately for *Ladies and Gentlemen*, there was a bus strike in London and the play didn't survive the effect of this on potential audiences.

Yet this production seems to have been another key moment in her career, and she is mentioned in all the reviews. She was described by one reviewer as 'an attractive minx in the Kay Hammond style', perhaps the first of several clumsy attempts to pin down her confident, sassy persona by comparing her to various established actresses, including such Hollywood comediennes of the day as Zazu Pitts and Una Merkel. As well as praising her for looks, her 'good sense of fun' and her 'volcanic performance', several drew attention to the unusual name. One even suggested that 'Since she is likely to make a big name for herself she would be well advised to change at least part of her present one.' The play, starring Isabel Jeans, was directed by Harold French: Googie was cast in *Ladies and Gentlemen* because French had seen her at work in a film.

French was probably referring to *The Girl in the Crowd* (1935), in which he had also appeared. In the second half of the decade, it would have been hard to miss her as she totted up nearly thirty films by the end of 1940. Many of these could be unkindly if accurately described as 'quota quickies'; films made fast to satisfy legislation and in many cases destined for rapid oblivion. *And* for the bottom half of the double-bill, the two-feature programme that was then the cinema's norm. However, enough of her films of the period remain to hint at the dominant figure she would become in her great run in '40s British cinema. Even when she is playing second fiddle to the comics of the day – George Formby or Will Hay or Arthur Askey – she is always more than mere adornment. She *is* that all right, but there is something knowing, something determined, a suggestion that, sexy as she is, she is not a girl to be taken lightly. There was nothing shy or inhibited about her then – or perhaps ever. In my first meeting with her, in 1990, she was talking about how the famously difficult film director Michael Powell had been rude to someone on the set of a film in which she was acting, and she stood up to him, ticking him off for this behaviour. She said, 'I was only nineteen, but I was as assured then as I am today.' Husband John, walking past at this moment, said out of the side of his mouth: 'And that's *very* assured.'

That 'assurance' just once led to a moment that may have embarrassed her. A notorious Hungarian producer of the 1930s, Max Schack, had called Googie into his office where they were arguing about her contract. The argument was not going well for her, so 'she threw in for good measure: "And you might stand up when a lady comes into the room." "I *am* standing up,' said Mr Schach, from behind his desk. And he was.'" He was a little less than five feet tall.

When Sergei Nolbandov had chanced to see her that night of her first speaking role on stage, the next morning found her at Warner Bros studios at Teddington, for what she expected was to be a film test. She'd been told to bring an evening dress and that she'd be given lines when she got there. It turned out that she never did do a formal screen test. A cocktail party scene was being shot for Powell's *The Girl in the Crowd*, and he asked her to get up and do the scene allotted to an actress already cast. Next thing she knew, he'd sacked the original actress, telling her with characteristic brusqueness that she was no good, that he hadn't time to put her through it again and again, and that she'd have to go. Enter Googie into the world of films.

It was clearly a matter of accepting whatever came along and making the best use possible of it. Difficult as it may have been for actors to work with Powell, as not a few would testify, Googie was lucky to come across him so early in her career – and he was lucky to have her, someone prepared to give as good as she got. Except in terms of its prolificacy, 1930s British cinema was perhaps not the best starting-place for an actress. Too often its products seem to have been hermetically sealed off from the realities of life; today, many of them, despite their incidental virtues, can feel airless, as if they rarely set foot outside of the studio. However, they undeniably provided steady work for a young actress determined to make her mark – and ready to dye her hair blonde and have her eyebrows plucked, if that was the popular, Hollywood-influenced choice of the day. Her ninth film was another 'quickie' called *She Knew What She Wanted* (1936), and its title might well have summed up Googie's career in the '30s and later. When I asked her whether her preference was for theatre or film, she stated unequivocally, 'My preference was for where the money and the work were'. From 1937, after a brief run in the play *Hand in Glove* at Richmond, films answered her needs and she did not appear again on stage until 1943.

Her first film is almost prophetically named, but she was not so much *The Girl in the Crowd* as the girl who *stood out* from the crowd. This is a 52-minute 'quickie', but, directed by Powell, it was likely to have a little more cutting-edge than most. When the film was released in May 1935, *Picturegoer* magazine couldn't help asking 'What is a Googie?' She would go on patiently responding to this and similar questions over the next thirty or forty years. Presumably she just knew on which side her contracts were buttered. When her second film for Powell, *The Love Test*, appeared, she was described as 'The quaintly named Googie Withers', adding that 'she gets laughs as well, as an all-embracing vamp.' Indeed, her wisecracking secretary is the liveliest thing about this film, which is a strained romantic comedy with uncharismatic leads. There were three more films with Powell, and if she often found him a difficult, even unpleasant man, she could hardly have had a better guide through the quickie thickets of the decade.

Her best opportunity was probably that of the hotel maid in *Her Last Affaire* (1936), which had been given a more lavish production than usual at Riverside Studios, and which generated more than usual publicity. Some of this paid special attention to Googie, who plays Effie, a pert and seductive maid in a New Forest inn. One account touted her as 'a young lady of eighteen summers, a young lady, moreover, who combines an easy talent for comedy with a natural inheritance of being easy to look at, and she astonished the old hands at the studio by being as fresh and full of fun after fifteen hours continuous work, as she was when she started.' There were several large publicity photographs featuring her, and when the film was released in 1936 she was several time singled out in reviews. To be noticed in her small role here says something for Googie's screen presence. The moment that people tend to remember from the film is that in which as Effie, bearing a tea tray, she discovers the body of the room's occupant. Effie sees a compromising note lying by the dead woman, secretes it in her apron pocket, looks about for other signs, then goes out with the tray. She then re-enters, lets out a scream of terror and drops the tray. This brief moment is played with brilliant comic timing, and *Film Pictorial* stated firmly, 'The honours go to Googie Withers, who gives a delightful study of the flirtatious servant girl.'

In all these mainly modest films, usually second features, she was clearly making the most of what came her way – and a good deal did. When you scan the credits of those films she made up to 1940, you realise that not many of the other actresses who regularly turned up in them survived the rigours of 'quickies' filming as definitively as Googie did. In some ways, too, she was luckier than many. Apart from Powell, her directors included several of more than average proficiency. There was, for instance, Anthony Kimmins, a naval officer in both World Wars, who directed Googie in *All at Sea* (1935) and in the George Formby vehicle, *Trouble Brewing* (1939). Kimmins, who became one of the McCallums' greatest friends, was a capable director of light comedy in the post-war period, and directed John in the Australian-set feature, *Smiley* (1956). There wasn't much scope for Googie in *All at Sea* but there would be more in *Trouble Brewing*. Bernard Vorhaus, who took off for Hollywood in the '30s after making several much better-than-average British second features that have only recently received their critical due, directed Googie in *Dark World* (1935). She was praised in this for her contribution to 'wise-cracking comedy relief'. The efficient B-movie filmmaker MacLean Rogers used her twice: in *Paid in Error* (1938) and (as female lead) *If I Were Boss* (1938), a prophetic title in view of some of the roles she would go on to make her own in the '40s. And there were three for the American director Thornton Freeland who filmed largely in Britain in the '30s and '40s, and who became a good friend: *Accused* (1936), really an 'A' film, starring Douglas Fairbanks, Jr; *Paradise for Two* (1937), a musical, which she disliked because she had to play a girl who danced very badly, made for Alexander Korda's up-market Denham Studios; and *The Gang's All Here* (1939), a comedy co-starring her with Jack Buchanan, one of the big names of the decade. About Buchanan, she recalled forty years later: 'I think I was about twenty at the time and Jack was about 40 and he had to say "We've been married 8 years darling haven't we?" and I'd say "No, 7". So I started to laugh on the set, and said "Look we can't say that! I would have been 12 if I'd married Jack 7 or 8 years ago. And he didn't like it. He got quite angry and he insisted on it being kept in. And there I was, I looked as if he'd married his daughter! It was absolutely ludicrous!' She was more aptly cast as the female half of a comedy duo (with James Hayter) in *Accused*, but her role was incidental to the main plot – and to the American stars, Fairbanks and Dolores del Rio.

Now, most of these titles will no longer be remembered, but, often in very good acting company, they gave Googie the chance, as she wisecracked her way through an assortment of chirpy blondes called variously Polly and Effie and Lottie and Toots, to establish a kind of persona. The very names of her characters seem to point to a certain cheeky independence that would characterise much of her '30s work, suggesting that this was not going to be a conventional, nicely-behaved leading lady. She was not going to be the heroine wilting in a dangerous situation while she waited for the hero to rescue her. Four of these swiftly and cheaply made program-fillers were directed by Powell, who would be important to her later career, and one that was distinctly *not* a quickie was *The Lady Vanishes* (1938), directed by Alfred Hitchcock. She is in the opening sequences, in her underwear at first, then in a no-nonsense plaid cloak. She is the friend of the film's leading female character Iris, played by Margaret Lockwood, and is gone from the film by the time its main action gets underway, but the memory of this confident young woman stays with us. If Iris had such a friend, perhaps there was more to her than we might have expected. As to Hitchcock, she said fifty years later, 'There was another very unpleasant man', but if she thought of Powell in these terms he did actually recognise her talent and in the next decade would be responsible for launching her major filmmaking phase.

Many of these earlier films wouldn't reward detailed attention, and some of them are in fact no longer available for scrutiny. But it's worth noting a few of them just to see how Googie left her mark on what must often have seemed unpromising material. One of them that she recalled with pleasure was *Busman's Honeymoon* (1940), a whodunit derived from Dorothy Sayers, which brought her into contact with US star, Constance Cummings, who gave Googie (playing sexy barmaid 'Polly') 'friendly encouragement' and became a friend for life. Even a contrivance such as Herbert Mason's *Strange Boarders* (1938), in which she had the second female lead, gave her the chance to suggest something going on behind the pert blonde façade. She plays a duplicitous maid in the boarding house in which Intelligence Agent Tommy (Tom Walls) is looking for information about an elderly woman run down by a bus while she was carrying important Air Ministry blueprints. This is a minor comedy-thriller and its outcome is both improbable and uninteresting. But Googie, whether sidling enigmatically around the boarding-house or beating the mealtime gong in a very unsubservient manner, or, in a slinky evening gown, going off to keep an assignation in a night-spot called the Tudor Club, manages to suggest the wits to cause trouble to those she has in her sights. It's a nice touch that she's at one point tied up and gagged with her own silk stockings.

In different vein, she played George Formby's romantic interest in *Trouble Brewing* (1939). It's hard now to realise just how significant a figure Formby was in the 1930s. All toothy grins, he would strum his ukulele as he got himself mixed up in plot complications through which he would improbably cut his way prior to ending up – and this was the most improbable of all – romantically embracing a young beauty who could surely have done much better for herself. It was said of such young women that, if you did a stint with Formby, you would go on to better things, and the examples of Dinah Sheridan and Phyllis Calvert gave substance to this notion. George's famously possessive wife Beryl kept him on a short lead and, it was said, timed with a stopwatch the obligatory clinch in the film's last moments. Googie must have given her more than the usual grounds for concern, not because of any romantic interest in gormless, toothy George, but because of a plot manoeuvre that required them both to fall into a vat of beer, complete with pyrene-induced froth, at the film's end. Googie later recalled: 'We were supposed to come up out of this beer and look at each other and kiss… We had to wait for the lights and the camera and they certainly weren't going to take us out of the beer because we were soaking wet. He quite inadvertently put his hand on my knee and suddenly felt a girl's thigh. Poor man, he hadn't been able to touch a girl for years… and then we had to kiss. And my goodness, was it a kiss that he gave me! But then Beryl was in on it like a flash. She said *"Cut"* after it had lasted about three seconds.' Even in all this nonsense, and some of it is still funny, Googie never suggests anything other than a girl who can look after herself.

Starring with Formby was a big deal for an aspiring young actress and it was a sure way of being noticed. And the same might have been said for her appearances with Will Hay in *Convict 99* (1938) or Tommy Trinder in *She Couldn't Say No* (1940) or Arthur Askey in *Back-Room Boy* (1942). Perhaps only devoted fans of British cinema remember these men today but back then they were immensely popular 'A'-movie stars, and it was shrewd of Googie to take leading roles opposite each of them – shrewd, that is, if she allowed herself *choice* in the matter. More likely, she was just going 'where the money and the work were'. In either case, they were brilliant exposure. Years later, though, when she was asked what it was like being a star in the 1930s, especially for one so young, she confessed that she'd found it demanding, because the films were all so quickly done, because she'd had no training, and because she was always just learning on the job.

Well, it must be said, she *did* learn. And she also learnt to relish the trappings that went with it, such as the recognition factor or the special treatment of cars being sent for her if she was appearing at previews and premières. She was earning a lot, by the standards of the day. She recalled that, at eighteen, she was earning about £150 a week; this was small compared to what Hollywood stars were earning, but handsome when compared with the average weekly wage of about £5. If she was earning a lot, she was also spending a lot on, for instance, the right clothes or jewellery for a particular occasion. She had, in a word, become a star. People can be 'made' into stars, she much later claimed, but they have to have 'something'. She undoubtedly had 'something', but she was about to change the way she presented it.

II

Difficult as he may have been to work with, Michael Powell was, as she later said, 'the man who really started my career, giving me my first job on *The Girl in the Crowd*, and the film that really set me off, *One of Our Aircraft Is Missing*.' This was in 1942 and Powell's and her accounts of how she reacted to getting the role of the Dutch resistance worker are nicely varied. In his autobiography, Powell wrote that 'like many actors during the national crisis, she was hard up and at her wits' end. She broke down and cried when I gave her the part. She had never played anything but comedy, but she had Dutch blood, her mother was Dutch, and I knew she could do it'. Significantly, Googie repudiated this account, was happy to go along with her pleasure in getting the role, but was not the crying type.

In this film, Googie has undergone a major image change. For one thing, and an important one, she is no longer blonde as she had been when playing all those amusing or vampish types she so often acted in her 1930s films. Further, the first shot of her in *One of Our Aircraft* shows her in murky surroundings in occupied Holland, hair in turban and wearing bulky work overalls. She doesn't appear until the last twenty minutes of the film, but *she* is what one carries away from it. Though the film has a distinguished cast, with major actors such as Eric Portman and Godfrey Tearle playing the British airman whose plane has been shot down over Holland, and most of the film is taken up with their attempts to get back to England, it is Googie's presence that stands out. She makes us believe in her authority and her cool courage. We don't doubt she could carry out the tricky manoeuvres necessary to ensure their safety and their getaway, and she loses none of her femininity in doing so. There is a dinner scene in which she is elegantly dressed and in which she says, 'It's nice to be a woman again even if it's only for half an hour'. You feel she's earned the tribute paid by one of the British airman who tells her 'We can't offer you [i.e., as member of the Dutch resistance] anything except our love, our gratitude, and our admiration for a brave woman in a fearless country', and there is something touching when, as she says farewell to the men, she kisses the most senior and he replies 'I suppose that's one advantage of being old.' She won an American Distributors' Award as Best Supporting Actress for her role in this, though was unable to go to the US to collect it. Her mother, then living near Denham, was given a small part in the film because there was a need for Dutch-speakers. Mrs Withers had a few lines and also coached Robert Helpmann, playing a quisling, with his accent.

It wasn't all work though. Googie was, and remained always, of a gregarious temperament. She loved parties and dancing (for fun, that is, as distinct from professionally); she loved country house weekends, and it's easy to imagine that this witty, lively young woman might have been sought after for such occasions. And there were romances as well. At one point in the mid 1930s she and actor Michael Wilding planned to marry, but the parents of both discouraged the match on grounds of their youth. Sixty years on, she recalled: 'We wanted to get married but we were much too young – I was 17 and he was 21 and poor as a church mouse. He was scraping a living by drawing on church pavements. He was terribly beautiful and a lovely person. We adored each other.' In the early 1940s, she lived for a time with Prince Leopold Loewenstein, who was separated from his wife. His son Prince Rupert, writing seventy years later, recalled how much he, as a boy of ten, had enjoyed meeting her, partly 'because I was fascinated by her being a film star and having seen a number of her films. She had become famous during the previous few years, appearing in *The Lady Vanishes* and *One of Our Aircraft Is Missing*. She was charming, pretty and also particularly kind to me.' She had also been 'a little in love' with the novelist Richard Llewellyn, author of the best-selling *How Green Was My Valley*: 'We had been what was then referred to as "going out together"... I enjoyed being with him, but he wasn't an easy man. He was typically Welsh, volatile, with a temper that flared easily, new-found wealth and an inbuilt conceit.' He turned up in London several years later, and during a break in filming *The Loves of Joanna Godden*, Googie went up to see him where he was staying at the Ritz. He was full of enthusiasm for his luxurious Hollywood life-style, which he wanted to share with Googie. When she made it clear that they had no future together, he left her with a silent handshake.

In late 1945, she had become engaged to the French Capitaine Jean-Pierre Le Mée, then a rising lawyer from a distinguished Parisian family, and they intended to be married in November. However, the wedding was postponed and, shortly after, cancelled. In Googie's own account of this liaison, she says that they called off the wedding three days before its announced date. Her parents were apparently glad, and finally Googie, who had been 'intrigued by the idea of living in Paris and of marrying a man who wasn't an actor', felt it all began to look 'like playing a part' – and a recipe for disaster.

She returned to the stage in 1943 to play Alice Foster, the female lead in Priestley's allegorical play, *They Came to a City* at London's Globe Theatre. The play explores the possibility of a different and more equitable post-war society, and its cast represents a cross-class microcosm of British society. Googie's character is a rebellious shop-girl and she and the anti-materialist Joe (John Clements) at play's end envisage a society that will enshrine the values of the visionary city. Googie was thrilled to have been asked to be in the play, because till then she had really been known as a *film* star, and 'Binkie' Beaumont was most likely wanting to use her film reputation for publicity. This was in the days of the blitz, when London was being regularly bombed. As it happened she did the play for two years, including going on tour with it. She joined the Stars in Battledress, a company formed to enable entertainers to play for the armed forces in England and Europe. Edith Evans urged Googie to join this company because it needed an ingénue. It had young actors like Peter Ustinov, but it lacked a pretty young actress and, after seeing *On Approval* on screen, Evans chose Googie. Googie was given the rank of lieutenant, and there was a great welcome for the troupe in Belgium, especially for the women in uniform.

As all the members of the concert parties were in the Armed Forces of Britain, there was no restriction on the location of concerts, as there would have been if they were officially civilian entertainers. She was performing in

Antwerp, which was subjected to a terrible onslaught of German shelling by V1s and V2s. In 2007, Googie recalled, on Australian TV's *Talking Heads*, how these raids went on night and day: 'It was a beleaguered city and the Germans wanted to get it back again … However, we survived until the Saturday matinee. The theatre was backed by a cinema, and on the top was the sergeants' mess… The bombing and everything, the noise was terrible. Suddenly there was no noise – then we were blown apart by a V2. I was off somewhere in a hole, and, when I crawled out of it, what had been an absolutely packed theatre was a pile of rubbish. And I knew that 1200 people had been killed, men who'd come to see the play. Only 17 of us, out of the cinema, the theatre and the sergeants' mess, were living'. Suddenly, she saw a bassoon emerging from the rubble: it was the only surviving member of the orchestra.

Googie's career was profoundly interrupted and her image modified by the experiences of the war. An Ealing Studios information sheet in 1946 said of her: 'The war has changed her probably more than any other star on the British screen – changed her into one of the most glamorous and undeniably capable straight actresses in the British film firmament.' In hindsight, it seems almost as if she felt the time had come to dispense with that '30s persona of the smart-talking blonde who gave men a run for their money. She made another film for the Archers, Michael Powell and Emeric Pressburger's company, in 1943, and again it was set in occupied Holland. This was *The Silver Fleet*, directed by Vernon Sewell, and she played Hélène, the wife of shipyard-owner Van Leyden (Ralph Richardson), who appears to be collaborating with the Nazi occupiers. He is branded 'quisling' and his wife has to entertain high-ranking German officers at dinner and to endure the contempt of the townspeople. Needless to say, the heroic Van Leyden has only patriotic interests at heart, and the film raises some interesting ethical issues about one's priorities in such a situation. Googie's role is more conventional than that of the resistance worker in the previous film, but she manages to give it some real distinction. For one thing, it's hard to think of another British actress of the time, except perhaps Pamela Brown, who might have been able to suggest so convincingly a sense of foreignness, and maybe that's where her Dutch heritage from her mother made itself felt. She also looks remarkably beautiful: the face has a delicacy that contributes to our sense of Hélène's vulnerability and growing dismay at her husband's lack of openness, and to her tenderness when she fully understands the extent of his sacrifice.

It may well have been her appearance in these two patriotically slanted films, with their strongly anti-Nazi sentiments, that accounted for one of the strangest items among her correspondence. This was a long printed letter from 'Reich Minister Dr Goebbels', sent to her in a hand-addressed envelope to her apartment at 33 Curzon Street, London, and forwarded to two further addresses. Its purpose was to reply to anti-German propaganda leaflets dropped over Germany re English 'affection' for the German people – and to suggest that the English should back off in this matter. Googie must have received this document because of her status as a well-known person by this time. Her response to it might have been interesting: she might easily have given Goebbels something to think about.

Her next role was in much cheerier vein, though in its way the film, *On Approval*, was quite daring for 1944. Based on Frederick Lonsdale's play, it records the decision of a couple who may be about to marry to spend a trial month together on an island, with inevitable complications. The complications include two others who may or may not be headed for matrimony. The demanding Maria Wislack (Beatrice Lillie) wants to test the company of Richard (Roland Culver), while American heiress Helen (Googie) is willing to marry the objectionable Duke of Bristol (Clive Brook). Partners are swapped by the end of the month, and circumstances combine to leave the less sympathetic pair on the island. The idea of a month 'on approval' may have been racy enough on stage in 1926 but was certainly still a matter to be discreetly approached in a 1944 *film*, as was the introductory sequence devised for the film. In this, a modern-day commentator groans, 'Not another war film' as shots of air and sea battle fill the screen before the story proper gets underway. Googie, in late Victorian costume and high-piled light-coloured coiffure, sashays her way across rooms and swivels her elegant person through doorways with a panache that enables her more than to hold her own in the formidable company of the film. Beatrice Lillie may have been the funniest woman in the world at the time, but Googie realised that she was essentially a one-woman show, unused to acting *with* other people. And Clive Brook was not without his share of ego: he'd had a long and successful career since silent days and had a stint in Hollywood in the 1930s. He fell out with Brian Desmond Hurst, the original director of *On Approval*, the production was then shelved, after which Brook took on the directing function as well as starring. Both Lillie and Brook were decades older than Googie, and Roland Culver was seventeen years her senior, and this led to some tense moments in a scene in which they are all supposed to be much older. One of the make-up artists on the film tactlessly said, as he went to work on the youthful Googie, that those other three hardly needed his skills. Even then, however, she seemed to have had a knack of working with a company, not needing to be pampered as 'a star', and this no doubt helps to account for how, in decades ahead, she was always well regarded as a team member.

It was surely reckless of Ealing to think in 1944 that a film version of *They Came to a City*, with its non-stop talk about ideas and ideals, was ever going to be a commercial success. And it wasn't. The stage cast was recruited to the film, which Basil Dearden directed, and though it has a certain historical interest today it is undeniably stagy, its characters too obviously representing types rather than individuals. Googie recalled that the cast were all paid very little but were promised a share of the profits, of which, she said, of course there were none. However, its importance as far as her career was concerned is that this first serious brush with Ealing (*Trouble Brewing* was made there by another company) meant that she was noticed by the studio that would come to be identified with the prestige arm of British filmmaking throughout the rest of the '40s and '50s – and she would become its major female star. Ealing's output was largely male-dominated, but in her four major films with the studio she established female images as potent as any in British cinema of the day. She always remembered her time with Ealing with affection, with all those bright chaps playing clever word games over lunch or after work at the pub, where they drank a great deal more than would have been acceptable to studio head, Michael Balcon, if he had known. In 2003, she described Balcon as being like a headmaster who would walk on to the set every morning to greet and inspect, but she felt he ran the studio very well and that it had the feel of 'a family'. And she also recalled the studio's Russian emigré publicist, Monja Danischewsky, who used to write articles for the press that went out over Googie's name, giving her, as she said, a reputation as a wit. In fact, of course, she had some legitimate claim on such a title. In 1947 an article entitled 'Acting for Stage and Screen' appeared under her name, and there are some provocative remarks about the demands of the two media – and certainly some wit, whether hers or Danischewsky's.

It wasn't just Ealing in general that determined a major shift in her film career; it was more particularly that she made three films for director Robert Hamer. She had the highest regard for Hamer, who she felt was more interested in and knowledgeable about acting and paid more attention to the women's roles than did any of the other Ealing directors. 'He knew what he wanted and he realised theatre acting was "bigger" and could bring it down for film.' Certainly the films she made with him gave her an imperishable presence in British film history. Her first with Hamer was in the portmanteau horror film, *Dead of Night* in 1945, in which she plays a strong-minded young woman who rescues her husband from the grip of a neurotic repression. Later in the same year, she is cast as a murderess in *Pink String and Sealing Wax*, which, many years later, she named as her favourite role, and you can see why. It gives her a chance – her first really – to take charge of a film. And in 1947, in *It Always Rains on Sunday*, perhaps her finest hour in the movies, she plays a bored and terminally grumpy housewife who shelters an escaped convict, her ex-lover, on the run.

It's hard to think of any other actress in British films who could have done such justice – let alone more – to that trio. When she smashes the antique mirror she has given her husband in the *Dead of Night* episode, you feel confident that his future is safe in her hands, now that she has forced him to confront the ghosts of the past. Her film persona makes her apt for this woman, who stands for wholesome adjustment, as one who can deal with neuroses and repression. In *Pink String* she cements her reputation for playing unusually strong-minded women without losing sympathy for them, even when her actions are extreme. Here, she is Pearl Bond, adulterous wife of an indolent and often drunken pub-keeping husband, whom ultimately she murders. Somehow Googie never loses her grip on the woman's strength and intelligence, so that when she hurls herself over a Brighton cliff at the end there is a sense of the life having gone out of the place. She has taken charge of her own life, and decides to end it rather than conform to the puritanical standards of the 'good' characters. She enormously enjoyed making *Pink String*, and a bonus of playing the dominant Pearl was that she got to wear an extensive and attractive Victorian wardrobe, 'which was all that was needed to complete my sense of well-being.' For one who loved clothes, this was indeed a real plus. At this crucial stage of her career she was fortunate indeed to have met up with Hamer and decades later she paid tribute to him as a really fine director who would see what an actor could do, and if it fitted in with his over-all vision for the film he'd leave it in. In other words, she respected him as a director who didn't seek to impose himself on his cast, and she rewarded him with several of the most striking performances any actress has ever delivered in British films. Driven by demons including alcohol, his untimely death robbed British cinema of a major talent.

Sandwiched in among these film roles was one of the stage appearances she most enjoyed, that of Amanda, when she took over from Kay Hammond in Noël Coward's *Private Lives* in a West End revival in 1945 at the Apollo Theatre, in the role made famous by Gertrude Lawrence. Coward, directing, was reportedly well pleased by Googie's playing as the mercurial Amanda, and it is easy to imagine how well suited she was to it. It drew on both her well-honed comedy skills and her effortless capacity to suggest women who knew what they wanted, and Coward liked the way she and her co-star, Hugh Sinclair, 'brought the love story out more'.

During the run of this play, she had an alarming encounter with a man named Danny Corrigan. When she was in a play, it was her habit to sleep in the afternoon till 6pm, when she'd be wakened in time to get to the theatre. One evening her alarm failed to go off, she overslept, couldn't get a cab in the thick fog, and when all her other possible contacts failed she remembered an

American she'd met once recently, who lived nearby and had on that occasion offered her a lift. Well, he came to the party – and to the theatre, where he brought her just four minutes before she was due on stage. He responded with loud laughter at inappropriate moments in the play and became violent and assertive on subsequent visits and had to be ejected from the theatre. In fact a Cockney, he had tried to give the impression of being a swarthy American film-gangster type, which was probably easy enough for him because he was in fact a criminal, shortly after imprisoned for embezzlement. Googie was grateful to be got to the theatre on time, but had a tricky time avoiding him thereafter, when he would claim she 'owed' him. For safety's sake, she always asked her tall co-star Hugh Sinclair to escort her from the theatre.

By now she had established herself as an actress to be reckoned with and, approaching her late '20s, as being in no hurry to rush into matrimony. She had worked hard to escape the typecasting as 'blonde nitwit' of her '30s films, believing that 'At least by nature I am a brunette'. Settled in a stylish apartment in Curzon Street, Mayfair, 'next to a delightful little area known as Shepherd's Market, where rather upmarket prostitutes of the day had their "apartments"'and later at 88 Portland Place, London, she was, in common with her film roles, never going to be the meek little woman waiting for strong male arms to protect her. In 1946, though, she appeared in a film at whose end she does opt for such arms (though on her own terms), and those arms belonged to an Australian actor called John McCallum.

Chapter 2

JOHN

John was born in Brisbane on 14 March 1918, which meant he was a year and two days younger than Googie, a fact he kept from her until they were well and truly married, five decades later referring to himself as 'Googie's toy boy.' In fact, in some of the interviews he gave when back in England after the war, his birth year is given as 1917. Was this just tact on his part? Unlike Googie whose parents had no connection with the world of entertainment and whose father at least was less than entranced by the idea of his daughter cavorting upon the stage, John was steeped in theatre from the start.

I

His grandparents had emigrated to Queensland in 1862 from picturesque loch-side Tighnabruaich, in the west of Scotland, where the graveyard houses the remains of many McCallums. They were in pursuit of better health for John's grandmother. Ironically, his grandfather died of sunstroke within six months of arriving in Brisbane while his ailing grandmother lived to be 94. Their son, John Neil McCallum Sr (1872–1956), was a theatrical producer and entrepreneur, as well as being an accomplished musician, his Scots Presbyterian mother having encouraged him to become a church organist. But the great influence on John McCallum Jr was less to do with church music than with the fact that his father was the first manager of Brisbane's famous 1800-seat open-air Cremorne Theatre. Built by one Edward Branscombe, this opened on 5 August 1911 and specialised in vaudeville (chiefly provided by 'Branscombe's Dandies') and musical productions, as well as Christmas pantomimes. It also sent touring companies to other states. In 1916, Branscombe sold the entire venture to McCallum, and in 1936, the theatre, which he had renovated in important ways, came under the management of McCallum Enterprises Pty Ltd.

The theatre, which had a somewhat precarious history, was home to an assortment of entertainment troupes of which the most notable was probably 'Pat Hanna's Famous Diggers'. McCallum also ventured into sound-film screening in 1934, and film really took over until 1940, the theatre having been leased to Metro-Goldwyn-Mayer. In England in 1936, he had a letter of introduction from the Managing Director of MGM's Sydney office recommending him to the London office as manager of the Cremorne, 'Brisbane's first-run house' for the production company. The letter also described the trip undertaken by Mr and Mrs McCallum to England 'where he proposes to settle for two or three years. Mr McCallum's mission to England is essentially for the purpose of developing the dramatic talents of his eldest son who, as a student of Shakespearean works, seems destined for a stage career.' After his time in England, John Sr gave a lecture back home on 'the gradual fading away of many of the Flesh and Blood shows and the rapid increase in cinemas and talkie theatres'.

So, both stage and screen were part of the growing up of young John, and his father was a major figure in the state's theatrical life and film distribution. John Jr was born on the opening night of one of his father's productions and with predictable good humour, if not great subtlety, a telegram came to his father congratulating him on 'two howling successes'. John Sr is a recurring presence in his son's life whereas his mother, by all accounts an accomplished amateur actress, figures much more sparsely. There is an account in the old Queensland newspaper *The Patriot* in which she is credited with having 'created the most expensive [theatrical] wardrobe Brisbane has ever known and set a standard that has never been lived up to by any other show than the famous Tropics, who used to cause gasps of admiring astonishment as they stalked or pirouetted in gorgeous raiment.' 'Johnny Mac' may be the name associated with the theatre and its wardrobe, but it seems as if the main credit for the famous 'wardrobe' properly belonged to *Mrs* Johnny Mac. She was also a devout Presbyterian but son John, though not a disbeliever at this time, never became a churchgoer in adult life.

Like Googie's early years in the idyllic Dorset seaside village of Studland, some of John's childhood was spent in the comparably sleepy little Queensland coastal town of Sandgate, where his father bought land in 1922. He'd found trouble sleeping after nights at the Cremorne and thought that the twelve-mile drive from Brisbane would relax him. He may have grown tired of the bumpy drive but he did love Sandgate and so did his sons. John Sr was sure the place would thrive as a resort and invested a good deal of money in it. He eventually became its mayor and president of its golf course, but it never really progressed because the Gold Coast took off as an alternative holiday venue in the 1930s. Ironically, Surfer's Paradise was given a major boost by an American, Bob Geraghty, who leased the Cremorne for five years during the war, and, as it turned out, this deal proved more profitable to the lessee than to the lessor. However, even though Sandgate didn't really prosper, the young McCallums – John would be followed by Ian and Don – greatly enjoyed their life there 'with tricycles under the house, a large garden, a bulldog and a Persian cat, and a wonderful old couple who had retired from the theatre.' These latter were Joe, a former stagehand who took them to play on the beach and catch crabs when the tide was out, and Annie, who'd worked in the theatre wardrobe and was now the McCallums' cook.

Even mosquitos and tropical downpours couldn't, many years later, spoil the seaside memories of Sandgate, where John first went to school. Being teased as a new boy and son of the mayor, as his father was, he launched an attack on what he thought was 'a menacing crowd of six-year-olds'. He butted the ringleader who fell into the adjacent lagoon. The headmaster threatened expulsion but he'd made his point with the 'menacing crowd', who left him alone subsequently. Life, he decades later recalled, was much more peaceful at his next school, St Wulfram's in Bournemouth, the first of the English schools his anglophile mother placed him in.

His mother, the former Lillian Elsie Dyson of Huddersfield, left England at nineteen to live in Australia, where she married McCallum Sr, but she often visited England, on one occasion enrolling John and brother Ian at Oatlands School. Mrs McCallum had serious aspirations for John: after the Harrogate prep school, he was to be moved on to Uppingham School, then to Oxford, the ultimate goal being the Diplomatic Corps. And it's easy to imagine the effortlessly courteous and astute young man he became taking this in his stride. However, the Depression intervened; back home the Cremorne was not flourishing; and they had to return to Australia. It is not quite clear when his parents became estranged, but there are references to her visiting John at Stratford at the end of the '30s and to the two senior McCallums' coming to visit him and Googie in the early 1950s. In the memoir he wrote in the 1970s, John remarked that he felt closer to Googie's mother than to his own. Nevertheless, he attributed to his English mother both his flair for drama and the fact that he spent some of his schooldays in England. She felt that if he were going to be an actor, his range would be increased if he had an English accent since Australian roles were then very thin on the ground. In fact, young John's education straddled two continents, as did that of his brothers.

After his first spending time at school in Chateaux d'Oex, Switzerland, his family – parents and their three sons, John, Ian and Don – moved to Harrogate in 1927, where, as noted, the two older boys attended Oatlands Preparatory School. Some later newspaper accounts have suggested that they were sent there as boarders, but it doesn't appear that the school was taking boarders. Mrs McCallum stayed on in England and a letter from John Sr to someone addressed as 'Attie' records that 'Jack and Ian have excellent reports for the half-term and are making very good progress at school. Don of course will be the happiest boy in England when he has his brothers for two or three weeks at Easter', their mother having taken a house in Blackpool for the Easter holidays. It was at Oatlands that young John acquired his taste for theatrical performance. While there, at the age of 12 he played Cardinal Wolsey in a production of Shakespeare's *Henry VIII* at the Grand Opera House, Harrogate. For this he won critical acclaim from the local newspapers, which rightly felt such a role made great demands on a boy of his age, the *Harrogate Advertiser* suggesting that, 'whether in Australia or later in England, he will be heard of again in theatreland'. He was about to return to Australia to take up his education there, but he had obviously made a real impression with his grasp of the character of the cardinal, achieving a realism that was pretty remarkable in one of his years.

The family having returned to Australia in 1930, he was subsequently educated at Knox Grammar School, Sydney, where he spent a year and recalled being bullied because of his 'pommy' accent, and, in his senior schooldays, at Brisbane Church of England Grammar School, where he became captain of the school. He also distinguished himself here in sport, in rugby and especially in cricket, as well as in acting. He represented Queensland's Public Schools in these games, and he remained always keenly interested in sport, particularly in cricket. He played cricket in various charity matches in England, for Stratford and later for Lord's Taverners, but that's to leap a decade or so, when he would have added golf (with a golf card of about 80 in 1946) to his favoured outdoor pursuits. On leaving Brisbane CEGS, he received a glowing reference from W.P.F. Morris, the Headmaster:

> He has passed the Senior Public Examination of the University of Queensland, and has held the offices of School Prefect and of House Prefect, being Senior Prefect in both cases in 1936. He has also been Captain of Cricket, and Sergeant in the School Cadet Corps... He has literary taste and refinement; and in the discharge of his duties he has been conscientious and painstaking. I believe him to be entirely honourable and trustworthy.

That's about a good testimonial as an 18-year-old boy might hope for, but in fact it does pretty accurately foreshadow the way John's life might develop, and the sorts of traits that would characterise so much of his professional career. He had also acquired an attractive writing style, winning the Jackson Essay Prize for 1935 and submitting a remarkably fluent House Captain's report for the school's magazine, *The Viking*. Forty years on this fluency would stand him in good stead in the memoir he wrote, and no doubt in other areas of his career.

In 1935, while still at Brisbane CEGS, he played the title role in what he later described as 'an ambitious performance of *Richard II*' for the Brisbane Shakespeare Society, also (energetically) acting as stage manager on this production. (This may be one of the very few occasions on which the actor playing this ill-fated royal was also responsible for the backstage organisation. Probably not Gielgud, for instance.) By this time John's sights were firmly set on an acting career, and there were further amateur productions, including the Brisbane Repertory Company's *Hamlet* at the Princess Theatre, Woolloongabba, in September 1936. Even as a small boy, he'd liked being called on to read the lessons in religious services at his Harrogate school. He liked the feeling of getting up in front of people and holding their attention. Years later he credited his Cardinal Wolsey at Harrogate with the first serious stirring of the histrionic juices. Whatever their source, he also had early theatrical training with Barbara Sisely of the Brisbane Repertory Company (playing Horatio for it, with 'an engaging freshness and youthfulness [really?]' while still at school), and, on leaving school in Brisbane, he went back to England and in 1936 enrolled in the Royal Academy of Dramatic Art (RADA), under Sir Kenneth Barnes and his sisters, Violet and Irene Vanbrugh (both born 'Barnes').

In the latter '30s, while Googie was playing what she described (a bit severely) as 'nitwit blondes' in her quota quickie films, John was engaged in serious drama training. He greatly enjoyed his time at RADA, where one of the attractions was that there were twenty young women to a class and only five men. In early 1938, he had a letter from the RADA secretary urging him to reply soon if he wanted to come back for the summer term or not, and there is subsequently a letter to his father saying how 'very glad' she is that his son is coming back because 'he is doing well and it will be to his advantage to get all he can in the way of tuition before accepting professional work'. A few months after this, in the Old Boys' Letters section of *The Viking* (September 1938), there is a long extract from a letter he wrote to the Headmaster about his progress at RADA. In this he describes the 'Public Show', the annual performance by RADA students before a distinguished audience, on this occasion held at the famous Theatre Royal, Haymarket. On this day he was lucky enough to be given roles in extracts from Dodie Smith's *Call It a Day* and as the Duke in an excerpt from *Measure for Measure*. As George Bernard Shaw and Marie Tempest were in the audience, he was clearly being noticed by some of the right people, and the 'Show' was favourably reported by the press. Then as now, RADA carried the right clout for those wanting to get on in the theatrical world. John had also had very valuable experience in his last term at RADA, with parts in Jeffrey Dell's melodrama, *Payment Deferred* (in the leading role played by Charles Laughton in the film version), in scenes from Shakespeare, in which he got to play Macbeth among others, and in a production of *Twelfth Night*. In a letter to Lynn Redgrave, he recalled how 'An ex-RADA company, we played [*Merchant of Venice*] a week at the Sorbonne', praising her mother Rachel Kempson as 'a most lovely Portia.' This production had been staged for London schoolchildren and then taken to Paris for two performances.

It would be two decades before Googie would have the chance to distinguish herself in Shakespeare, by which time John's interest had been caught elsewhere. While she was becoming a consummate – perhaps *the* consummate – British film actress, John was equipping himself for a stage career. There will be something like a crossover of paths in this matter in the decade ahead, with Googie taking to the stage and John becoming a film leading-man. But at this point, in the years leading up to World War Two, he was working hard to establish a presence on London and provincial stages. In a late 1990s interview, he recalled that 'There was no film training at RADA in those days at all, which was surprising. We used to go down to the BBC now and then and have someone give us a bit of technique about broadcasting, but not about film'. For many theatre people at the time, film, though financially more rewarding, was still considered as lower in prestige than the stage. Film would have to wait a couple of decades to find in television a medium for *it* to look down on. However, undaunted by this perception, Mr McCallum Sr wrote to Darryl F. Zanuck, founding boss of 20th-Century Fox studios, enclosing a photo of John, which was returned with an answer telling him that Zanuck 'doesn't hire people with so little experience but to let them know when he gets a part in London'. Well, John never did work with Zanuck (Googie did in 1949), but that 'experience' referred to in the letter was about to begin.

John's first professional appearance was at the People's Palace, Mile End Rd, East London, and he subsequently gained repertory experience with the County Players at Tonbridge Repertory Theatre, Kent, before – in a stroke of great good fortune – joining the Stratford-upon-Avon Festival Company in 1939. The Tonbridge papers reviewed him as giving 'a confident and firm performance' in J.B. Fagan's comedy *Improper Duchess*, and felt that he 'displays an amazing personality as Robert Caplan', the leading role in J.B. Priestley's *Dangerous Corner*. (As with Googie's, his brush with Priestley in the '30s did him nothing but good.)

The range of plays and roles in which he appeared at this time is remarkable. In Ian Hay's *The Housemaster* he convincingly subdued his natural vigour to 'acquire that stoop and bent head so typically scholastic.' He was also 'a fine romantic lover' in Noël Coward's *The Queen Was in the Parlour*, gave 'a brilliant interpretation of the sex-obsessed Rev. Alfred Davidson in Somerset Maugham's *Rain*, was a 'superbly disdainful Demetrius in *A Midsummer Night's Dream*, and the villain with 'a cold menace in his voice and a brutality in his bearing' in Patrick Hamilton's Gaslight. Not a bad line-up for a young actor to show what he could do. In *Gaslight*, the duplicitous maid was played by Joan Hopkins, whom John, sixty years later, referred to as 'a girlfriend' at the time. Regarded as an 'outstanding newcomer', she was an actress eloquent of face and voice who went on to secure a modest, but firm place in British films of the '40s and early '50s, notably as Princess Charlotte in *The First Gentleman* in 1946, but she seems not to have acted again with John.

In Douglas Murray's play, *The Man from Toronto* (filmed in 1932 as a vehicle for Jessie Matthews), he won a review that 'was not tremendously surprised to see from the programme that Mr McCallum is an Australian, for there was nothing small or insular about his acting.' By this time, John was a strapping, handsome six-footer-plus and his attractive physical appearance, allied to a solid theatrical training, gave him a strong stage presence, and it is not surprising that Stratford should have beckoned at this time – as would films in post-war Britain. He was engaged to play at the Memorial Theatre for the entire 1939 season, having been signed up as a result of the Director and Producer of the theatre's having seen his 'Antonio' in *The Merchant of Venice* at the New Cross Palace. The Tonbridge Company was not happy to lose John, or fellow actor Michael Gwynn, to Stratford but gamely wished them well there. While there he was paid £3/10/0 per week and managed to live quite well on it, with enough left over from food and lodging to pay subs at the golf club, and to play tennis and cricket as well. The *Brisbane Courier*, reporting on John's progress, of course commented on his 'carrying on the stage tradition of the family', though the acting strand of that tradition belonged to his mother, not to his father whose legacy would be more specifically felt in John's later managerial career.

At Stratford, he played the usual selection of small parts that one might have expected of a young actor. He was the Herald in *King Lear* and Francisco in *The Tempest* for example, and as with many of similar age at this time career aspirations had to take second place to more pressing engagements. After this time at Stratford and small roles at the Old Vic, including one in *King Lear* again, in a company including John Gielgud and Peggy Ashcroft, he made his London West End debut in a long-forgotten piece, Priestley's *Cornelius*, in 1940 at the Westminster Theatre. (Another aspiring young actor in the cast was Derek Van den Bogaerde, whose post-war hour would come as Dirk Bogarde.) Decades later he recalled that, when he was playing golf one Saturday morning at Stratford, the actor Michael Goodliffe appeared with the news: 'German tanks have gone into Poland.'

In 1941, the theatre of war found him back in Australia. When war broke out, he went to Australia House in the Strand, London, where he found that to join up in the Forces he (with his brother Ian) would have to fund his own passage home. John's mother was living in Linden Gardens, Notting Hill, when war broke out, and she went back to Australia with her sons in a convoy that went via the Atlantic and the Panama Canal. John praised his mother's courage, as she accompanied her sons on this potentially dangerous voyage. Back in Australia, he enlisted in Paddington, New South Wales, in the 2/5 Field Regiment of the Australian Imperial Force (AIF), which claimed his attention for the next four years, much of it, spent as a gunner in New Guinea. This particular regiment saw action in Egypt and Syria, as well as Borneo and New Guinea, but the latter seems to have been the scene of John's participation.

It is difficult to find much detail about his time in the army, and all his obituarists, myself included, tended to elide those years between leaving his burgeoning stage career in England and starting up again in Brisbane. Certainly, he never spoke about the war years in any of the conversations I had with him, and this seems to have been the case with such interviews as survive. However, we know that he was in 1942 stationed for gunner training at Hume camp, near Albury, where he made the acquaintance of the artist Donald Friend who described him as one of the only three in his platoon for whom he 'gave a hoot'. Decades later, John recalled playing Antonio in a wartime production of *The Merchant of Venice*, for which Friend did the sets. John was involved in the military action against the Japanese at Milne Bay, which was fought in a tropical downpour, and it was a medical board that ended his stint as a soldier in 1944. There is another anecdote which records that singing was not his forté but pays tribute to his speaking voice at a wartime concert at the military camp in Cowra, New South Wales. Peter Snodgrass writing about this in *The Land* several years later recalls how, as reluctant General-in-Charge of concerts, he was forced to audition a number of only modestly talented recruits. 'On the stage was a young gentleman who began to make a very loud noise. I asked the pianist what the artist was alleged to be doing. He told me that it was singing. I couldn't and wouldn't believe it.' On subsequently hearing John *speak*, he felt he had 'rarely heard such beautiful speaking.' When John took the stage, after the singing fiasco, with a rendering of the Agincourt speech from *Henry V*, he held the audience spellbound – and stirred the troops to 'a frenzy of enthusiasm'. As far as existing records suggest, John never again sang on the stage, making do with acting and speaking and leaving the trilling to others who were better at it.

Suffering from malaria, he was demobbed in 1944, and returned promptly to the theatrical career he had put on hold five years before. In this period, the name he is most associated with is that of fellow Queenslander Gladys Moncrieff. If she is not much remembered now, 'Our Glad', as she was widely known, was an indisputably big star in the mid-century, hugely popular with theatre audiences as she sang her way through operettas and musicals such as *The Maid of the Mountains* and *Rio Rita* (both in 1945), in both of which John was cast opposite her. She had actually, as part of her war effort, entertained troops in New Guinea, but I have found no reference to John's having been one of those troops so entertained.

In *The Maid of the Mountains*, he played the bandit chief Baldassaré, who wins the love of Teresa, the bandit maid, and with whom, after many trials and tribulations, he finally escapes from his Devil's Island prison to make off with his beloved. Sounds a bit clunky today? Perhaps, but back then there was scarcely a bigger theatrical draw in Australia than Moncrieff. Whereas Baldassaré is a non-singing role for which John was no doubt cast at least partly on the basis of his imposing appearance, 'Our Glad' was no beauty but sang her heart out – and *into* the hearts of millions – in a range of popular numbers. John played the conniving General Esteban, unsuccessful suitor to Moncrieff's Rita, in the triumphant 1946 production of *Rio Rita*, in which she sings and he has to make do with acting. John retained warm memories of working with Gladys Moncrieff whom he later recalled as having 'a wonderful rapport with Australian audiences, who adored her... She was splendidly vulgar, loud and cheerful, and she returned the affection which audiences gave her'. Appearing opposite such a diva at such a time can only have been beneficial to an actor trying to restart a career after a four-year break.

As well as the high-profile entertainments with Moncrieff, he also had other useful experience in these immediate post-war years. For J.C. Williamson's, with whom he would later have so important an association, he produced *The Wind and the Rain* in 1945 with the Minerva Company at the Theatre Royal in Sydney, and played in such popular commercial plays of the day as *Susan and God* and *Claudia* at the Comedy Theatre in Melbourne. If Mrs McCallum had been right in her pre-war assessment of the limited scope for a theatrical career in Australia, the local *film* industry was barely visible in the late 1940s. This being so, John was lucky to have been given a couple of chances in this medium. (Whatever other sources say, he was *not* involved in the 1936 film *Heritage*, an ambitious adventure drama directed by Charles Chauvel.) He was approached in the mid '40s by the Commonwealth Film Unit to speak commentaries for two modest 'acted' documentaries, *Joe Comes Back*, in which he also played a soldier returning from the war and settling again into civilian life, and *South West Pacific*, both made essentially with propaganda intentions. Other actors such as Grant Taylor and Peter Finch were also involved in these. Perhaps John's clear, unaccented and unaffected voice accounts for his function in these short films and as narrator of the well-loved children's adventure, *Bush Christmas* (1947). He was in England by the time the latter was made, but knew the director Ralph Smart, who asked him to do the voice-over for nothing, as a gesture of support to Mary Field, who ran the Children's Film Foundation for the Rank Organisation.

He also appeared in one feature film, *A Son Is Born* (1946), directed by Eric Porter, a somewhat hoary melodrama of family passions and generational conflicts. In this, John, greyed at the temples to suggest mature years and sporting a pipe and an improbable moustache, is involved in a divorce settlement, which he has helped to bring about, then marrying the woman in the question. (Incidentally, there is a tiny moment in the film where his wife mocks his attempt at singing. Was there some kind of in-joke intended here?) Later in the film, he has to slap twice a surly Ron Randell, playing his stepson, and in this and several of his British films later in the decade he was called on to knock his co-stars about convincingly. The film is quite handsomely produced and has a cast full of stars of the future, including Muriel Steinbeck, Peter Finch and Ron ('Smithy') Randell as well as John, and still works as well as many of the Hollywood melodramas of the day. But the McCallum career path was about to make a major divergence.

II

He had read that Trevor Howard, an old friend, from pre-war days at Stratford, was doing rather well in films, having made a big success in 1945-46 as Celia Johnson's would-be lover in *Brief Encounter*. This fanned the flames of film ambition in John McCallum, and instead of going on tour to New Zealand with Gladys Moncrieff he found himself drawn to the idea of pursuing his career overseas. He must have felt sufficiently secure in May 1945 to turn down an offer from E.J. Tait, Manager of J.C. Williamson's Theatres, of a 'further option of twenty-six weeks' on his contract. He had been paid a salary of £20 per week in Sydney, £30 outside Sydney, which was good money for 1944, with a guarantee of 20 weeks.

It was becoming clear to John that, if he stayed indefinitely in Australia, much as he was enjoying the life, he could end up just doing more of the same. Many years later he recalled an episode that helped confirm him in his decision. Having been demobbed, suffering with malaria, he'd been warned to be careful about his alcohol intake, as indeed for the most part he was. However, on the night of the Melbourne Cup, 4 November 1945, he suffered a very severe hangover, which was unfortunate since he was due to perform that evening in *The Maid of the Mountains* with Moncrieff on stage at His Majesty's Theatre, Melbourne. He'd had a spectacular win at the races - £1,800 in fact, far more than he'd had in his life up to that point. This victory had led to an unwisely extended visit to a pub, and then, in his theatre dressing-room, to a head-spinning bout of the shakes. To add to his dismay, he found he'd been robbed, probably in the crowded pub, of well over half of his winnings. Nevertheless, with the help of Herbert Browne, the Company's tenor, who came to his dressing-room and, seeing John's condition, wondered if it's 'just the booze or a touch of the old anopheles', he managed to make it on stage. At the end of the second act, after singing 'Love will find a way', Moncrieff would fall into his arms and he would gently lower her to the floor as the curtain fell, to rapturous applause from the much-moved audience. On Cup Night, this was more difficult for him, made more so by the fact that she had broken her leg, and by the memory of the curtain's having been raised too early a few nights earlier to reveal her being lifted to her feet by three stage hands to take a bow. Applause was now mingled with rowdy laughter. (A choice recollection of John's: When she left hospital after breaking her leg, she received huge floral tributes some of which she festooned about her ample person. A Melbourne newspaper reported this under the headline, 'Gladys Moncrieff leaves hospital, orchids pinned over her crutch.')

Somehow, he staggered through the Cup Night's performance but this experience, when he had to be nudged along by Browne, sharpened his sense that musical comedy was not his genre, that he was, in a sense, being carried by real singers. So when the prospect of the New Zealand tour came up, and at a salary quite handsome for the times, he reflected: 'I had a wonderful job, I had a wonderful life, and a wonderful girl in the chorus – she went on to become a J.C. Williamson's star – who I thought I was in love with, and who thought she was in love with me [but] neither of us wanted to get married'. He foresaw that when the Company returned from New Zealand, it was likely to be just more of the same, more musical revivals, more radio and so on, and it no longer seemed challenging enough.

Further, in Australia at this time was American screenwriter Jesse Lasky Jr, son of the influential Hollywood pioneer and producer, Jesse A. Lasky. Lasky Jr had been in Australia in the US Army and he had seen John in the acted documentary, *Joe Comes Back*. He obviously thought John had a future and encouraged him to try his luck in the film capital. This proved to be easier said than done. Lasky warned him that he'd have to get a 'quota number' to work in the US, but, as Australians were issued only about fifty of these per year, John's hopes were not high. To his surprise, three months later he was granted a quota number by the American Embassy in Canberra. Then he found that he couldn't get on a boat to Hollywood because the ships were full of returning GIs. He even approached the Seaman's Union to see if he could work his passage, but all the vacancies were filled by ex-naval personnel returning to merchant ships after the war. So he decided to approach 'abroad' via England, managing to get a steerage passage on the *Aquitania*, with £800, the unstolen remains of his racetrack winnings. He knew England and liked the idea of stopping off there, and then crossing the Atlantic. The problem then was that he couldn't get across the Atlantic either, because the boats were full of war brides heading for the States to see what they'd married into. Up to a point, it could be said his subsequent career – and happiness – was set in motion, partly by post-hangover reflection, but nudged by Howard and Lasky, even if these two were unaware of their influence. Whatever the relative impacts of these various influences at work on him at the time, his decision was made. If he'd gone directly to the US, who knows which bright star of the Hollywood galaxy of the day might have caught his susceptible eye?

Having, as he thought, merely stopped off in England en route to the US, his agent put it to him that he might consider staying, especially as British cinema was enjoying a period of high productivity and prestige. The war had given it a fillip and it had maintained this ascendancy in the post-war years, when a new realism characterised some of its best achievements. Arguably, these were, in that resonant phrase of the 1940s, the British cinema's 'finest hours' – years, really. At the moment, his agent said, there was a part going in a film called *The Root of All Evil*. He went to test for a small role in the film, but director Brock Williams found that 'He showed such ease before the camera and ability to handle lines that I recognised immediately he is wonderful star material. I tested him the same day for the big part.' And so he ended up with the larger of the two leading males role opposite Phyllis Calvert, then a big name in British cinema, and co-starring Michael Rennie, at that stage an established leading man, having made film love to that *Wicked Lady*, Margaret Lockwood. A small coincidence: both Rennie and McCallum had spent some years of their education at Oatlands School in Harrogate. Australian papers reported his success with pride and avidity. There were headlines such as 'Australian Actor Gets Big Film Lead' and 'Handsome Sydney Actor Wins Star Film Role'. Whereas 'Sydney' is credited with John's origins, another clipping refers to 'Brisbane Actor in New English Film'. By this time, his mother was living in Sydney, with his brothers, but his early days were most closely associated with his Brisbane birthplace. Someone has been scrupulous in preserving all these items, though not always in giving their sources and dates.

Having been in England before the war meant that he was not a stranger to the acting scene there, but all his pre-war work had been in the theatre, with no experience in film, so that he was very fortunate to nab a leading role with a major actress, and for the then very successful Gainsborough

Studios. Gainsborough had been responsible for a string of hugely popular melodramas such as *The Man in Grey*, *Fanny by Gaslight* and *The Wicked Lady* which had made household names of the likes of Calvert, Lockwood, Jean Kent, Stewart Granger and James Mason. John could hardly have fallen more firmly on his feet in the British film scene in early 1946.

And speaking of names, Googie wasn't alone in having people try to persuade her to change hers. John was told by Gainsborough publicists that fans would have trouble spelling his, and like Googie he refused to change. It wasn't only fans, though, who would misspell his surname. Several newspapers referred to him as 'McCullum' or 'M'Callum' or 'M'Cullum'. He was warned that he would end up being known as 'Whatcha M'Callum', but he remained unmoved on this matter. In fact, well before his first British film was released and as a result of careful publicity, he had already acquired a substantial fan following.

His handsome masculine presence was going to be a welcome addition to the ranks of British leading men. Stewart Granger and James Mason would shortly succumb to the blandishments of Hollywood, John Mills stood for a different sort of everyman hero, and Dirk Bogarde hadn't yet appeared on the scene, so that this may well have been a very opportune moment for an intelligent and personable new leading man to get a career moving in British film. Moreover, though arguably his screen presence hadn't quite the edge of danger associated with Mason or Granger for instance, he was offering something a little different from those others. There was an openness about him, an air of the Australian sportsman, along with an English way of speech acquired during his early schooldays in Harrogate and honed at RADA in the 1930s. Obviously quite at home in England in the latter 1940s, he nevertheless carried with him a whiff of difference. Perhaps it was also something to do with what writer Sewell Stokes called 'The look in his eye', which persuaded the writer that John McCallum was 'the young actor most likely to become a top-ranking star'. It is a watchful, intelligent 'look' indeed, but, whatever combination of personal advantages and training he could draw on, he was certainly about to be taken up in a big way by British films.

It was one thing to find himself starring with Phyllis Calvert; it was another to make do with a screenplay that reviewers variously described as 'preposterous', 'witless', and 'feeble', and John himself years later dismissed it as 'a terrible film'. Based on a novel by crime writer and Yorkshire historian, J.S. Fletcher, the film doesn't have much that's new to say about the well-worn notion that money isn't everything, that in fact too much of it is apt to corrupt whatever is best in human beings. It could be said that this is a moral dictum that can't be restated too often; equally though, it may need to be dramatised with more freshness and vigour than it gets here.

The Root of All Evil may recall Joan Crawford's Hollywood classic *Mildred Pierce* (1945), in which a woman cuts a swathe through unsatisfactory men and achieves striking business success. Calvert, who was sick of her run of goody-goody heroines, here plays Jeckie Farnish, who realises her father's indolence has been responsible for their farm's failure and who, as their fortunes plummet and her engagement to a rich young man ends, announces: 'From now on I'm going to manage the farm.' She is 'going to turn a somersault … from now on it's going to be head over heart. There's only one unforgivable sin – poverty'. From this low point on, there is a newly purposive look to Jeckie, who is seen in increasingly smart costumes, admired by girls in the street, a more sophisticated hair-do, lots of smoking, and no-nonsense talk as she deals with men both spineless and aggressive. As well, there is a sharper contrast made with her sister Rushie (Hazel Court). Rushie ('Rushie'? 'Jeckie'?: who was naming these girls?) settles for a conventional marriage, but Jeckie will eventually have to attend to Rushie's wisdom, 'Life's not all business'. A brief affair with a caddish visiting man (Michael Rennie), who nearly runs her down in his flash car (almost certainly a 'roadster'), hardens Jeckie further. Though there is some feminist sympathy for Jeckie's enterprise, there is no question of her being allowed to get away with her money-making schemes, as a man might, and in the end she will find comfort in the arms of Joe Bartle (McCallum – mistakenly spelt as McCullum in credits) and is forced to say, 'I've come home and I'm sorry'.

Yes, it's a pretty simple-minded morality tale, but this doesn't mean that it didn't give John some valuable exposure. Though reviewers sharpened their scalpels to take the film apart, they dealt more leniently with the actors, the *Times* going so far as to suggest that it was 'not their fault that their gestures seem divorced from all reality', and the *Yorkshire Evening Post* wrote that 'it shows you can have excellent acting in a second-rate story.' In general, John's personal notices were satisfactory – the trade journal *Today's Cinema* claimed that 'newcomer John McCallum revealed considerable promise with his sympathetic handling of the rustic lover role'. He is dressed and shot in ways that stress his rural decency in contrast with the unreliable city-slicker type played by Rennie. There was, too, a good deal of useful publicity relating to his hectic fight with Rennie, one journal running a double page of shots from this sequence. This no doubt bolstered the virile McCallum image that was being promoted in the fan magazines. One columnist, writing of his abstemious habits (non-smoking, drinks sparingly) ended by saying that he 'seems serenely unconscious of the fact that he leaves the ladies languishing in all directions.' Celebrity reporting has come a long way since then.

Watching *The Root of All Evil* today, one can be a little less harsh about its shortcomings as they appeared to contemporary critics. It is not a complex film but the Calvert character does get to show some serious muscle as a woman determined not just to accept what life hands out but to make something more durable of it, and on her own terms. It moves towards an unnecessarily melodramatic oil-fire climax when it could just as easily – and more convincingly – have relied on the working out of the pattern of human relationships it has set up, but it stands up quite well in comparison with the Hollywood counterparts of the period. John, who had been expecting to sail to the US as soon as the exodus of GI brides slowed to a trickle, was now committed to staying in England. He was lucky to survive the film's critical onslaught, and perhaps even luckier that, by the time it was released, he was well and truly involved in his next film. Just as Phyllis Calvert's character had found final solace in his manly arms, so too would the heroine of the new film. The actress who would play her was Googie Withers.

Chapter 3

JOHN AND GOOGIE
AND JOANNA GODDEN

'I said "Who the hell is he, I've never heard of him" and she [my agent] said "He's an Australian and he's come over here and he's done two films here and he's very good, and we think that he's right for the part". So I said "Well he'd better be". So that's how I heard of him and I went over from Hollywood to London and I went down on location to do *The Loves of Joanna Godden* and that's one of many stories there. I went upstairs to change because I'd just flown in and a little old man was standing at the bottom of the stairs.'

Googie was in Hollywood *not* signing a contract when she got a cable from Ealing Studios saying her next film was to be *The Loves of Joanna Godden* and that her leading man was to be an actor called John McCallum. The name meant nothing to her, his first British film not having been released at that point. She explained later that she preferred being free-lance and disliked the idea of a long-term film contract which, in her independent way, she would have found constraining, saying 'I couldn't bear to be tied to one of those interminable Hollywood contracts and be compelled to go into all kinds of films'. She also disliked Hollywood as a place and saw little future for her relationship with Richard Llewellyn who was enjoying some success there as a screenwriter. To bolster her courage for flying back to England, having had a rough and alarming flight *to* the US, she used her remaining funds to book into the cheapest room in New York's Waldorf Hotel. On arrival there, she was shown to a luxurious suite with a magnificent view of the city. She was sure a mistake had been made. It had. The Waldorf had confused her with the then-prominent American actress, Jane Withers, but on finding its mistake the management asked her to accept this accommodation at the price of a single room, since the rest of the hotel was fully booked. It was probably easy for her to adapt to these circumstances.

When she returned to England, she went down to the village of Peasmarsh in the Romney Marsh country and found herself at the Pelsham Hotel, formerly a privately-owned stately home, in which some of the company were to live during the location-filming. After establishing herself in her upstairs room she came down to find a small grey-haired man waiting at the foot of the stairs. 'I'm John McCallum,' he said by way of introduction, neglecting to add for the moment that he was in fact the father of the actor of the same name who was to be her co-star. The elder McCallum always wished he'd had a camera to create a permanent photographic record of Googie's reactions to his announcement.

The many accounts of this meeting fail to specify whether it was deliberately set up or whether it was simply a matter of chance. Either way, it is a choice bit of detail in the lives of the couple who were about to come face to face a few minutes later. Googie may not have had any idea as to who John was, but he certainly knew *about* her. He had first seen her on the screen in *The Silver Fleet* at a showing for troops in New Guinea during the war (with its tale of treachery and heroic sacrifice, it was just the thing to keep their spirits up – or not). In a 1955 interview in Sydney, he recalled that 'When she came on one of the Diggers sang out [with an antipodean way of cutting to the chase], "All right, you beaut – you'll do"'. But just after he arrived in London in early 1946, he also saw her in the flesh when she played Noël Coward's volatile Amanda in the successful revival of *Private Lives* at the Apollo Theatre. Having, like so many Australians in Britain in the post-war years, been able to afford only a gallery seat on this occasion, he then made an important financial investment when he found he was to have a part in her next film, *The Loves of Joanna Godden*. 'I went back and saw *Private Lives* again – this time from the front row of the stalls to get a good look at her.' He liked what he saw from this vantage point.

The Loves of Joanna Godden was adapted from a once popular novel by Sheila Kaye-Smith, published in 1921. Kaye-Smith was a very prolific author and *Joanna Godden* was perhaps her most famous book. The film version added '*The Loves of...*' to the title, no doubt in deference to the box-office, and it was a change noted sniffily by several reviewers, but one of the great strengths of the film, as of the novel, is its evocation of the Romney Marsh countryside, overlapping Sussex and Kent. The novelist H.E. Bates (abetted by Ealing screenwriter Angus McPhail) wrote the screenplay and made some significant changes in key plot manoeuvres, but there is still a remarkable sense of this strangely empty but curiously seductive stretch of land.

Much of the film was made on location and the filmmakers pay tribute in the opening credits to 'the many friends in Romney Marsh for their unfailing help', and 'The People of Romney Marsh' are listed as cast-members at the end of the film. One local cast member was Ernie Fisher, a farm labourer from Lydd, who had a role as a shepherd in which he had to give Googie 'a good ticking off' on a matter of farming practice. Asked how he felt about speaking thus to the film's star, he said 'That'll be easy after dealing with all those Land Girls'. His wife disapproved of his new career in films and berated him when he arrived home late, following a few beers with the crew, saying, 'No more filum acting for you... Coming home all hours, full of beer and conceit, and talking about Googie Boogie Withers.' After his brief acting career, he was reported back at work on a farm near Lydd. The people of Lydd on the Romney Marsh were described as 'the life-blood of this film', and the stars would show their gratitude by making the local screening a glamorous occasion.

Both John and Googie, and their co-star, Jean Kent, remembered forty years later how much they had enjoyed the film's location-shooting: 'We were living in the most beautiful house that had belonged to a family who had lived there for many, many years and who couldn't afford any longer to keep it going, and so they turned it into a sort of hotel. It wasn't *really* a hotel, but a sort of place for 'Paying Guests' and they took twelve of us; and they had, would you believe, a cook and butler called Neat and Tidy, and that's where our base was. It was so comfortable, and they lived there still too, the people who owned it, so it was like being there in a house party the whole time. We'd go out and work in the Marshes, and we took months to make the film, but three months of it was spent on location which was just divine.' That's Googie's account, but Jean Kent's was much the same, including recall of 'Neat and Tidy', though Jean couldn't help wondering if the names were really a 'con'. Apart from rain, inseparable, Jean said, from any location-shooting, it was a more or less idyllic time. But even rain couldn't really dampen things. On the first day of rain and with filming cancelled, Jean remembered: 'Googie said, "Let's have a bottle of champagne"', as they settled down to play gin rummy, 'then a couple of the film crew came in and suggested another bottle, and a bit later John arrived and bought a third. By the end of the afternoon we were merry as grigs.' Sometime later, Googie and John returned to Peasmarsh, East Sussex, where they'd stayed while on location, judging the 'village fancy dress competition', in a typical act combining good will and good sense.

Joanna Godden was, in hindsight, almost the ideal vehicle for bringing John and Googie together. There was also quite a bit of publicity about how Googie had changed course and matured as an actress, as in one article headed 'Comedy Queen Turns to Drama'. Following the novel's outline up to a point (a crucial one, too), it cast Googie as a forthright, very capable woman who takes on the running of her late father's farm and insists on her equality with the men who are apt to be patronising about a woman doing 'a man's work'. There is a codicil to her father's will to the effect that she should marry Arthur Alce (John), a neighbouring farmer. Well, her affections are diverted in other directions – first to a shepherd (Chips Rafferty) whom she employs and to whom she is briefly attracted, then to a member of the local gentry (Derek Bond) who gets himself drowned (not all that convincingly). Arthur then lets himself become beguiled by Joanna's minx-like younger sister, Ellen (Jean Kent), even to the point of marrying her. But that's of course not the way it ends. Unlike in Kaye-Smith's novel in which, to my surprise in reading it about ninety years after its publication, Arthur dies and Joanna is left, pregnant by someone else, pregnant but determined to face whatever the future holds. A 1946 film was unlikely to end in this advanced feminist way. Instead, the naughty sister runs off, and Joanna finally surrenders to Arthur's embrace – *but* she is still wearing a rather masculine-looking shirt and tie, as if to say, Don't imagine I'm about to come over all 'little-woman' and start doing as I'm told.

The film was directed by Charles Frend, whom Jean Kent remembered as 'a quiet sort of fellow', but some sequences were directed by Ealing's ace, Robert Hamer, when Frend became ill. Googie had a high regard for Hamer who had led her down her murderous path so brilliantly in *Pink String and Sealing Wax* and would guide her and John through their finest film together, *It Always Rains on Sunday* in 1947. There were other classy credits associated with *Joanna Godden* including a musical score by Vaughan Williams and glorious black-and-white cinematography by Douglas Slocombe, evoking the beauty of the Romney Marsh countryside and its wide skies. Sheila Kaye-Smith went down to see the scenes of Christmas morning being shot and commented on 'a race between the camera and the budding trees, which were already beginning to show an un-Christmaslike appearance – to say nothing of daffodils in the churchyard, which worried the producers a bit.' She saw the finished film at a special screening at the Lydd Cinema to which all the locals who had taken part were invited. 'It was all flowers and flags, with the stars in attendance. ... As for the film itself – well... there is some lovely photography & splendid acting, but I disclaim all responsibility for the story'. She rightly allows that it follows the first three parts of her novel, but that 'the end is quite different', though she appears not to have been too agitated about this.

Rain to one side, the filming of *Joanna Godden* was an enjoyable experience for those involved, and during this time John and Googie became firm friends. In his notes for the second volume of memoirs that was never published, he wrote warmly of getting to know Googie at this time. He found her to have 'authority, intelligence, humour, confidence and a consummate knowledge of film acting.' He also found that 'she talked a great deal, and talked well, and that she listened well too.' Even then, though, he sensed that, 'if your opinion differed from hers, she was utterly convinced that she was right and you were wrong.' They spent a lot of time on location walking and driving, and talking the while, checking out each other's views on such potentially contentious, divisive matters as politics and smoking and God. In other words, they were sufficiently interested in each other to want to understand where the other stood on these and other such issues. On politics, Googie had become inadvertently and improbably involved with the Communist Party while filming *Pink String and Sealing Wax*, when she got to know the elderly character actress Mary Merrall. Googie and a friend had been to see a play at the Unity Theatre in London, and she'd been with her father to a concert at the Albert Hall to raise money for the Russian war effort. Hearing of these two accidental brushes with the 'Left', Miss Merrall tried without success to recruit Googie to the party. John, later rather conservative politically, in the days of *Joanna Godden*, was revolutionary in the sense that he told Googie he favoured the doing away with political parties, leaving the way open for individuals to be elected on what they believed and on their merits. On religion, John had become a non-believer whereas Googie *wanted* to believe and loved the theatricality of the church. As for smoking, he was a non-smoker while, in those days, she puffed her way through about sixty a day.

These were just some of the conversational topics they canvassed in this period of getting to know each other while the filming ran over schedule as a result of the inclement weather on location. They took to going out together in London and elsewhere, stressing that 'There is no truth in a rumour that we intend to marry', as John was quoted as saying in an interview reported in the *Sydney Mirror* in June 1947. Well, maybe there was no truth in it at that time but there soon would be. He responded to her liveliness and, in their first filmed scene together, the occasion was a quarrel and he later described his impression of 'a woman of mettle'. Years later, in various interviews, he would make clear that he was never going to be interested in a docile woman who was 'always apologising'. 'My wife never apologises, even when she's wrong', he once claimed. There was no suggestion that Googie would take umbrage at such a pronouncement!

In the last moments of *Joanna Godden*, Arthur says to Joanna (having earlier said it to the flighty Ellen), 'There's no bounds to what we can do.' This line rather aptly anticipates the sixty-odd years of partnership that lay ahead.

Given how fresh and attractive the film looks now, it is surprising to find what a mixed reception it had from contemporary reviewers, most of whom had more praise for the film's pictorial beauties than for the personal story. Dilys Powell, respected critic for *The Sunday Times*, was impressed with the look of the film in Douglas Slocombe's cinematography of the wide spaces and skies and with Vaughan Williams's musical score. However, she claimed that Googie, whom she valued as an actress, couldn't persuade her that 'she knows any more than I do about the Southdown or the Blackface'. This line was also adopted by the *Evening Standard* reviewer who wrote that 'The human relationships offer little excitement', but 'Dungeness, and the ever-changing pageant of English rural life' were 'tenderly and poignantly captured' by director Frend, himself 'a Kentish man'. And the *Tatler* waxed lyrical with 'here the cameraman stakes a claim to be given a place alongside the poet and the painter. To the grave beauty of this procession of sun and cloud, furrow and pasture, Dr Vaughan has wedded some notable music.' C.A. Lejeune, then-popular reviewer for London's Sunday *Observer* found 'the new title ... tasteless and misleading' because, 'Every time something in the way of a lover ... pops up for Miss Withers', he is 'sternly put down and returned to [his] muttons.' Lejeune tended to care more for being 'witty' than judicious, but this time she is in line with several others in praising the film's attention to 'the English scene, the spread of the downs, the salty pebbled headlands along the south shore, and the quiet grazing of flocks,' and in finding the human interest 'practically nil'. One of the film's key sequences, very near the end, involves the putting down of a flock of sheep infected with foot-and-mouth disease. This was staged in a way that points to the film's concern for realism, though Ms Lejeune complained thus: 'It is not my idea of entertainment to see sheep, even the simulacra of sheep, dying singly at lambing time, or burnt by hundreds after foot and mouth disease.'

Perhaps it was fortunate for John and Googie that Ealing had them pencilled-in for their next co-starring venture before *Joanna Godden* was released and the reviews were out. This may have been particularly so in John's case. Indeed, his preceding British film, *The Root of All Evil*, had been even less of a critical favourite, but Ealing obviously had faith in him and cast him opposite Googie again in *It Always Rains on Sunday* before either of his earlier films had been seen. Skilful publicity had ensured that he was familiar to fans from umpteen photographs, stressing his 'ruggedly handsome' appearance in assorted press reports, one of which ended with 'I almost forgot to tell you that John is unmarried!' In hindsight, one could add that time was running out in this regard. There had been as well a great deal of publicity surrounding the production of *Joanna Godden*. In fact, in spite of the carping about the personal story, there were still enough positive notices of the star performances to justify Ealing's confidence in them. The *Tribune*'s reviewer wrote that 'The part of Joanna Godden is admirably played by Googie Withers, who is now the strongest of our young character actresses'. Sixty-odd years on Googie seems remarkably assured as the woman determined to manage her life on her own terms, even if one lady reviewer quibbled that it was 'hard to believe in a woman farmer who drives to market in outfits suitable for a Royal Garden Party'. The weekly entertainment guide, *What's On* found her 'wholly delightful as the self-determined young woman with ideas ahead of her time', and wrote of John's playing of Arthur Alce, 'I like his wholly masculine, firmly-set personality … and this, allied to first-class acting ability, should take him a long way.' He echoed producer Sydney Box's belief that John was 'one of the ten British stars of tomorrow'. The popular fan magazine, *Picturegoer*, devoted a whole-page article to John under the title 'Australia sends us another star'. That is, he was becoming well known before British filmgoers had even seen him on the screen. Like Googie, he seems always to have been co-operative with the press, as if understanding fully its importance in launching a film career.

With *Joanna Godden* well on the way to completion and with the announcement of their next co-starring film, *It Always Rains on Sunday*, to be directed by Googie's favourite, Robert Hamer, the future must have looked promising at the end of 1946. As for their Christmas plans, they may still have been persisting in their denial of engagement rumours, but John, with his father, was taking his car to Paris and the plan was to pick up Googie and her mother there and drive them to Riviera. The local Romney Marsh papers reported this, and indeed took a delighted interest in having the stars and the filmmakers in their community. There were happy reports of John and Chips Rafferty and others of the cast playing in a cricket match between the local team and the film-location team. This was the sort of activity, which both John and Googie would throw themselves into, with every appearance of enjoying themselves, in both Britain and Australia. It was no doubt good for business but there was always a sense of unaffected pleasure in the way they went about it. In the 1940s, British film studios expected their stars to take up the publicity banner, as it was obviously in everyone's interests – stars', studios' and the public's – and, by the time the McCallums went to Australia in 1955, they were old hands at it. For instance, by the end of the '40s, Googie knew how to receive with aplomb a bouquet at a preview, hand it back to the cinema manager out of view of the audience, and then to receive the same floral tribute at the next preview on the same night, the while expressing surprise and delight all over again.

Within eighteen months of finishing work on *Joanna Godden* the real-life portrayers of Joanna and Arthur would be 'pulling together' on their next projects, professional and personal.

It Always Rains on Sunday was one of the most powerful and intelligent British films of the high period of post-war production. It was based on a novel by Arthur LaBern, a popular hard-hitting author of the time. By coincidence, the next film of *Joanna Godden*'s third star, Jean Kent, was also based on a novel by La Bern, *Night Darkens the Streets*, filmed as *Good-Time Girl*. (How the times have changed. Whatever became of 'good-time girls'?). *It Always Rains on Sunday* kept the original title but updated the pre-war setting to an East End marked by post-war bomb damage and spivs flogging black-market goods to a luxury-starved community.

Googie and John would go on to co-star in five further films (she would also be a guest star in one of *his* starring vehicles and would star in one directed by him) but it's arguable that *It Always Rains* gave Googie at least the great role of her film career. She plays Rose Sandigate, discontented wife to the much older George (Edward Chapman) and stepmother to his children including the stroppy Vi (Susan Shaw), who may well reflect the younger Rose's yearnings. Into a rather gloomy Sunday morning erupts a figure from Rose's past, a former lover called Tommy Swann (John), now an escaped convict on the run.

Many years later, the French director Bernard Tavernier, when asked for his ideal film double-bill, cited the 1957 American western *3.10 to Yuma* and *It Always Rains on Sunday*, saying: 'I absolutely love *It Always Rains on Sunday*. Here is a very violent and bleak story. It's about a small neighbourhood during a Sunday in post-war Britain… Hamer was a rare director in England at the time, who was willing to deal with the sexual element in his films…' Often when one mentions Ealing to filmgoers with long memories they will sigh nostalgically and recall their fondness for the famous comedies, such as *The Lavender Hill Mob*. Few would be likely to name *It Always Rains* as one of their favourites, and certainly it is a much tougher, less instantly likable film than many conjured up by the idea of 'Ealing'. Some of us, however, regard it as one of the finest of all British films. There may be a strong thread of melodrama running through it but everything is embedded in a most powerful sense of reality, of a difficult, busy, frustrating world. It's also the film that establishes John and Googie as a team to be reckoned with; it makes plain that *Joanna Godden* was no flash in the pan as far as they were concerned.

Tavernier referred to the 'sexual element' in the film. The American censor, Joseph Breen, who had been much disturbed by the corrupting effect of Margaret Lockwood's cleavage in *The Wicked Lady* in 1946, was apparently deeply worried about a scene in *It Always Rains* when John, clad only in his trousers, engages in a passionate embrace with Googie who then falls backward on the bed. And this is the bed she shares with her much older husband. In order to set Mr Breen's mind at rest, 'The players had to go through their paces once more. This time Googie broke away from

John before the "cut" came.' It's easy to forget how prissy America – or its censorship at least – was in those days. The fact is that much of the tension of *It Always Rains* comes from the fact that Googie's Rose has by no means forgotten the passion she once felt for Tommy, even though she is aware of the threat he now poses to such stability as her everyday life offers. She and John invest the scene with a potent, believable sexuality that was by no means common in British cinema of the time.

It's not just a simple-minded matter of conflating art with life here. Googie had always been able on screen to suggest the sensual potential of the characters she was playing, but perhaps not until John came along did she meet with a significant challenge. He makes Tommy Swann a real threat to Rose's life. In Rose's memory sequence when she first hears of Tommy's escape, he is depicted as a flashy wide-boy type, sure of his sexual charisma and its impact on the barmaid Rose was then. He represents another, more exciting world for Rose, and significantly in this sequence Googie has returned to her 1930s blonde image. It's a way of suggesting how far Rose has changed to her present somewhat surly brunette self – and it reminds us (as it did several reviewers at the time) of the 'days when she was given the part of the mischievous blonde, in farce after hardworking farce' as one wrote.

Whereas the film, with many strands to its plot as it works its way through the events of a wet Sunday, involves Googie in scenes with others such as the dull, decent husband to whom she will finally be grateful and the stepdaughters, one nice, the other on the sluttish side (this one charmingly addresses Rose as 'You fat rotten cow', which Breen also objected to), John's scenes are almost entirely with Googie. Until near the end. When a nosy reporter comes to the house and Rose is dealing with him, Tommy knocks her down as he makes his escape. But the escape only gets him as far as the railway yards where he is captured by police, after a brilliantly shot chase conducted in the marshalling yards at Temple Mills, Stratford. Years later John recalled how the director, Hamer, 'a perfectionist... took five weeks to shoot that end sequence in the railway yard. We took awful risks – going under moving trains and running on top of them, things like that.'

By the time this exhausting shoot was finished, John was looking somewhat gaunt – and unshaven – when he escorted his former Australian leading lady Gladys Moncrieff to the London première of *Joanna Godden*. Because of the filming schedule for *It Always Rains*, he was required to keep this less-than-immaculate appearance. At an East End screening of *It Always Rains*, when Googie introduced John as her future husband, there were cheers but someone in the audience who knew how John had felled her with a blow in the film shouted out, 'Don't sock her in the jaw any more!' In another newspaper article, there was a still from the film showing John with his hand over Googie's mouth and the caption was: 'Latest picture of the happy couple.' Googie, on another occasion, remarked of the scene, 'A fine start for our married life'.

In spite of those newspaper reports of their 'being seen together frequently around town' and of John's insisting that 'we have a lot in common and like each other's company. We are doing our second film together and I think Googie is a fine actress', he was still quoted as saying there was 'no truth in the rumour that we intend to marry'. Well, that was reported in June 1947, by which time they were actually living together, but by the following November it was official and the scenario for the next sixty-odd years was set in place. They became engaged on 24 November. John met her with a proposal when she returned home from New York and Googie was widely quoted as saying, 'I gave my answer during the interval of *The Taming of the Shrew* which we saw the same night – but we did not see the funny side of it till afterwards.' Googie was never in any sense a 'shrew', but equally she was too firm-minded and self-reliant to need or respond to 'taming' – and John was far too affable, in any case, to be a 'tamer'. There is actually another account, in an interview fifty years on, that suggests the proposal was put when John was watching the Royal Wedding and, at the moment of the young Princess Elizabeth's saying 'I will', he rang up Googie, put the question and received an answer which followed the Princess's example. We may simply have to live with the uncertainty surrounding this crucial moment.

It Always Rains on Sunday had its first London release on 25 November, just a day after the engagement, which received an amazing amount of newspaper coverage, in both London and provincial papers and of course in Australia. Much was made of the hope that it wouldn't rain on Saturday as they planned to marry just two months later at the fashionable St. George's Church, Hanover Square, on Saturday 24 January, 1948. In that era publicity now seems remarkably polite but enthusiasm for the couple still comes through. Googie at 30 and John at 29 were clearly not youngsters rushing headlong into marriage, and the reporting of the imminent event reflects the sense of two people who've come to know and respect each other after working together in the demanding climate of filmmaking. Many of the accounts stress the fact that they had made three films together (the mermaid comedy, *Miranda*, was finished but not released till the following April), as though to suggest that this is not just a celebrity match but the happy fulfilment in personal terms of what has been a rewarding professional partnership.

By the time of the wedding they were very well known as film stars. Having thrown themselves into the publicising of their films, and with every sign of enjoying themselves (whether they were or not), they attracted large crowds whenever they appeared in public, whether it was a charity performance of *Hamlet* attended by royals, or a charity cricket match at Oxton. Googie had known the value of publicity from the early days of her dizzy-blonde 1930s films and John, a shrewd businessman among other talents, quickly adapted to the film star's public role. In the lead-up to the wedding there were at least three personal appearances, associated with screenings, at Dalston, Woolwich and Camberwell. By this time they'd acquired a large troupe of friends, to ask all of whom to the wedding would have required Westminster Abbey, according to one comment. So, the chosen three hundred were invited to St George's at 3.30 pm, and afterwards to Claridge's, while another large crowd waited outside for a sighting of the popular couple.

Among those guests well-known at the time were directors Ken Annakin, Charles Frend, Robert Hamer, Anthony Kimmins, and Basil Dearden, producers Sydney Box and Betty Box, cinematographer Douglas Slocombe, actors Dame Edith Evans, Raymond Huntley and many more. It is worth listing such names to suggest how this couple had made friends with so many they'd worked with. The weather sadly was not kind and did lead to much punning along the lines of how it always rains on Saturday, as for example, in *Sunday Graphic* which ran a very large picture of the happy couple and some further ones of Googie gamely smiling from under a large umbrella, as she emerges from church.

In the official wedding photos, the work of the celebrated 'Baron' and his assistant, young Anthony Armstrong-Jones, there are plenty of shots of Googie's parents, Captain and Mrs Withers, and of John's father with whom John had some time before lived in a hotel at Lancaster Gate, but none of his mother. Not even in the Tatler , which ran a double-page spread of pictures from the occasion. She was living at the time in Manly, Sydney, and the *Sydney Sun* had written that she 'will come to England, probably by plane, for the wedding.' Earlier, John had expressed the hope that she would overcome her dislike of flying and that she would bring a family diamond ring with her for Googie. In fact, she did not get to the wedding, but watched excerpts from it as a newsreel item in a Sydney cinema, and a few years later when she was referring to Googie, in flattering terms, it sounded rather as if this was after their first meeting. John's parents appear to have become estranged, as indeed did Googie's, but it is hard to be certain of when or even on what grounds from the remaining information. Maybe the knowledge of crumbling marital partnerships on both sides of the newly married pair would in the decades ahead work positively for them.

The honeymoon was spent first in Bournemouth, at the Norfolk Hotel, where they first met the actor Jack Hawkins and his wife, Doreen, who was expecting their first child. Googie would later work with Hawkins, and the two couples became life-long friends. The next stage of the honeymoon was spent in the quiet village of Cong in Western Ireland, where Googie scored a hole-in-one in the first golf game she ever played – and then gave it up for life. Even on honeymoon they weren't entirely free from the exigencies of stardom and found themselves making a public appearance at the Theatre Royal in Dublin. Where to live as a married couple was the next matter to settle. Googie had for some time been living in what a rather gushing reporter described as 'an enchanting flat in Portland Place'. However 'enchanting' it was, they felt it was not really big enough for two people and they settled then on a tall Georgian house in St. John's Wood. Googie greatly enjoyed – and had flair for – decorating the various houses they lived in. Here in Avenue Road, she had the drawing-room, a lofty apartment, papered and painted in ivory and gold, with Regency furniture and comfortable chairs covered with green brocade. The windows looked on the large smooth lawn and surrounding flower beds, giving scope for John as an enthusiastic and knowledgeable gardener. The numerous journalists who would seek them out over the decades ahead would all comment on these complementary home-making skills, which no doubt played their roles in this long-lasting partnership.

Meanwhile, *It Always Rains on Sunday* with its richly textured picture of lives in the post-war East End was attracting praise from discerning critics, though C.A. Lejeune's delicate sensibilities were again upset, this time it seems because the film is concerned with the sorts of people she wouldn't want to have tea with. Her particular distaste was for the 'spivs' who plied their trade in the markets and pubs on this East End Sunday. She is sure that 'there are a great number of people who positively loathe and detest a film about a spiv. I am one of them, and when I encounter a film like *It Always Rains on Sunday*, in which every other man is a spiv, and every other woman his dupe or victim, it is clear that the merits of this piece of work will appeal to me but faintly.' It's hard to believe now in what esteem she was once held, but fortunately her ineffably genteel, middle-class revulsion from the world of this film (inaccurately as she describes that 'world') was not universally echoed – and, to be fair, she does allow the film some virtues, when she grudgingly writes: 'The playing, too, is not uniformly bad', but without mentioning either of the recently engaged stars! Fortunately, from the point of view of not casting a blight on their recent real-life co-starring role, there were plenty of other reviews, which applauded the authenticity of the picture of the life explored in the film. One reviewer, not for a major daily or Sunday paper, perceptively noted the way the film avoids 'piling on the gloomy effects just for the sake of gloom' and how its 'humour is not artificially superimposed, one feels, but springs from the innate character of the people – they are, after all, the same people who withstood the worst of the blitz and joked while the bombs were falling.'

For the McCallums, this was a very significant production. It established them as a major acting partnership – this had been glimpsed in *The Loves of Joanna Godden*, certainly, but the later film gave them opportunity to enact a raw, sexually-based passion that was not common in British film at the time. It put them at a considerable remove, in public response too, from the famous contemporary duo of Anna Neagle and Michael Wilding. (Nothing to disturb Miss Lejeune there.) By this time Googie had built a substantial reputation as a serious dramatic actress on screen, having put her 1930s image well behind her. There were many notable actresses in British cinema at this time, but none dared to be quite so bold, so brazenly sensual. She once said when I put this to her, 'If you're toff you can act common, but if you're common you can't do toff.' There may not be any reliable research on this matter but she undoubtedly could do both 'toff' and 'common'. John was equally able to shed his gentlemanly demeanour in the interests of playing convincingly the sort of wide boy who grows into a robbery-with-violence convict and won't stop short of knocking down the former lover who has been trying to help him. Somehow, the range of films they were able to do together seems to presage the long and productive personal as well as professional life they were just setting out on. Marriage and respected stardom meant that 1948 got off to a great start for them. An early 1948 film poll would shortly place them as 5th (Googie) and 8th (John) in the 'Top Ten British Film Actors and Actresses'. This can't have hurt their chances for the year ahead.

Chapter 4

A VERY BUSY COUPLE

Marriage certainly didn't slow down the careers of either John or Googie. It was never likely that Googie, any more than Joanna Godden or any other of the independently-minded women she'd played so successfully, would settle into quiet domesticity. Nor would John have wanted her to do so. They both had strong views about the viability of combining marriage with careers, and the years immediately following were some of their most productive.

In these years, from early 1948 to late 1954, it is not only remarkable how much work they did and how varied it was, but they were again and again interviewed about their views on marriage and households – and running two careers in each of these. Their replies no doubt reflect astuteness on their parts: they knew the professional value of keeping in the public eye. They were obviously not going to be railing against each other or the institution of marriage in the press, but there is a persuasive consistency in the way that they talk about each other and their work. They sound like two people who respect each other's individuality while utterly valuing the partnership.

John told a reporter in the *Daily Herald* that he thought Googie was a perfect wife because 'She's good-tempered; always looks nice to come home to and go out with; tact comes easy to her; she's a good manager, both professionally and in private life, and she's warm-hearted and affectionate'... But he added, 'Don't tell her this', in case it "undermines his position in future arguments"'. A little later in an article headed 'The Same-Job Wife Joins In', Googie was on record as saying 'I try to see that John has a separate professional existence... any man who boasts that his wife is his severest critic is either a fool or a liar.' If this particular 'severest critic' cliché were enacted in real life, she contended, 'the marriage would collapse in no time'. The pair attracted a great deal of newspaper and magazine interest during these years immediately following their marriage, partly no doubt because they were very active professionally during this period and perhaps also because they always gave articulate copy to their interviewers. And as Googie said, 'Being "in pictures" together, John and I share the same gossip, the same views, we are constantly meeting and working with people in the same business.'

The next two films they did together were popular enough at the time but now seem a comedown after *Joanna Godden* and *It Always Rains…* Both are feather-light comedies based on popular if undemanding stage successes. The mermaid comedy, *Miranda*, was finished by the time they were married and released in the following April. When a doctor on holiday in Cornwall is beguiled into bringing the eponymous mermaid back to London, passing her off as a wheelchair-bound patient, he causes problems in his own household and further afield. As you might expect, from such an unusual house-guest. Googie plays the doctor's sophisticated but increasingly suspicious wife, while John plays her best friend's slightly bohemian artist fiancé. Given that Miranda is played by the very fetching Glynis Johns, her effect on the men she meets comes as no surprise. Googie brings a practised coolness and timing to her role, and there are moments when her humour gives a bite to a scene as she observes men falling for Miranda, and John, after a couple of rough-hewn types in his previous films, has his first chance at film comedy. The film attracted quite a bit of publicity about the use of the studio tank, the mermaid's fish-tail (the final credit indeed reads: 'The Mermaid's Tail by Dunlop'), and for the use of London locations (outside Buckingham Palace, Chelsea Embankment). However, most of the material about the cast relates to Glynis Johns and Margaret Rutherford as the eccentric nurse who delights in her fishy 'patient'.

Some reviewers welcomed the film as 'a good change from violence and spivs, and from the gloom which has pervaded the British cinema for so long', and as 'a relief to be able to sit back and have a good laugh. *Miranda* is a cascade of comedy'. These outnumbered the couple that took exception to the final shot of the mermaid sitting on a rock with a baby as 'giv[ing] a distinctly unpleasant tinge to what had seemed innocent fun'. What would such genteel reviewers have made of today's idea of sex comedy where it all hangs out – quite literally in many cases?

Neither John nor Googie is in any way stretched by the demands of their roles in *Miranda*; nor are they by their next joint film venture, and this kind of light romantic comedy was arguably not John's forté. *Traveller's Joy* draws its not-too-hearty laughs from the plight of post-war British travellers trying to enjoy themselves abroad on the inadequate sterling they were permitted to take out of the country. Googie and John play a couple called Bumble and Reggie Pelham (names that could only have derived from a West End comedy of the period). They play with easy confidence but it is probably true that the best laughs come from their American co-star, Yolande Donlan, and a roll-call of British character actors such as Dora Bryan and Maurice Denham. I suspect John was being loyal to his employers when he described it as his 'favourite role'.

Much of *Traveller's Joy* was set in Sweden, and the luxurious Gustav Adolph Square hotel, Stockholm, was recreated at Shepherd's Bush studios in London. Filming began in January 1949, but was held up when John became ill with jaundice. Production had to be shut down after the shooting of all possible scenes without him, and Sydney Box, head of production, claimed that the cost of a week's hold-up was more than £12,000. Googie also became a bit unwell after overdoing the eating of Swedish *hors d'oeuvres*, about which matter one reporter rather ungallantly wrote: 'Googie Withers is no believer in half-measures' and this had 'led to her tucking-in in a scene for the film'! She did, in fact, famously relish her food. Their first wedding anniversary fell on 25 January, 1949, and the *Daily Mirror* noted this with a photo report of Googie's serving John food in bed, with champagne, to celebrate the first of what would prove to be sixty-two such milestones.

Googie's next film, *Once Upon a Dream* (1949), is a mildly amusing comedy of misunderstandings but hardly worthy of the actress who'd made those strong features at Ealing. Indeed, No. 1 box-office star Margaret Lockwood had reputedly turned it down before it was offered to Googie, and one critic wrote of it: '... even the adorable Googie left my withers unwrung'. She plays an army officer's wife who dreams she has fallen in love with her husband's batman, towards whom she is alternately imperious and seductive. Though the story is feeble, Googie manages what few other British actresses of her day could: that is, she is properly saucy and knowing as she plays with the idea of a woman's sexuality and how it might be open to the same persuasions as a man's. This doesn't mean that the film is a clarion call for Women's Lib, but only that she could carry off the mix of seductiveness and wit with a panache that reminds one of the great heroines of American 'screwball' comedies of the 1930s. At one point during production, Googie (with director Ralph Thomas, and co-stars Griffith Jones and Guy Middleton) was trapped in a lift at Shepherd's Bush Studios. She tore the nightgown she was wearing as she squeezed out the opening, missed lunch, and had to take a bath and have her clothes cleaned before shooting could resume. Given her passion for hats she must have been pleased with the extravagant concoctions designed for the film by Julie Harris: when she was interviewed in 1949, Googie was emphatic that 'A woman should never be without one. Shoes, gloves, handbags, stockings … the whole thing is incomplete without a hat, just remember that'. Strong views she may have had on such matters, but Oscar-winning Harris had only happy memories of dressing her in this film and in *Traveller's Joy*: 'I don't recall any scenes, no stamping her foot and saying "I won't wear that", and she was a good size to dress, not one of these little midgets. We had a good rapport and became friends.'

Squeezed in between the making of these undemanding films, she was also involved in such varied activities as judging the Bakery Beauty Queen at the Bakery Industries Ball and, next day, serving on the Liberal Party's National Committee. Does the latter suggest some serious political affiliation in her past?

The Rank Organization, to whom John was under contract, clearly thought it was on to a good thing. He had acquired a certain matinee-idol standing, through the skillful handling of the press, and Rank rather rushed him through several other films at this time. The *Yorkshire Evening Post* noted that 'John McCallum is fast staking a claim as personal appearance champion of the Rank Organisation', while *Movie Magazine* hailed 'Britain's New Male Star – John McCallum'. Singly or with Googie, he was constantly being photographed at film premières, or playing in charity cricket matches, or giving views on actors' profit-sharing, or 'Working with the wife', or finding himself listed in Britain's top ten film actors.

In between the two comedies with Googie, he appeared in starring roles in three other films. The first was the racetrack thriller *The Calendar*, based on a play by the prolific Edgar Wallace. John plays a likable but impoverished ex-Captain who has got himself engaged to a blonde siren played by Greta Gynt. Anyone familiar with British films of the later 1940s would realise that no good would come of that – she was always far too soignée and sleek, as if dressed by courtesy of the black-market, and with an eye to where the money was. Fortunately, after a series of reverses on and off the racetrack, there is a softer target for his affections in the person of the actress Sonia Holm (his girlfriend in *Miranda*, and in *Joanna Godden*, until Googie's Joanna edged her out).

Again, there was much publicity, this time mainly re locations at Epsom and Hurst Park Racecourse and the use of real jockeys, as well as to do with the building of a replica of the owners' stand at Ascot. But this attention to details of place did the film little good. The then-influential critic Paul Dehn headed his review 'A Waste of Celluloid', going on to say that Wallace's story had been 'brought up to date by inserting a shot of the King and Queen at Ascot. In all other respects its characters are as obsolete as cloche hats and not half as amusing.' That other influential critic, Richard Winnington, deemed it impossible to make a film from Edgar Wallace's 'mildewed sporting farce.' Seen today, the film does look predictable and pallid, but John cuts a handsome figure (especially in morning dress in the Ascot scene) as the increasingly desperate hero, and the reviewer in *Sound* felt that John 'certainly looks the sort of chap you'd like to be', while *The Star* labelled his performance as 'pleasantly wayward'. This is obviously unremarkable stuff, but if you were building a film career the exposure was doubtless valuable, as was the publicity you got from being billed as 'This Week's Profile' in *Northern Scot*, even if they'd misspelled your name as John M'Callum. Then in autumn 1948, *Movie* magazine announced him as 'Britain's New Male Star'. Remember, this is the high point of cinema-going attendance in Britain and to be the subject of such flattering notice can only have been valuable in career terms.

More attractive was the film he made largely on location in Yorkshire. This was called, if you can believe it, *A Boy, a Girl and a Bike*. In the twenty-first century it may be hard to imagine a film with such an ingenuous title, but, unpretentious as it is, it has a real charm about its dealings with a rural cycling club, and was originally to be called 'Wheels within Wheels'. It's about as far as one can imagine from the special effects-driven blockbusters of today when the bikes would no doubt be required to hurtle into all kinds of computer-generated disasters.

The entire film unit moved from Gainsborough's London studios to go to the North Yorkshire market town of Grassington, for five or six weeks, then shifted to Halifax. There was much press interest in the location shots of the Charles Fox Memorial Race and in the casting of Halifax girl Margaret Avery as the teenage Ginger. Some exterior scenes were shot in the rocky limestone of Craven Dales and Wharfedale, and Halifax and Hebden Bridge provided the industrial background. Shoring up local interest, the film's racing adviser was the team manager of the Halifax Racing Cycling Club, and local members appeared in cycling scenes. So did John and other actors who had to throw themselves into this unaccustomed sport if they weren't going to look like rank novices among the local cycling stars. One journal reported that 'Patrick Holt rides like a seasoned racer [and] J McCallum, cast as a convert to cycling who ultimately becomes an expert, is equally adept.' John, now with several notable episodes of film fisticuffs behind him, this time has a dust-up with Patrick Holt, who is his rival in several respects in the story, both on the track and in romance. The cause of romantic rivalry was played by Honor Blackman, future Pussy Galore in the Bond saga, *Goldfinger*, but then just starting.

Not that the shooting all went smoothly. There was a lot of bad weather leading to quick takes when the sun shone, and there was the danger of racing-bikes skidding on wet roads. The *Yorkshire Evening News* reported that

'A cloudy day in the Dales costs £200'. This paper also reported two days later that 'Googie comes to Yorkshire', and it's to her presence on location that we owe a choice recollection. Also in the film's cast was future blonde-bombshell type Diana Dors, in one of her earliest roles and before she was a name and face to be reckoned with. One night the cast and crew were relaxing at a local pub, when Googie noticed hordes of customers besieging Dors for autographs. Considering how unknown Dors was at the time, Googie was puzzled and decided to check out the situation. She returned to her party to report, 'She's signing herself Lana Turner!'

As always when the McCallums were on location, John threw himself into the life of the Yorkshire Dales communities in which they were filming. Here, for instance, he was reported as opening a Road Safety Exhibition at Brighouse and presenting a cheque at the Regal Cinema, Skipton, on behalf of the Cinematograph Trades Benevolent Fund. The film was modestly well received, and now seems to have acquired a certain nostalgia element, for the rural beauty of its uncluttered roads and an era when cycling was just a fun pastime, not having yet acquired all its environmentally correct associations. Also, the element of skullduggery – fixing a bike's brakes to cause a problem, a bit of illegal bookmaking – now looks simplicity itself. John remembered it forty years later with affection: 'It was a lovely little film, and a lovely location. There we were, just after we were married, up in the Yorkshire Dales, which is still our favourite part of northern England.'

Rank then moved John into *The Woman in Question*, a more ambitious production, directed by the highly regarded Anthony Asquith and starring popular '40s star Jean Kent, with whom John had appeared in *Joanna Godden*. In the new film, Jean, in a role originally intended for Bette Davis, plays Astra, a fairground fortune-teller who is strangled and whose life is explored from the viewpoints of five different people who've had dealings with her. John was a cheerful, drunken Irish sailor, one of her many male friends, a role which one reviewer felt he 'unhappily overplayed'. Years later, Jean said that she felt 'the nearest to what she [Astra] was really like was probably the character in the John McCallum episode – the good-hearted, don't-care-very-much sort of girl. This is the point I started from.' This is a film whose reputation has grown with the years and, given that Rank was pushing John through films at this stage, capitalising on the attention he was getting from the press, he was fairly lucky with the range and quality they offered.

Valley of the Eagles, an adventure set in Norway and Russia, with Cold War overtones, and largely filmed in Norway and Sweden, saw John, as some reviewers pointed out, somewhat improbably cast as a Swedish scientist, but the film had its quota of action, given a political as well as a romantic slant, and visually it is dominated by some spectacular snowy vistas, threatened by eagles and avalanches. John's scientist has discovered a way of converting sound waves into electrical energy, but his faithless wife and his assistant make off with the secret to Russia. It all ends well of course for the free world, scientific advancement and romantic pairing. Googie went along to the location for some of the time, perhaps, as she hinted years later, to keep an eye on John's very attractive leading lady Nadia Gray.

Sources as disparate as the *Hollywood Reporter* and *Bulawayo Sunday News* (Southern Rhodesia) praised John's performance, even if he didn't look the part. Actually he plays some quite interesting variants on the kinds of heroes or villains he'd done in his preceding films. With little touches of grey at the temples, some curious vocal inflections, and the wearing of spectacles (a sure sign of serious purpose in the films of the day), he brings a touch of gravitas to the role of the top-level scientist. Also, these strategies help him to play convincingly a little older than his thirty-two years. Of course, he'll shed most of these ageing signs to emerge as an action hero when the time comes, and to be ready for the final clinch (with Nadia Gray, as the Laplander heroine). He had, after all, an image to live up to. When his engagement had been announced at the same time as that of husky actor Kieron Moore, one headline ran: 'Two British screen "he-men" name their wedding days.' His he-man status must have been tested by the location work in which one reporter wrote that 'John McCallum experienced all the risks and difficulties of an Arctic expedition.' That probably overstates the case, but Pinewood Studios, where the interiors were shot, would certainly have been cosier.

Two films that drew on his Australian background made an improbable pair. They were *Lady Godiva Rides Again* (1951) and *Melba* (1953). The first is a satirical romantic comedy taking swipes at anything in sight – British railways, drab British Sundays, sleazy beauty contests – with John playing an Australian pineapple-grower who rescues a naïve young provincial woman from the perils of stripping for profit. It has its funny moments but these are not enough to hold it together. Googie has an uncredited 'guest appearance' in this, in a 'film-within-the-film' called 'Shadow of the Orient.' More dignified, if not all that much more interesting, was a largely fanciful biopic of Australia's most famous diva, Dame Nellie Melba, played without much panache by American Patrice Munsel. John played the unrewarding role of Charles Armstrong, whom she married, and the film was received with generally scathing disbelief. For instance, one review, headed 'No Peaches for Melba', felt it was 'largely ridiculous when the singing stops.'

Fortunately his other 1953 release, *The Long Memory*, gave John one of his very best roles – that of the tormented detective in a difficult marriage. This was directed by Robert Hamer who had been so influential in Googie's career and was responsible for the masterly *It Always Rains on Sunday*. The film offers a complex exploration of guilt and blame, and required John to suggest deep unease beneath the restrained surface when a man released from prison (John Mills) comes looking for vengeance, perhaps against the detective's wife who had framed him for the murder he hadn't committed. The film got off to a fashionable start with the Duchess of Gloucester at the première in aid of RADA, and John went to well-publicised previews in Glasgow, Newcastle, Bristol and Leeds. He also received laudatory notices from most reviewers, eliciting praise from the *Sunday Times*'s astute Dilys Powell and from Leonard Mosley in the *Daily Express*, saying that '… as a Scotland Yard detective, John McCallum creates sympathy, strength and affection.'

Somehow, while all these films were appearing in rapid succession, John also found time to fit in several stage appearances. In 1948, with permission of the Rank Organisation with which he had a seven-year contract, he returned to the People's Palace, Mile End Road, East London, to play Dick Dudgeon in Shaw's *The Devil's Disciple*. This was a sentimental journey to the theatre that had given him his first professional chance back in 1939. The *East End*

News reported that John gave 'a splendid performance and full value to one of melodrama's most interesting heroes', and the *Sydney Sun* loyally offered the headline 'John McCallum a Hit in London Stage Play'. There were two other stage ventures (again with Rank's permission) slotted in among all the filmmaking: *Western Wind* at the Piccadilly Theatre, in September 1949, and *View Over the Park* at the Lyric Hammersmith, inAugust 1950. None of these plays can be said to have taken off, but the mere fact of his involvement in them, along with his first television work, indicates how much in demand he was at this point, the demand fuelled by his film reputation. The television debut was in a BBC play called *Interlude in Eden*, by James Parish, with John playing 'an ex-RAF officer who nurses his secret that he has only a few months to live'. It went to air on Sunday 10 April, 1949. It had been very well publicised, but was not very well received, dismissed as 'a flabby work' by *The Observer*'s C.A. Lejeune in a rare sortie into television reviewing. Googie had been seen on television as early as 1937 when she appeared in a programme simply entitled *Songs*.

While all this filmmaking was going on for John, Googie returned to the stage in a now-forgotten play called *Champagne for Delilah* at London's New Theatre in June 1949, after opening in Leeds. This play, a comedy that made its fun at the expense of stage and film people, was written by Ronald Millar, with whom both John and Googie would be reunited a little later. It had a strong cast including Nigel Patrick and Irene Worth as well as Googie, and its failure to run must have been a disappointment to Googie who had not appeared in a play since *They Came to a City* in 1943, which had also been first staged in Leeds. Her most significant production at this time was that of daughter Joanna.

In spite of what looks like a hectic professional time on stage, film and most recently television, there was also – and always – much more going on in the lives of this busy couple. For one thing, there was the matter of houses. Having lavished a good deal of attention on the elegantly appointed house in Avenue Road, St John's Wood, they had planned to let the top two rooms because, as a working couple, they didn't need a whole house to themselves. But the arrival of Joanna changed that. She was born at the Welbeck Street

Nursing Home, London, on 27 June 1950, and named for the film that had brought her parents together.

Joanna's arrival, much noted in the press, led them to settle on the top storey for a nursery. Whether Googie's mother, who was living with them, fancied the stairs as a regular access to the black-haired granddaughter is not recorded, but she did live with them for much of the McCallums' married life and gave great support to the hard-working pair. Inevitably there were the odd inter-generational conflicts, about for instance when babies should be fed, but the two strong-minded women seem to have valued each other's presence. There would also be nannies to help out on the domestic scene, and Googie, while she enjoyed motherhood, was never going to give up her career to be a stay-at-home wife. Being interviewed at this early stage of Joanna's life, in an article entitled 'So Googie put on an apron' she revealed that she had plenty of film scripts sent to her but none of them seemed quite right.

If none of the film scripts appealed to her, the stage was offering more attractive opportunities. In April 1952, she appeared at the St James's Theatre, London, after a provincial tour, as Georgie Elgin in Clifford Odets' *Winter Journey*, as the wife of a once-famous actor whose career has been imperilled by alcoholism. The director of the possible comeback play believes Georgie is the real cause of Frank's problems and this makes for serious tensions between Georgie and him. This was the first of several co-starring roles with Michael Redgrave, with whom she had fleetingly appeared in the Hitchcock film, *The Lady Vanishes*, in 1938. For much of the play's length Georgie seems an unsympathetic character, and more than one woman in the audience was heard to whisper 'She's a nasty piece of work'. But Googie was never one to shy away from depicting some of life's harsher realities (in past films, she'd done murder, for heaven's sake), and she made this seemingly weary woman, trying to safeguard her husband from his darker possibilities, in the long run admirable in her tenacity, and she won almost universal critical plaudits. This was her most demanding stage role to date (she would play it again in Australia) and epithets like 'memorable', 'wonderfully eloquent' and, several times, 'superb' pepper the reviews.

All may have worked brilliantly for audiences but *Winter Journey* was not without its offstage dramas. For one thing, Redgrave and the American actor Sam Wanamaker, who was also directing, clashed frequently in their views about what should be done and how. According to Googie, Wanamaker disapproved of Redgrave's drinking, and the conflict between them at one point led to their throwing chairs at each other. As for Googie, she had a domestic crisis. Her understudy, Patricia Marmont, recalled how Joanna, aged two, was with them on the pre-London week in Bournemouth:

> She fell and cut her forehead and had to be stitched by a brilliant surgeon who was the father of one of the 'Two Fat Ladies' who years later did the cookery programme. Poor Googie was hysterical and we tried to calm her by saying that having hysterics wasn't going to make it any better. I think I went on just for the matinee. First, it was a matter of trying to find me who was out sightseeing, and they finally caught up with me and took me to the theatre for a run-through, so I didn't have much time to think. But thank heavens I knew the part, which quite often on tour people don't get a chance to because they're too busy rehearsing their own parts. Sam said "Whenever you come to scenes with me, if you skip something I'll follow you. Don't bother about moves." The hiatus moment I remember was when I had to help him into a jacket that's hanging on a chair and I hadn't noticed a sleeve was hanging inside out, so there was a fuss getting him into it. It threw me terribly.

Joanna still recalls having to be held down while the surgeon did his work because she wasn't given an anaesthetic. So, quite early on Googie was getting experience of the dual role of actress and mother.

On a larger scale of collateral dramas, there was also an enormous downpour of rain that crashed through the roof of the St James's Theatre on 6 June 1952, not surprisingly bringing the performance to a halt. The storm that raged across Britain from the west caused all manner of chaos, including the flooding of a hospital basement ward and the stranding of 15,000 people in the Battersea Festival Gardens where the storm created a lake marooning them. At the theatre, Googie in a light summer dress was dodging round the puddles on the stage and shouting her lines so as to be heard over the thunder and rain. The *Daily Express* next day reported that Sam Wanamaker had announced the halting of the performance at 9.15 for fear of lights fusing, while Googie said, 'Michael and I were trying to keep straight faces and to concentrate on our parts – but every time we looked into the wings we could see people with umbrellas up or floundering about in oilskins'.

Fraught as the peripheral circumstances were, the play went on to real success, and both Michael Redgrave and Googie stayed with it until 4 October when they were released because they were both too tired to continue in the play any longer. They were each playing very demanding roles, so this is not too surprising. Tired she may have been but three months later she was back on stage in perhaps the most challenging role of her career. This was Hester Collyer, in Terence Rattigan's *The Deep Blue Sea*, one of the toughest roles for women in 20th-century British drama.

In this lacerating study of an unequal relationship between a married woman and perennially immature ex-RAF type, the challenge for Googie was not just in the rawness and anguish she had to convey but also in the fact that the role had been created by Peggy Ashcroft to great acclaim, and she had been briefly replaced over the Christmas period of 1952 by Celia Johnson. Nevertheless, following in these pairs of revered footsteps, Googie somehow contrived to make the part her own, as critics who came back for a second look found. An interesting note was struck by the reviewer who felt that 'She is not quite so poignant as the other two, but she somehow makes it more credible than they did that such a woman could love such a man so desperately.' Jean Kent, her co-star from *The Loves of Joanna Godden*, who had also played Hester on a South African tour, bore this out. She had seen all three of the distinguished London leading ladies and had no hesitation in proclaiming Googie's the finest, saying that she felt Googie suggested most powerfully the kind of passion that drives Hester. A year later Googie would reprise the role on television, for which she won the TV Producers' Guild award for Best Performance by an actress – and Leonard Mosley's tribute in the *Daily Express*: 'Her performance, in my opinion, was the most moving piece of acting we have ever seen on TV', and at the end of the year

TV Mirror featured her as cover-girl and 'Actress of the Year'. Heady stuff indeed, but it needs to be remembered when we come to the upheaval of the following year.

'The main thing in a woman's life is to have a home, a husband and children. I would drop acting and sweep streets, rather than sacrifice my home,' Googie (in semi-contradiction of some of her other utterances) told an interviewer in January 1954, just a few weeks into her triumph in *The Deep Blue* Sea. Fortunately such deprivations and rigours never proved necessary, but, on the domestic front, life was taking a major turn. The McCallum family was moving house from St John's Wood to go to Denham in Buckinghamshire, where they settled for 'The Mirrie', a handsome two-storeyed farmhouse with a spacious garden for Joanna – and their boxer dog, Mutz – to run wild in. Both John and Googie loved the countryside, but because of the demands of their professional lives they needed to find a place that was also within easy commuting distance of London. Denham was just about ideal from this point of view, as some of their friends, including John and Mary Mills, had found.

As she told several interviewers for women's magazines, Googie liked 'experimenting' in the matter of home decoration, in colours and materials, and said she would happily have changed colour schemes every two years – if it weren't for a sense of thrift. As they had a maid and a secretary at this point, necessary for them to maintain their acting careers, that 'sense of thrift' may have been a necessary precaution in other matters. They found, for instance, that keeping hens was an expensive pursuit, with four eggs a day costing about 13s6d to produce. The twelve-roomed house boasted some promising vines, which led Googie to enthuse, 'We've been reading up on wine-making,' though they seem not to have established their own label. Maybe she was being extravagant in her claims about giving up acting in the interests of 'home', but both she and John seem to have embraced turning 'The Mirrie' into a home both elegant and supremely comfortable, geared to the needs of two professionals who nevertheless wanted more from life than just what those admittedly rewarding professions yielded.

The papers, and especially the women's journals, were happy to record the minutiae of their lives. The *Woman's Weekly*, in a long article replete with coloured illustrations of the house, even tracked Googie as she went about shopping in nearby Gerrard's Cross. For readers insatiable for such detail, she told her interviewer about how she and cook-housekeeper Dorothy would work out the list of what was needed and then off she, Googie, would go to do the buying. It seems to chime with her gregarious nature when she said, 'Although I could do all the ordering by telephone, I prefer to choose things myself... I suppose it's because of my Continental ancestry that I like to go and look and prod', and there are pictures of her discussing a salmon's weight with the butcher, while the interviewer snaps the moment. In May the following year, *Homes and Gardens* ran five pages of sepia photographs of the imposing interiors and elegant exteriors of 'The Mirrie'. It was a long way from the zealous charting of the sex lives of the famous that now demand our attention on the covers of popular magazines.

Throughout their long careers, though Googie and John enjoyed working together, they never made it a condition of the employment of one that the other should be part of the hiring arrangement. However, both were drawn to *Waiting for Gillian*, the first play they ever did together. She had miscarried her second baby shortly before this, which may have been a further incentive for her wish to take on Ronald Millar's adroit adaptation of Nigel Balchin's novel, *A Way through the Woods* (filmed fifty years later as *Separate Lies*). The play opened at the Opera House, Manchester, on 12th April 1954, before making its way in to the St James's Theatre, London. With its basis in a hit-and-run accident and marital infidelity, it had a mixed reception from the critics, regarded by several as being somewhat old-fashioned in its values but reliably enough constructed. There was a good deal of praise for the acting. *The Times* was typical in its reaction: 'Miss Withers imposes what emotional power she can on the part, but... she is given no words to express her emotional turmoil. Mr John McCallum makes something that is not boring out of the prig who is willing to shed his priggishness.' If there was some consensus that Googie's role was underwritten for the sort of demands it seemed to make on her, or for the kinds of strength she so easily imparted, most also agreed that John, on the West End stage for the first time in four film-packed years, made something compelling of a prosaic, good man.

Absent from the West End he may have been, but John managed to squeeze in among the many films a play called *Night of the Fourth*, a thriller by Jack Roffey and Gordon Harbord about 'split personality', which opened in Edinburgh on 13 April, 1953 and toured extensively but failed to make it into London. Starring with the notable Hungarian actor Paul Lukas, John played a police superintendent and, while his performance generally attracted favourable notice for its quiet conviction, the *Manchester Evening Chronicle* reviewer wrote that his 'distraught appearance … on discovering that he might be the criminal looked to me more like the plight of a man ready to visit his dentist with a bad filling'. No such cavil prevented his being besieged by delighted female fans when the play reached Bolton, where he met again his brother-in-law Colonel Harry Withers whose military headquarters were in Bolton. In an interview at this time, he put forward the view that people 'often make better stage actors and actresses by virtue of their film experience …[in which] every fleeting expression, every twitch of a muscle is seen by the audience and magnified many times larger than life. This teaches absolute control, a feat which is just as useful in the theatre.' This may not have been a popular point of view with the theatrical fraternity, but it does suggest an actor who has thought about his profession. Years later in Australia, Googie made a similar comparison, speaking as one who had learnt her trade in film and then found naturalistic techniques that she could readily apply to the stage.

In this hectic period of their lives, the first six years of their marriage in early 1948, you feel there must have been an element of the workaholic about them, considering they were also starting a family and setting up house in a very substantial way. One old friend indeed confirmed this trait in Googie in particular, but felt they both had great stamina, even if John might sometimes have settled for more restful periods. Those first six years of their married life were astoundingly busy, professionally and personally. Each of them went on to do other films, including some of their most notable screen performances, and there was radio and television work. And it's not as if the domestic scene was being neglected; nor were the numerous social and/or publicity occasions either.

After the comparatively frothy romantic comedies of the late '40s, Googie had two remarkably strong roles in contrasting films: the *film noir* gangster drama, *Night and the City*, in 1950 and, in her last great screen role, the hospital drama, *White Corridors*, in 1951. *Night and the City* remains arguably the finest British *noir* thriller, much of it shot in Soho, the docklands area (before their being reclaimed to yuppie prosperity) and the Covent Garden streets, and it's hard to think of another British actress who could have endowed the character of Helen Nosseros with such sensual command as Googie brings to it. She plays the unfaithful wife of nightclub owner Phil Nosseros: of course she's unfaithful, as he's played by Francis L. Sullivan, the best fat actor in British films, and she has her eye on an American hustler, played by Richard Widmark, who's aiming for a life of big-time skullduggery in the wrestling world. The American beauty Gene Tierney is billed above Googie but she is given almost nothing to do, while Googie takes charge of every scene in which the scheming Helen appears. The *Monthly Film Bulletin*, though, felt it gave her too little scope, and was generally sniffy about the film's attempt to transplant the American style thriller 'wholesale', claiming 'loss in the all-important quality of atmosphere'. Time has not supported this negative view.

This was a film Googie valued, though recalling her scenes with Sullivan as 'rather an unpleasant experience, principally because I'm a bit squeamish and he was very fat, and sweated a lot. I had to put my arms around him and cuddle his head.' She enjoyed working with the American actors – Widmark and Tierney – who exhibited 'none of that "big American stars" act about them,' and she admired the director Jules Dassin, a refugee from the Hollywood anti-communist blacklist and the vile Senator Joseph McCarthy. He was one of a number of American filmmakers thus forced into exile who found refuge and work in England. Some scenes of *Night and the City* were filmed in Soho and Googie remembered that most of the Soho criminal types were the real thing: 'They had been picked out by Jules, and they were ponces, racketeers, very dangerous men most of them – but they just loved being in the film.'

Back in California when the filming was over Dassin wrote to Googie that 'Your f-----g censorship is destroying *Night and the City*. This is literally true and unfortunately they have most attacked the relationship between Nosseros and Helen... Helen in the English version will make no sense at all.' He goes on to implore Googie – '<u>You</u> are the only one who can help' – to 'be creative, be daring' but 'You must do this without mentioning my name' for if it was known that he had urged her to intervene at high levels to get the censorship cuts reversed he would be 'persona non grata with 20th Century-Fox and maybe in Hollywood.' This was all surprising to Dassin because, he claimed, US censorship was 'notoriously the most narrow in the world [but] has passed the film without a single cut.' The film was finally released in England in April 1950, but it's hard to determine the extent of Googie's influence. The final result is one of the toughest, most compelling *noir* thrillers made in any country, whatever may have fallen victim to the censor's scissors. For Googie it represented a return to the more demanding territory of her earlier '40s roles after the romantic comedy respite of 1948–9. It was also her nearest brush with Hollywood as Fox was involved in setting up the production, but she was never seriously lured by the idea of the film capital, though she might well have made a potent 'bad woman' in the sorts of tough melodramas that were being made there in the '40s.

To prepare herself to act convincingly as Dr Sophie Dean in *White Corridors*, she went into Richmond Hospital every day for a month to watch doctors and other staff at work. 'I was determined to look as if I could hold a stethoscope and take someone's pulse, as if I was a surgeon.' This is a film which sets out to give a realistic idea of life in a busy hospital, and there are also several personal dramas going on as well, including the relationship between surgeon Sophie Dean and the research pathologist, Neil Marriner (James Donald), whose life she saves when he accidentally infects himself with a serum he has developed. In a 1998 interview, Googie described this as her favourite film, recalling that *Nature* magazine 'which was a worldwide scientific journal, saw the film and gave it very good notices… and recommended it for all aspiring young people who wanted to become doctors'. One of its episodes was so realistic that it caused director Pat Jackson to faint during the filming. The film's reputation, like that for *Night and the City*, has grown with the years. It was quite well received at the time and the US trade paper, *Variety* felt that 'it's in the strong-meat class as entertainment, and … it merits specialized booking in America,' while the *Monthly Film Bulletin* praised its professionalism as 'set[ting] a new standard for popular entertainment in films of this country.'

The last two films Googie and John made together before setting out for Australia at the end of 1954 were a distinct falling-off from the standard of their earlier co-starring ventures – and both were about horse-racing. These were *Derby Day* (1952) and *Devil on Horseback* (1954). *Derby Day* is a multi-story piece in which Googie and John, on the wrong side of the law, are almost the only redeeming feature. The film represents director Herbert Wilcox in decline as he puts his wife, Anna Neagle, and her regular co-star (and Googie's former boyfriend), Michael Wilding, through some very tired – and tiring – paces. Nearly forty years on Googie remembered it like this: 'Well, it was one of those things, it was a fill-in thing really. John was under contract to Herbert Wilcox to do two or three films and Herbert just thought it would be rather fun if I came along and played his girlfriend, and so we did it, but I don't think we were mad keen about it, and I hate it now when I look at it.' The reviews were full of facetious headings like 'A good bet for the summer', 'No winners', and 'A cert', but the Withers-McCallum plot strand was the only one to elicit any critical praise.

John's films for Wilcox, to whom he was under contract in the early '50s, were perhaps dim enough to make him think of the Australian venture, which was looming. *Derby Day* was a non-starter, as the reviewers might have said, and the other two – *Trent's Last Case* (1952) and *Trouble in the Glen* (1954) – were not much better. Wilcox, by the early 1950s, was past his most successful days, when wife Anna Neagle was a box-office queen. By John's account, he was 'a dear sweet man' but his working day was by now not much more than a gentle movement towards the champagne he routinely served late morning, after discussions with his ace cameraman Max Greene (aka Mutz Greenbaum), followed in the afternoon by shooting some 'terrible stuff'. *Trent's Last Case*, based on E.C. Bentley's fine detective fiction, works moderately well, with a scene-stealing turn from Orson Welles. 'Stealing' was the key term: John, who admired Welles and worked with him again in *Trouble in the Glen*, recalled ways in which he would ensure that attention in any given scene was focused on him. Wilcox hadn't the slightest chance of directing Welles against the actor's own wishes, and John, though he got on amicably with Welles, said he 'was one of those actors you act against, not with.' In one scene, he was supposed to give John, as his old Oxonian secretary, a package and 'he said "I'll hold it back John. That way the audience will wonder what this damn thing is. We'll keep it to the end of the scene", but he also knew that they were looking at him the whole time because he had this in his hand, you see!'

As for *Trouble in the Glen*, John enjoyed working with veteran Hollywood actor, Victor McLaglen, as gypsy father and son, but the resulting film is probably the one he would most have preferred to forget. Not only was Wilcox in decline but leading lady Margaret Lockwood, so popular in the '40s (and, like Googie, Karachi-born), made several films under contract to Wilcox – the two with John, plus the excruciating *Laughing Anne* (1953) – none of which restored her to box-office favour. But it could also be argued that British cinema in general, after its wonderful efflorescence in the post-war years, was running out of steam. The other film John and Googie made together in 1954, *Devil on Horseback*, was a modestly pleasing racetrack drama, which of course attracted critical headlines such as 'Odds-On Favourite' and 'On to a Good Thing'. The film is now unavailable for screening, so that one can only take contemporary reviewers on trust, when, say, *Today's Cinema* described it as 'Entertainment off the beaten track for popular audiences,' or *The Daily Recorder* considered that 'Googie Withers as the owner gives her usual faultless performance, and John McCallum as the high-minded trainer gives the picture a surprisingly elevated moral tone.' *Variety* thought that John and Googie were 'nicely teamed in the romantic leads... although only given moderate scope.'

Sandwiched in among all these plays and films, with excursions into radio and television, there was also a lot of other life going on. Mere pregnancy didn't mean that Googie was just sitting at home and knitting small garments. She did a good deal of radio work when she was carrying Jo because for that, as she said, 'It doesn't matter how you look'. She had the lead in Somerset Maugham's *The Letter* for the BBC's Light Programme, 11 November 1953, and in 1954, she did a major TV drama set in the French Revolution, Fritz Hochwaelder's *Public Prosecutor* with friend Jack Hawkins, which was received with more respect than enthusiasm. Googie recalled herself 'acting away like mad' unaware that the camera was no longer recording her but had faded away to make way for Winston Churchill's Guildhall speech on Lord Mayor's Day. Googie, who was not generally given to star tantrums, was outspoken about the difficulties of maintaining an acting performance on live TV, 'with men crawling about on the floor shifting props.'

But apart from these professional engagements and the premières and previews and touring associated with these, they were continuing to be involved in social activities such as John's doing a guest stint at the National Press Club or Googie's going to the races and indeed owning a race-horse, or arranging a birthday party for little Joanna at which the guests included the small children of the Jack Hawkinses and the Richard Attenboroughs. Speaking of 'little Joanna' she made her film debut in 1951 as the baby (well, what else at age one?) in the Festival of Britain film, *The Magic Box,* in which she joined her parents who played sitters being photographed in a studio in Bath. John, always mad on sport and especially on cricket, was again and again involved in charity matches as when he opened the batting for the Shakespeare Memorial Theatre and Stratford-on-Avon Cricket Club against the Lords Taverners' team, in September 1952. And there was a family holiday in Torremolinos, Spain, early in 1953, chosen 'because it is small and unsmart.' Their stamina must have been astounding to fit in all they did, in and out of the spotlight.

During this period, John, despite his success in films, really hankered to go back to the stage. In a 1993 interview, he claimed that he never really 'knew how to work the camera,' and that from his pre-war Stratford days he most wanted to be a classical actor. The London office of J.C. Williamson's, Australia's major theatrical firm, made overtures that were attractive and opportune: attractive in the variety of plays offered to the pair and opportune because, while both were at a peak of popularity in Britain, it was clear that the British film industry was in a sort of doldrums and the McCallums were not likely to be attracted to the 'angry-young-men' theatre which was soon to bring sweeping changes to the London stage. But, undeniably, the first six years of their marriage had been wildly productive, professionally and personally: they would embark on their Australian venture while very much in the ascendant in England.

Chapter 5

HEADING SOUTH

It used often to be said, and with some truth, that stars of overseas theatrical distinction only came to Australia when their drawing power was on the wane in their country of origin. This was probably the case with such names as the Frank Lawton-Evelyn Laye duo or Jessie Matthews who, in the early 1950s, came trailing clouds of what had once been glory to appear in such plays as, respectively, *September Tide* (1951) and *Larger than Life* (1952). But, as with the Oliviers in 1948, this could not have been said of the Withers-McCallum partnership. They elected to leave England when they were almost at the peak of their popularity and achievement.

So why did they choose to leave and what were they actually leaving? There was an enormous amount of newspaper coverage of their decision, not all of it absolutely consistent, but then that is apt to be the way of such prolific reporting. For one thing, Googie's second pregnancy had miscarried in earlier 1954 and, though the family was happily settled in the beautiful, much-written-about and -photographed house, 'The Mirrie', at Denham, with Joanna at four-and-a-half having young friends in the village, perhaps this disappointment might have encouraged Googie to embrace the idea of something entirely new. On the other hand, she had just scored her greatest theatrical triumph to date in *The Deep Blue Sea*, initially on stage and then on television when one critic described her performance as the 'greatest' seen to date on the small screen. Further, she had turned down the offer of the leading role in the US stage import, *Wonderful Town* (the musical version of the comedy, *My Sister Eileen*), claiming that she felt it should be played by an American actress. Some publicity mileage would be made of her opting for the Australian tour instead of this plum West End role. And

John, having survived seventeen films for either Rank or Herbert Wilcox, had secured a firm niche as a reliable leading man, not just in the movies but on stage and television as well. He, though, had been away from home for nearly eight years by the end of 1954, so that it was not unreasonable that he might feel drawn to the far south if rewarding opportunities could be found. He also wanted reunion with brothers Don and Ian, whose wives he had never met.

Whatever the forces influencing the Australian tour, no one could have said that they were seeking to prop up ailing careers by taking a punt on a different cultural terrain. John was quoted later as saying that he felt British cinema was 'running out of steam', in the mid 1950s, and there is some evidence for this, in the plethora of forgettable war films and brightly coloured comedies that were being churned out, before a new realist wave commanded attention with films like *Room at the Top* towards the end of the decade. John's own account of this claimed that: 'The bubble had burst in the British film industry, hundreds of thousands of pounds had been lost by producers, and studios were retrenching, or closing down altogether. The Rank Organization dropped nearly all its contract artistes.' Certainly his and Googie's last films together, as we have seen, were run-of-the-mill material compared with their earlier big successes. In all the recorded interviews before they left, and there were many, they seemed to be approaching their antipodean venture with real enthusiasm.

Their arrival at Fremantle on the *Orsova* on 31 December 1954 was widely reported, with such headlines as 'Actor Returns After Eight Years' (*Newcastle Morning Herald*), 'Actor Husband Returns With Actress Wife' (*Bendigo Advertiser*) and 'Success Story Of An Australian Actor' (*Kalgoorlie Miner*). In all of these provincial papers, as well as in the metropolitan ones, there is a recurrent note of Australia reclaiming its own. Much was made of John's good-humoured remark to the press about how he'd left Australia with 'a passport and one suitcase' and was returning, eight years later, 'with four women and 15 trunks'. The 'four women' were Googie and Joanna of course, and Googie's mother and Joanna's nanny. Approached for his views about women, John claimed, 'I'm looked after like a pasha by my four.' The stated aim of the trip was to spend a year touring Australia and New Zealand with the plays *The Deep Blue Sea*, Alan Melville's new comedy *Simon & Laura*, and Clifford Odets' *Winter Journey*. In fact, the last named wasn't performed in Australia until 1960, perhaps because the other two had proved so successful that the Australian tour lasted a year, instead of the planned eight months, and was followed by three months' touring both islands of New Zealand.

During the voyage itself, Googie and John appear to have been popular among the ship's diners and winers. These included the author A.P. Herbert who wrote a poem that sings praises of Googie and of which a copy autographed by other passengers remains intact. It is called, in reference to one of the meanings attributed to 'Googie', 'Dove Day':

> 'Googie!' many folks have cried,
>   'Not a worthy name –
> One so sweet and dignified -
>   Bound to be a Dame!'
> …
> Good old customs still survive
>   Bombs and Boogie woogie
> Let us all, in '55,
>   Try to be a googie

These first and last verses of the five-stanza doggerel suggest the kind of affection in which she was held – and the prospect of Googie as 'Dame' must have seemed almost inevitable then if she'd stayed in England. But there would be other compensations. There was another poem by someone cryptically signed 'OMAR', and entitled 'On the Occasion of John and Googie Disembarking at Sydney, 7th January 1955'. This rather undistinguished offering takes the precaution of including the couplet:

> But if you think our rhyme is thin
> Please blame it on the coastal gin.

It ends its paean of praise to 'our shipboard friends' with this:

But let it be voiced to the realms above,
We'll miss our dear John and his little White Dove.

While one wouldn't want to make high claims for the literary merits of the poems, they do stand as a small testimony to the popularity of the pair – and as a forerunner of the way in which Australia and New Zealand took them to their collective hearts.

After putting in briefly at Melbourne's famously dignified Windsor Hotel and before the plays opened in Melbourne, the McCallum entourage spent two weeks with John's parents in Manly, New South Wales. Relations between the senior McCallums had been strained for some time and they spent long periods apart; for instance, in the 1930s when Mrs McCallum and the boys were some years in England or at one point in the 1940s when John and his father were living in a hotel in Lancaster Gate, London. Then Mrs McCallum failed to make the wedding in London but turned up several years later to be charmed by her daughter-in-law. It is difficult to trace the degree of estrangement that existed but they were apparently living in the same house in Manly when son John and his household arrived in January 1955. One family member has suggested that John Sr discouraged closeness between the sons and their mother. His father died in the following year, and, in view of the close bond between father and son, John must in hindsight have been glad to have had some time with him on his return to Australia. There was also the pleasure of reunion with his brothers, also living in Manly, and their wives whom he hadn't hitherto met; Googie had met Ian in England but not Don. And according to the *Woman's Day and Home*, 'Ever since they married, Googie has wanted to come to Australia to see this country her husband is always skiting about'.

One way or other, everything seemed to be conspiring to bring this successful couple to Australia at this time. Not only were they to co-star in two plays which had box-office success written all over them, but John was also to produce them and to have final say in the choice of supporting cast. (The term 'producer' then carried the significance that 'director' would in later decades.) As well as all the newspaper coverage of their arrival, by lucky chance a radio recording of their British stage success, *Waiting for Gillian*, was aired just after they set down in Sydney, having been recorded in England shortly before their departure. There were articles about Googie's passion for hats, about how she 'likes cooking and antiques' and about how this 'Actress likes husband to be boss' (Googie wouldn't always have expressed such an opinion so firmly), and, as the year wore on, there were articles about Joanna's life here ('Bedtime for Joanna'), in the *Women's Weekly*, with photos of her saying goodnight to her parents, her Grandma (Withers) and Granddad (McCallum), and a double-page spread of photos illustrating the article, 'John Shows Googie the Sights of Sydney' in the then-popular illustrated weekly, *Pix*. And there was a further one in which John is quoted as saying how much they'd like to make a film together in Australia before returning to England. Well, this would have to wait for a further fifteen years.

The journal *AM* ran a piece headed 'Melbourne's blaze of West End stars'. In fact, 1955 was something of a banner year in Melbourne theatre. As well as 'one of the best-known married couples on the British stage and screen', as author Ian Aird described the McCallums in the *AM* piece, there were also Sir Ralph Richardson, famous on stage and screen, and wife Meriel Forbes, with Dame Sibyl Thorndike and Lewis Casson, performing two other Rattigan plays, *Separate Tables* and *The Sleeping Prince*, at the Princess Theatre around the corner from the Comedy Theatre where John and Googie were performing. Decades later Googie would recall the domestic brawling of the Richardsons, which sometimes spilled over into verbal hostilities in presence of others like the McCallums. Then there were Katharine Hepburn and Robert Helpmann doing *The Taming of the Shrew* and *The Merchant of Venice*, Marsha Hunt in *The Little Hut*, an Italian opera company, and others as well. Arguably, none received quite such non-stop attention from the press as our couple and, almost certainly, no single performance attracted quite such rapturous notices as Googie's in *The Deep Blue Sea*.

Astutely, John, in conjunction with the Tait family who ran J.C. Williamson's theatre chain, decided to start the season with *Simon and Laura*. Nevin Tait, Williamson's London representative, also agreed to John and Googie's request that the firm buy *The Deep Blue Sea* as well for the Australian tour. As the season was to start in the heat of February in Melbourne (on the hottest day of the year as it happened), it may have been felt wise to start with, in audience terms, the less demanding of the two plays. Googie was quoted as saying: 'I thought it better to face an audience for the first time in a comedy role complete with glamorous gowns in *Simon and Laura*, rather than have the curtain go up on *The Deep Blue Sea*, with my head stuck in a gas oven, and my face green from supposed suffocation.' One journalist, H.A. Standish, detected an element of patronage in this comment and, in a piece headed 'Hint for Googie Withers', offered this riposte: '… apparently she has been told that Australians need to be wooed with laughs before anyone would even consider confronting them with more serious plays… Did Miss Withers' advisers ever stop to tot up the numbers of enthusiasts who support our small theatres just because, with all their limitations, they do succeed in giving us a reasonable proportion of interesting, challenging plays?'

Standish may well have been right not to let Googie's easy remark pass without comment, but, whatever the thinking behind the choice and opening order of plays, the season proved a triumphant success, first in Melbourne and then in other state capitals. *Simon and Laura* was a skilfully timed piece by popular playwright Alan Melville, whose previous success, *Dear Charles*, starring English actress Sophie Stewart, had played in Melbourne the year before and was still touring Australia and New Zealand in 1955. The timeliness of *Simon and Laura* had to do with its satirical approach to the world of television, which was much in the air but not yet in the sitting-rooms of Australian audiences. John's views on the future of television in Australia were sought at this time, with his recommending half-hour shows with great Australian backgrounds and sunshine. All this was no doubt good publicity for the play. It revolves around the eponymous couple who appear in a popular sitcom as an ideally married couple, in real life as well as on the small screen where their lives are depicted in weekly doses that seem like a distant ancestor of reality television. In fact, when the cameras are not on them they fight noisily and more or less constantly, often with missiles called into play. The point is that the television company needs to promote the myth of their domestic bliss.

The play had been commercially successful in London in 1954 with (Australian) Coral Browne and Roland Culver in the leads, but the casting for the Australian tour no doubt gained an extra piquancy from the fact that Googie and John were not only married in the sitcom and in the surrounding 'life' in the play, but also in *actual* life – and widely known to be 'happily married'. There's a tiny detail in which it may be that Melville was gesturing to the McCallums when, in a publicity moment in the play, he has someone say that Simon has given Laura 'the new Parker '51[pen]' for her birthday. In fact, one of the McCallums' many extra-curricular activities had been advertising the new 'Parker '51' which John *had* given Googie for her birthday. Perhaps this ad, in the early 1950s, was well enough known for the reference to carry a nice touch of recognition.

Simon and Laura isn't a great comedy but its central situation – the bickering couple who act out an idyllic marriage for the TV cameras – and a good sprinkling of funny lines found very willing Australian audiences, even in the summer heat. It had always been John's aim as producer to fill the cast with local talent and the excellent company he found for the tour bore out the wisdom of this decision. These included prominent performers such as Charles 'Bud' Tingwell, becoming well known in films, popular character actress Letty Craydon, and attractive New Zealander Bettina Welch, well regarded in Australia for her work in such plays as *Blithe Spirit* and *Edward My Son*. These, and several others, also appeared in *The Deep Blue Sea*, and, as these two plays were performed all over Australia and New Zealand for about eighteen months, this meant steady employment in what must always be a precarious profession. *Simon and Laura* ran for thirteen weeks in Melbourne which was not surprising given its light-hearted appeal and star voltage, the imminence of television perhaps giving it an extra shot in the commercial arm. Less expected but just as gratifying, *The Deep Blue Sea* went on to enjoy a similar run before the two plays and the company took off for Sydney, John and Googie driving there, with an overnight stop near Albury, thus giving Googie a chance to see the countryside of which she had heard so much.

The critics were kind to *Simon and Laura*, though at least one suggested that Googie and John's 'parts must have made very little demand on their capabilities', and another felt that John's 'playing has more naturalness', whereas Googie 'gives to her every gesture a deliberate and witty staginess, a consciousness that she is a leading lady.' By the time the tour reached Brisbane, there was a good deal of stress on the return of the home-town boy, but one hopes that the distinction drawn between his and her playing did not lead to dissension of the Simon-and-Laura type in the domestic scene that was always being promoted in the public eye – not so much by the principals as by the press. When it came to *The Deep Blue Sea*, the critical response was uniformly laudatory, and it's possible that critics weren't always alert to the kinds of discipline involved in the effective playing of comedy. Googie herself, interviewed years later, expressed the view that 'comedy requires enormous concentration', whereas a drama, like *The Deep Blue Sea*, is 'easier because the aim is to take it out of the audience rather than the actor.'

However, the Rattigan play is indubitably a powerful piece of work and more notable in *its* genre than *Simon and Laura* was as a sophisticated comedy. The role of Hester Collyer was one of the most demanding – and rewarding – for an actress in a new play of the 1950s, and her performance was described as 'a moving and almost unbearably tense study of emotional strain'. Hester is a married woman who has fallen passionately in love with Freddie, an attractive, younger man who is less committed to their relationship. *The Listener-In* considered '"Googie" scores a triumph' but also applauded John for his Freddie, 'an opportunist to the life'. When the company moved to Sydney in July, then on to the other capitals, there were similar paeans of praise for the pair. This report of the play in Sydney was typical: 'Throughout Googie Withers never makes a false move – no unaccountable gesture, and John McCallum's Freddie is impeccable'. There is plenty more evidence that could be cited to verify this widespread approval. The critical and commercial success of both plays must have gratified them both – and J.C. Williamson's.

But as well as doing eight performances a week on stage at Sydney's Theatre Royal and trying to keep things steady at home for Joanna, they were both wildly busy in an extraordinary range of social and charitable affairs, as well as being interviewed on every conceivable aspect of their lives. After reporting a Town Hall reception when they arrived, the newspapers of the day recorded the following, among others no doubt: their visit to 2CH radio studio; the Royal Empire Society's reception; their heading the bill at J.C.W's Benevolent Fund Matinees at the Royal; the 2nd/Fifth Regimental Association Ball at the Paddington Town Hall; opening the Victorian Drama League Conference on aspects of the theatre, both amateur and professional, guest speakers at an Over-Seas League luncheon; the All Nations Ball; Googie's opening the Spring Fashion Parade for the Royal Society of the Blind; John's lecture, 'Acting Here and Abroad', for the Arts Council lunch; her opening of Legacy's 'Floral Fiesta' exhibition; the Elizabethan Ball; Googie's talk on how 'Australian men are spoilt by their women' at a Feminist Club lunch; and Googie at Ladies' Day at Randwick Race Course. Apart from the last-named (on 4 October 1955), all the others were crammed into July and August of 1955. When I mentioned to one of their later associates, director John Sumner, how Googie always seemed to be enjoying herself on these occasions, his reply was: 'Yes, I think she mostly did – and when she didn't, she was just a very good actress.' As well as all the above, they also found time to fit in a Lux Radio Theatre broadcast (15 November) of Somerset Maugham's *The Letter*, in the Rainbow Room of the Australia Hotel, Melbourne – and to advertise gin and [Schweppes] tonic as a poolside refresher.

A great deal of this sort of activity, pretty much replicated in the other state capitals, was no doubt in the interests of keeping the pair in the public eye and of keeping patrons queued at the box-office. However, there seem to have been a great many purely sociable events as well. In Melbourne, they took a house in Hill Street, Toorak, at that time the hub of the city's social life. They were taken up by Melbourne's best-known hostesses, such as Dame Mabel Brookes, wife of former tennis champion, Sir Norman Brookes, and their photos on such occasions were frequently to be found in the 'Social Pages', a phenomenon long gone from the newspapers. Googie famously loved entertaining and was incurably gregarious; John professed to like a quieter life, but he also realised the benefits of being known around the places where they were performing – and, remember, he was also directing the plays. While he may have preferred more restful nights at home, he was business-man enough to understand the commercial demands of his profession. On several occasions, they entertained the whole company at their home, and this seems to have been an ongoing habit of Googie's especially. Though she was apt to be seen outside the theatre socialising with the upper echelons of society, she was always known as a good 'company' actress, with no patience for the hierarchies of her profession, so that she was as likely to make a friend of her understudy as of her co-star.

There is no doubt that the McCallums had chosen their plays wisely and the Sydney season was even longer than the Melbourne. While there, and following their usual preference to avoid hotels for longer stays, they lived at Whale Beach in a house lent by the actress Gwen Plumb, who happened to be in England at the time. During the Sydney season, John was also filming by day. It was actually a British film in which he was involved. This was *Smiley*, based on the novel by Queenslander Moore Raymond, about a small boy desperate to own a bicycle. The project had been lying around for some time in producer Alexander Korda's offices at London Films, Denham, when it occurred to him that the time was ripe for its filming. Both Ralph Richardson and John McCallum were by chance in Australia; Chips Rafferty could be easily located; Aboriginals could be found as extras to give a look of outback authenticity; and he sent director Anthony Kimmins, long-term friend of the McCallums, to Australia to set it all in motion. Two small boys were needed and found without much difficulty. They were freckle-faced Colin Petersen as Smiley and Bruce Archer as his mate Joey, and the plot revolves around the (mis)adventures of Smiley as he goes about trying to raise the money for the bike. One of his escapades brings him into conflict with the villainous, opium-dealing pub-keeper played by John (sporting a bounder's moustache), reverting to the low-life types he'd played in England, while Richardson was the local vicar and Rafferty the police sergeant.

The film is somewhat over-plotted and morally simplistic, and the plethora of phrases like 'too right' makes it sound a bit archaic now. However, ingenuous as it is, it was indulgently received in the UK when released in June 1956. Several reviewers, rightly suggesting that Petersen stole the show, compared the two boys to Mark Twain's Huck Finn and Tom Sawyer, and applauded the agreeable use of Australian scenery and its good humour.

Peterson went on to find fame as drummer with the Bee Gees pop group. The *Daily Worker* felt that the film offered 'a pleasant evocation of the simple virtues and villainies of life in the back-blocks. Some of them are perhaps too simple, but the kindliness of the film provides compensation for the lack of polish.' *The Evening News* predicted 'a great success – and, I hope a sequel.' This hope was gratified two years later with *Smiley Gets a Gun*, but with a largely different cast and John was not of their number. *Smiley* was his last feature-film role, though there were several TV appearances in the 1970s.

It was late December before they – John and his 'four women' – set out for Brisbane, the next stage of the tour, and, as in Melbourne, opening on a night of blistering heat, at Her Majesty's Theatre on 24 December. John had been familiar with this theatre since his youth, when it was the rival to his father's Cremorne Theatre. There was no doubt a good deal of nostalgia at work for John during this time, and plenty of photo opportunities in which Googie was being shown the ropes of John's Queensland youth. Joanna, now five-and-a-half, was taught to swim while in Brisbane, and while her parents were engaged on stage or in promotional and other activities, they had the comfort of knowing she was well looked after by her nanny Helen Gilligan, and grandmother Withers.

Predictably the publicity in Brisbane was perhaps even more intense than in the other cities. As the *Telegraph* said, 'John is today in the truest sense "home"', with mention of 'a cup of tea with the Lord Mayor' (striking a rather frugal note as civic receptions go) and pictures of Joanna romping about; on the following day it was anticipating 'A Real Aussie Christmas for Googie Withers', while noting the 'bright frocking' on display at the opening of the play'; and on this day the *Courier-Mail* recorded Googie's liking for 'mink, caviar, and champagne. I don't get them all the time but I like them' and John's intention to 'head for Redcliffe – and mud crabs.' It was not surprising that they attracted so much attention, with John recalling his father's theatre, now a car park, or more interrogation re Googie's name, or an article in which 'Stage star shows how to make a soufflé', or how her mother 'Hides from publicity', a trait which her daughter fortunately had not inherited. When *The Deep Blue Sea* opened early in January 1956, it attracted the same critical applause as it had further south, with the *Telegraph*'s reviewer going so far as to say that 'it enriches one's understanding of humanity'.

In various interviews, Googie said they had travelled about 50,000 miles during this antipodean venture. There may be a certain rounding-off effect in this figure but indubitably they did cover massive distances. Joanna recalled that John liked driving but that, in later life, car trips could be a bit fraught, with Googie's sharp reiteration of 'John!', followed by a reprimand such as 'I don't like the music. Could you please change the station?' Following the Brisbane season of the two plays, they – John and the 'women' – drove down the cooler coastal road to Sydney where they boarded ship (the *Orsova* again) for New Zealand. Their first port of call was Auckland, where they were to play at *His* Majesty's, not 'Her', Auckland alone not having acknowledged a change in name since the theatre was established in the time of Edward VII. A problem arose very quickly. An Australian dock strike meant that the scenery and larger props for *The Deep Blue Sea* were still in Sydney and had to be replicated in Auckland in the space of a few days. They were 'lucky to have opened with *Simon and Laura* which had a much more elaborate set and a lot of authentic-looking TV equipment which could never have been duplicated here.'

Immediately on arrival there was the usual barrage of press reporting. The plays opened on 31 January 1956 and the following day the Mayor gave a reception for them. Googie told a reporter how she had met and admired lots of New Zealanders, often during the war, and was impressed with 'their generous dispositions and obvious happiness with life'. Well, why would potential theatregoers *not* take such a recollection to heart and flock to the box-office, as they did? Furthermore, she was willing to open herself to describing her love of luxury living which turned out to be a matter of 'the three B's' – breakfast in bed with a book – offering an idea of 'luxury' that was within reach of many. There was also a lot of emphasis on the domestic side of the McCallum entourage, Googie being accompanied by her mother and 5-year-old Joanna, an animal-lover who professes a desire to visit the

Auckland Zoo. Joanna also told a New Zealand reporter that she wants to 'be a policeman to help Daddy with his parking tickets.' Googie told another reporter that, though John had been filming while on stage at night, she couldn't because of her crowded engagement book: 'It's a succession of talks, addresses and luncheon dates... I think it's the least an actress can do to make herself available in this sense to her public. They, after all, give you their loyalty and support.' Both she and John were certainly making themselves 'available' to the public, in addresses to Rotary Clubs or giving talks to the nurses at Auckland Hospital, or appearing at the New Plymouth Floral Festival or 'Travel Clubs', or in Mayoral receptions at many of the towns they performed in. It all reads like a punishing schedule, which, as far as recorded reports suggest, was carried out with good humour and good grace. On one occasion, John hit back politely but firmly. A newspaper editorial suggested he'd been given 'a little off-stage prompting' with regard to his curtain speech in which he urged Palmerston North to 'hang on' to its Opera House. He replied firmly that he had not been 'prompted', except by his own perception that too many British theatres were shutting down under the impact of television.

Certainly, though some famous figures (such as Dame Marie Tempest) had adorned New Zealand stages early in the century, there had not been much recent incidence of world-famous theatrical names. Even so, the interest raised by this tour was remarkable. As the Company ('probably the happiest company on record' is how one of its oldest members described it) travelled the length of the two islands, performances, in the thirteen towns visited, were reviewed in all the provincial papers, as well as the recording of innumerable meetings with the press. The starring couple endeared themselves with their image of a typical home-loving family off-stage, regretting having left their Denham home and two boxer dogs behind, and adamant that, though Joanna showed talent as a dancer, 'all schooling must be completed before [she] thinks seriously of dancing or any other form of stage career.' If there is nothing remarkable in such public statements as these, that may be part of the reason they were so well received: they may have come trailing clouds of glamour but at core, these quoted comments often seemed to suggest, they were a recognisably ordinary couple with concerns that anyone might empathise with.

Along with such matters there were also insights into the professional lives of touring actors. For instance, take Googie's belief that 'A stage actress can't afford not to appear in film. Her name might be quite unknown outside her own country, but films give her a world audience.' Or John's views on stage acting: 'The producer has the last word and if he is wise he will let actors work on the play by themselves for about ten days. The actor needs that time to get into the part, but detailed characterisation can wait till later.' In other words, whether by chance or more careful consideration, they offered again and again a balance between everyday and celebrity preoccupations that proved attractive to New Zealand audiences from Auckland to Invercargill.

As to the plays themselves, the critical reaction more or less followed the pattern established in Australia. There was the predictably happy response to *Simon & Laura*, seen as a modern adaptation, in terms of television, of 'the good old story about the mettlesome stage stars who pose in public life as the ideal married couple but quarrel in private like a pair of Kilkenny cats', with praise for the stars 'at the height of their powers' and for the rest of the Company. But as was the case elsewhere, the superlatives were saved for *The Deep Blue Sea*; indeed, one used the phrase 'superlative entertainment', while another called it a 'thrilling performance of Rattigan play'. One of the more thoughtful assessments was from the *Auckland Star*, which recognised that, while Googie's performance as Hester was likely to dominate theatregoers' perceptions of the play, John's playing of 'selfish, stupid, irresponsible Freddie' is done with 'such vigour and sensitivity that the audience is never out of sympathy with him.' Many years later, he told me that he feared he was miscast, that London's Freddie, Kenneth More, was nearer to Rattigan's conception. Perhaps so, but in retrospect John's Freddie seems less stereotypical, less obviously raffish and RAF-ish, a more substantial figure against whom Googie was given more to react.

The rest of the Southern Hemisphere tour involved seasons in Adelaide and Perth in May and June 1956. In Adelaide they performed at the Theatre

Royal, an old wooden building dating back to the turn of the century, whose resilience in the event of an earthquake some decades earlier John described in these terms: 'It had no real foundations, and just sat on the ground' and following the quake, 'the whole theatre just moved a few feet one way and then moved back again, with only a crack in the proscenium arch to show that anything had happened.' After staying first at the venerable South Australian Hotel, the McCallum caravan came to rest in a house in the foothills of the ranges that circle Adelaide. After the train journey across the Nullarbor Desert, with an Australian Rules Football team for noisy company, the tour finished in Perth – where the family had arrived a year and a half earlier. While they were in Perth, John's father suffered a stroke from which he never fully recovered and he died nine months later. John flew to Sydney to bid farewell to the parent who had been such a source of encouragement and support to him.

Googie, now pregnant again, and John, with Joanna, grandmother and nanny, left Fremantle in July 1956 to sail back to England. The tour had been an unqualified success and its results were to be far-reaching. Shortly before leaving, John had had a brief conversation with Frank Tait in the Melbourne airport in which he'd asked John if he'd consider joining J.C. Williamson's as joint managing director. This meeting would have a decisive effect on the McCallums' subsequent lives.

Chapter 6

INTERLUDE

Farewelled by the company they'd been leading, the McCallums left Fremantle in pouring rain on the *HMS Himalaya*, and arrived at Tilbury Docks, London's principal port, a month later, on 15 August, 1956. Their return was predictably noted by the press, with Googie, now six months pregnant, assuring reporters that 'it might be nice to have a boy but we don't really mind' . She was possibly less pleased by the headline that read 'The Actress Having A Baby At 39 Comes Home'. She stressed that John wasn't 'the sort of husband who insists that he must have a son'. As it happened, it *was* a boy, Nicholas, who was born on 14th November. Pregnancy had not been a pushover for the McCallums. Before Joanna's arrival, they had had difficulty in conceiving, until their friends Richard Attenborough and his wife Sheila Sim recommended that Googie should stand on her head for twenty minutes after the necessary preliminaries to possible pregnancy – and this advice had worked. Googie then miscarried in early 1954. Back then, having a baby at 39 was less common than it is now, and when their third child Amanda was born Googie was 43. She was not about to let a little matter of approaching middle age stand in her way. One article describing how Googie 'and her popular husband have just returned home from their triumphant tour of Australia and New Zealand' wrote idiotically that, 'though Googie has a gay personality, she is very shy of publicity.' Googie was shy of publicity the way cats are afraid of mice.

As well as giving out cheerful news about the expected child, Googie, supposedly resting during the last months of the pregnancy, was coming to terms with her Australian experience. No doubt this involved a lot of reflection on her part, but it also meant a great deal of verbalising for the publications that thrived on the views of such outspokenness. Googie always gave 'good copy', but that is not the same as saying that the views she expressed were consistent, or even based on anything as substantial as information or evidence. Never mind, they made lively reading.

Several themes recur in these accounts in which she gives her impressions of Australia. She is adamant that it is the best place on earth for bringing up children, offering them a sunny climate and a freedom they'd be unlikely to enjoy in England. On the other hand, they seem to be exempt from what she considered the precociousness of their similarly placed American counterparts. A good deal of what she has to say about the raising of children has to be placed in the context of a career which involves her in keeping unusual hours and often being away for long periods. At this point, there is only one child, Joanna, whom she'd taken on tour to New Zealand, with Googie's own mother to help. But even in the decades ahead when there were three young McCallums to consider, she maintained her view about the desirability of Australia as a place for raising children. It could be said she was in a privileged position with the help not only of a compatible grandmother as part of the entourage but with live-in nanny and housekeeper. As the children grew older they would be placed in boarding-schools, but none of this is to suggest that the family was ever other than close-knit. Privileged, certainly, but full of affection and, as Googie said some years later, she missed them more than they missed her, which says something for the sort of continuity and security in which they grew up. Once when she'd been away for a few weeks on tour and when Joanna was still very young, she found that Joanna had got so into the way of kissing her mother's photo goodnight that she had some hesitation about switching to the real thing.

One of the other matters on which her opinion was regularly canvassed, or at least one on which she had plenty of views that she was willing to share, was that of the position of Australian women in their society. Now, there's no suggestion that she's basing these views on carefully considered research or that they derive from a wide social spectrum, but they do reveal a woman willing to take ideas on board and give vent to them. On some occasions, she would suggest that Australian men take their wives for granted, weren't sufficiently interested in giving them opportunity, either in careers or other activities, to express themselves. She was one who said she would go mad if she had to spend three months without some rewarding work to do, that she couldn't have operated as one of those 'charity wives', who spent their time doing good works. This was a rather risky opinion to put forward as she had often been the guest of honour at charitable galas and moved in the social circles, in Melbourne certainly, where such wives operated.

On the subject of Australia at large, she was similarly expansive. In general, her feelings about the country were so glowing that she came to be thought of as a sort of unofficial ambassadress. She was concerned to correct anything she heard that seemed to put down Australia as short on culture and felt that Australians themselves did not sufficiently promote the virtues of their native land. Sometimes she would take a different tack if talking about, say, the theatre arts in Australia, suggesting these would benefit by Australian actors' going overseas for experience, or by encouraging famous British or American players to come to Australia to help lift the theatrical standards there, by giving opportunities for local talent to display itself and have the benefit of playing with acknowledged masters. She was generally so enthusiastic about Australia that, when she once rather put her foot in it, she was mortified. An interview she had given was headlined: 'Googie: Back from the land of the friendly Philistines'. In handwriting on a copy of this article, perhaps intended for John, she says, 'Hate the headline. Was furious really. Phoned Betty Best to scotch it for Australia'. She sought to distance herself from the remark in a later article, in which she said her comment that 'some Australians were philistines' had been taken out of context. It was part of 'a long and otherwise adulatory song of praise for Australia and Australians'. In the widely quoted comments she had to make about her first visit to Australia, it is clear that, though she had missed some aspects of her English life, she had in the main been very happy there. In the light of events in the next two years, she would need to be coming to some sort of terms with her antipodean experience, and perhaps the enforced rest time of the pregnancy enabled her to focus what that experience had meant to her.

A less attractive aspect of the return to England in mid-August 1956 was the tax situation. If John and Googie hadn't wanted their expected child to be born in England, they could have followed their accountant's advice and stayed away for a few more months, because as John wrote: 'If you are out of the country for a year you don't have to pay tax on what you earned the previous year.' As there was no way of delaying Nicholas's birth, due in November, they were hit with an enormous tax bill, which involved 'hand[ing] over all our savings to the Commissioners for Inland Revenue.' Fortunately John was able to resume working very promptly, while presumably Googie was putting her feet up, though somehow that image doesn't seem to fit her style.

His first job (25 November 1956) was in a television production of Ibsen's *Pillars of Society*, in which he appeared as a shipbuilder who is faced with the consequences of a youthful indiscretion just as he is about to bring off a property deal. There was also a television play with American actress June Havoc and Bryan Forbes whose very title seems to have eluded John by the time he was writing about it twenty years later – and of which it is hard to find any trace. Then in the Christmas season, he played both Captain Hook and Mr Darling in *Peter Pan* at London's Scala Theatre. None of these engagements was perhaps exactly what he would have chosen, though he enjoyed doing *Peter Pan*, recalling the moment when, as Hook, he gloomily tells the audience 'No little children love me', to which six-year-old Joanna in the audience called out 'I do!' to the delight of the audience. Presumably, though, with the tax situation, 'The Mirrie' to keep up, and Googie for the time being unavailable for stage or screen, it was important for him to take what was going.

Their spacious and beautiful house, 'The Mirrie', in Denham, had been satisfactorily let to an American family during the McCallums' time in Australia. One of Googie's great pleasures was always in the renovation and decoration of houses, and she had spent a lot of time and thought – and money – on this particular house. The McCallums always enjoyed living in the country even though it meant a lot of driving, often 80 kilometres late at night after theatrical performances in London's West End. And when they were playing at, say, Stratford or Chichester or Melbourne, their preference was always for renting a house, especially one at some distance from city centres, rather than staying at hotels.

By April 1957, Googie was back on stage – remember, she'd 'go mad if she didn't work for three months' – in *Janus*, co-starring with John, who later in the year embarked on a much more commercially successful venture. This was Lesley Storm's popular comedy, *Roar Like a Dove*, in which he played Lord Dungaven from September 1957 till he left the cast in the following July, when career-changing ventures were in the air. He played a Scottish laird desperate for a male heir but whose American wife refuses to try after producing six girls in a row. What had seemed such sparkling comedy in its first year had become tired by later in 1958 when Patrick Barr, a reliable rather than scintillating actor, had replaced John. Yet, John and Googie would subsequently present the play with éclat in Australia in the following year.

It is not easy to find what Googie was doing during this time. Joanna was back at the Denham school she'd attended before leaving for Australia, and there were nanny and housekeeper to help with the running of 'The Mirrie' and the infant Nicholas. Jean Miller (now Fox), the nanny who was with the McCallums from 1956 till early 1959, recalled them as being a 'wonderful family to work for – so normal!' She'd been warned not to expect a trail of film stars through the house, though she certainly did meet some. A half-century later she recalled their lives at Denham, where their neighbours on one side were John and Mary Mills and their children, but the McCallums and the Millses didn't see too much of each other, Jean feeling that they respected each other's privacy. On the other side of 'The Mirrie', the neighbour was ex-war ace, Air Vice-Marshall Sholto Douglas, with whose nanny Jean became good friends. Establishing as regular a home life as their schedules permitted was always a priority of the McCallums, and ensuring continuity of staff was an important element of this. On one evening, Jean was led to threaten discipline to a disobedient Joanna, who kept leaving her bed and coming downstairs to see what was happening on the television. After two warnings,

Jo came down again, and Jean administered the old-fashioned hairbrush treatment. 'Next morning I made a point of seeing Googie (still in bed) to tell her about it before Joanna could, and she accepted my account without any difficulty.' Jean was unable to accompany them when they returned to Australia, because of her own family difficulties. She was replaced then by the Irish nanny, Helen Gilligan, who had been with them when Joanna was born and who later stayed with them for some years before marrying a policeman, who was posted to New Guinea and Helen left with him. Googie was frequently on record as saying that family came first with her and there is evidence to support this attitude. Certainly Helen Gilligan found this so: though, as she said, 'a place lit up when Googie entered', she also found her and John 'caring, natural and easy to work with'.

In 1958, Googie made her Shakespearean debut with a season at Stratford-upon-Avon. In *Hamlet* and *Much Ado About Nothing*, she was reunited with Michael Redgrave, with whom she'd last played in *Winter Journey*. It's tempting to discern a tendency to increasing seriousness at work in her career, from the chirpy blonde second-leads of the 1930s, through the series of strong-minded women she played in the Ealing films of the '40s, the anguished women of *Winter Journey* and *The Deep Blue Sea* in the earlier '50s, and now at last two great classical roles. Of her performance as Gertrude in *Hamlet*, it was interesting to find that she kept notes of how she saw this character, as though, if she had no personal insight into why the Queen behaves as she does, she wouldn't be able to make the role convincing to the audience. And given that her Hamlet, Redgrave, was nine years older than she, there was no doubt some serious work, and not just make-up, required to make the relationship of mother and son credible. Among her surviving handwritten notes on the subject are such comments as 'She [Gertrude] finds his melodramatic behaviour exasperating' and she sees the Queen as 'a kindly, slow-witted self-indulgent woman in no way emotionally or intellectually the equal of her son. Hamlet finally forces her to feel guilty'. There was more in this vein, sufficiently revealing to make one wish other famous actors had left examples of their cerebrations when preparing to play classic roles.

This *Hamlet*, produced by Glen Byam Shaw, then the sole director of the Shakespeare Memorial Theatre, was a personal success for Michael Redgrave whose performance I saw and recorded at the time as 'a continuous excitement – he gave us a genial, manly but not unthoughtful Hamlet and the moments of grief were profoundly moving'. The play was set with a few austere columns, some rich drapes and the odd chair but as one writer has said, 'the stage was often reduced to an enormous bare space... with static groupings like an old-fashioned opera production'.

One of Googie's recollections of playing Gertrude involved her final scene with the poisoned chalice. The actress now known as Dame Eileen Atkins was cast as 'First Gentleman', the role having been re-gendered for her to become a lady-in-waiting to Gertrude. Let Eileen Atkins' account stand:

> We were all in costumes and jewels and I was the first person in the company to get some awful flu that was going around. I'd gone on at the matinee of what we'd call a preview now, then public dress rehearsal, and, right at the end when Gertrude had taken the poisoned cup and fainted, I fainted right on top of her. Googie was very sweet about it and said, 'I think it was rather good', people will be thinking 'There's the serving lady fainting at the sight of her mistress dying.' But I did feel rather awful at having done it, and in the evening we did another of these public dress rehearsals and I kept repeating over and over in my head, 'You must not faint'. Well, Googie went down and this time I was sick all over her. She was wearing a thick, jewel-encrusted dress, and I could not believe how nice she was about it. She did say afterwards that she hoped I was pregnant, but I wasn't – I was just the first one to get the virus that then went all around the company, so everyone saw that I couldn't be blamed. I couldn't imagine any other leading lady behaving as she did.

Such accidents to one side, Googie did well enough in the reviews but her triumph was as Beatrice in *Much Ado*, and it is easy to imagine the wit and feminine vitality she might have brought to the role. John quotes what the actor Robert Speaight, 'in the unusual role of critic, wrote about her – "A star danced when Miss Googie Withers was born, and we have been waiting for a long time for her to play Beatrice. She has in her a vein of pure gold, and she mints it into a memorable performance'". The theatre director W. Bridges-Adams wrote of this production: 'Beatrice (Withers) and Benedick (Redgrave) were balm and joy. Having seen Ellen Terry – but not Irving, and not having seen Peggy Ashcroft and Gielgud, I pronounce them about the best ever.'

It is perhaps the Shakespearean role she was born to play, and it is regrettable that she never had the chance to do it again, apart from the excerpt in the Australian anthology production, *The First Four Hundred Years* in 1964. She might also have made a great Lady Macbeth or Cleopatra if these chances had come her way, but perhaps, like most actors, she had to be content with what came along, and certainly a significant variety of roles did. All these roles can do with a touch of imperiousness and Googie was well able to call this into play – on occasion in life, as well as on the stage. Maybe her imperiousness more than met its match in Dame Edith Evans, Nicholas's none-too-attentive godmother, who planned to arrive at Stratford station and ordered Googie to collect her at 4pm, though Googie had a play to perform that evening.

While Googie was starring at Stratford, the McCallums had taken a cottage about four miles out of town. John wasn't always there because other matters were preoccupying him that required his presence in London, but on more than one occasion, Jean Fox recalled, they would have the whole company out after the show for a party. This sort of sociability came naturally to Googie, as did her democratic way of not observing a hierarchy in the company, a fact commented on by several who worked with her. Jean Fox remembered the 'tremendous fun for a young nanny' of meeting, say, Dorothy Tutin (Ophelia in *Hamlet*) or Richard Johnson or Timothy West at such parties. She also recalled going with John to the opening night of *Much Ado*, when Googie, dressed in Victorian crinolines, caught her dress in the railings of a spiral staircase as she descended. So, with considerable presence of mind, she just sat on the stairs and twiddled her dress free as she went on with her lines.

Following his brief discussion with Frank Tait while he was in Australia, John wrote expressing his interest in the offer Tait had made. 'I think that really a managerial job is something I've always wanted to do. I was brought up on the management side through my Father of course. He made a success of it and I only hope I can.' As we shall see, he did achieve success in this role, and the matter was settled. In a letter written from 'The Mirrie', John, then starring in *Roar Like a Dove* at the Phoenix Theatre, London, asked Frank Tait if he could postpone coming to Australia until September 1958, to take up the offer at J.C. Williamson's. He didn't want to leave Googie with the children for nine months in a house near Stratford where 'she is doing two heavy Shakespearian parts.' While presumably doing eight performances a week, John would also acquaint himself with the firm's procedures by spending time in its London office where Nevin Tait, Frank's brother, was in charge. He had reached agreement with Nevin to stay in the cast of the play until September when he would leave for Australia. This would give him time to arrange the sale of 'The Mirrie' and to oversee the packing up of their belongings for shipment. This would have been too much for Googie to manage alone, based as she was in Stratford for the season. It also meant that he would be separated from Googie and the children for only three rather than nine months.

This arrangement also suited the management at the Phoenix as the cast of *Roar Like a Dove* was due to break up in October in preparation for opening on Broadway. In a nicely businesslike touch, John adds in his letter to Frank Tait about wanting to stay till September: 'And, also, of course, the play is doing such good business (£4,700 a week), that, as long as I stay, I am doing rather nicely from it!' This was no doubt a consideration not to be taken lightly by the McCallums who had been seriously hit by tax on return to England the year before. He says he is 'itching' to get on to the job in Australia and, in the meantime, will, at Nevin's suggestion, get to know the working of the London office, on the corner of the Haymarket and Panton Street. His first job for Williamson's was the casting of its imminent Melbourne production of *My Fair Lady*, including Bunty Turner as Eliza Dolittle.

Selling 'The Mirrie' was a major affair, both financially and emotionally. It fetched £11,500 and, as Joanna says, they never made money out of selling their houses, until their very last move. As John would find out, buying a house in Australia was to prove a much more expensive business. For Googie, on record as giving priority to family, this opportunity for John to take up a managerial position with J.C.W. was a serious test and it is one which she passed without question. The English papers sought her views on the prospect of emigrating to Australia. She told a *Daily Express* reporter: 'I am quite prepared to back John to the hilt in this new venture. There is no question of my trying to stand in the way.' She also added 'I shall probably do some acting over there once we get established.' In a longer article for the same paper, she conceded: 'Of course it will be an awful wrench to leave our house in Denham, just as we have finished making the garden. But this is a chance for John that may never come again.' Another report was headed: 'A decision that shocked my friends', but once her mind was made up she never seems to have regretted the 'decision'.

As several writers have noted, until now it was usually Googie who was in the position to choose roles, whose stellar situation was the more secure of the two, so that there was some irony in the fact that, just at this point, John was starring in a big West End success. This was a role that he might have repeated on Broadway if the Australian opportunity had not beckoned at this time. As an Australian newspaper wrote some years later, 'For Miss Withers accustomed to the excitement of theatre and film stardom in a sophisticated capital, the move must have been undertaken with some misgiving.' However, she certainly did 'do some acting' when she finally arrived there in early 1959, and she was steadfast in her view that, though intensely European herself, Australia was a great place in which to bring up children. And, recognising the unpredictable nature of the acting profession, she told writer Godfrey Winn: 'John and I are among the luckier ones. He will have a steady and permanent job, our children will grow up in a wonderful country.' Googie was also smart enough to realise that, with John co-managing a large theatre chain, she was likely to cop some interesting work – and said so to the press on several occasions.

John left England the day after Googie's triumphant opening night in *Much Ado* (and after the post-opening night party which lasted till nearly 3am). He flew to Australia via the US where he checked out the latest offerings on Broadway as part of his preparation for joining J.C.W. as joint-managing director, and this would become standard practice during his years in this position. Frank Tait met him at Sydney airport and they went straight into business discussion. Googie, who hated flying, came by sea on the *Dominion Monarch*, accompanied by the two children, Mrs Withers, the nanny Helen, the family boxer Mutz, and presumably by an enormous quantity of luggage. John joined them in Perth, the dog was put in quarantine in Melbourne, Joanna was enrolled in St Catherine's school in Toorak, and during the exceptionally hot summer of 1958–59 the family took up again the threads of the life they had lived in Melbourne two years earlier.

Chapter 7

GOING SOUTH –
AND STAYING THERE
(MORE OR LESS)

If the 1950s was the decade that clinched Googie's position as a major stage actress as well as honing her image as a formidable film star, the '60s was really John's decade. It's not that Googie didn't go on doing notable work in several continents, but that John's career took a couple of really decisive turns, as a result of which he made a contribution to the Australian performing arts that has perhaps never been fully recognised. While Googie was undoubtedly a consummate performer in all the acting media, John would add to *his* acting credentials those deriving from his roles as theatre administrator, play-producer, film director and television producer and director, and even as playwright.

An Australian actor met in Piccadilly Circus just before John left England in late 1958 said to him: 'I hear you're going back to the Bush. You won't stay, you know. You will miss all this too much', gesturing up towards Shaftesbury Avenue, in which the theatre signs beckoned. Quite shortly after arriving in Sydney then going on to Melbourne, he was struck by the kinds of theatrical activity available to the public, and wrote that 'there is more live theatre going on in Melbourne or Sydney than in any other city in the English-speaking world outside London and New York.' There follow quite a few generalisations about what Australian audiences want – to laugh, to enjoy themselves – and don't want – 'anything pretentious or artificial'. He refers to a list of recent successes ranging from J.C. Williamson's Shakespeare Company, performing four plays in Adelaide, Melbourne and Perth, to Ray Lawler's new play, *The Piccadilly Bushman*, also sponsored by J.C.W., at Melbourne's Comedy

Theatre, and directed by John. It was doubtless judicious of him to draw attention to some of the latest successful ventures by his new employers, but there was indeed a sense of Australian theatre's embarking on an unusually productive time in its history.

At this time, J.C. Williamson's – 'The Firm', as it was known – was arguably the most wide-ranging and ambitious theatre company in the world, owning seven theatres in Australia and New Zealand, and leasing three permanently and a further ten periodically. In the sheer scope of its operation it outdid the likes of Tennent's in London or Schubert's in the US. In an article John wrote at the time, he recalled his own childhood in the theatre world of Brisbane where his father was in (more or less amicable) competition with J.C.W. 'Being brought up in the Theatre in Australia is almost synonymous with being brought up with J.C. Williamson's, because it is by far the oldest and largest management in Australia.'

John began his relationship with J.C.W. in London, familiarising himself to some extent with the firm's workings in the offices supervised there by Nevin Tait. Arrived in Australia he became Joint Managing Director with Sir Frank Tait, and the two became fast friends. Frank Tait's daughter, Isla Baring, recalled that:

> It was a great thing for my father: instead of that burden he had with trustees and so on, and people he'd been with for 100 years, he had a nice bit of young blood who was knowledgeable about everything in the theatre and also intelligent. John had a very good business head as well as being a very good actor, and they got on terribly well. It was a wonderful combination and they used to go swimming together in the Melbourne City Baths to relax after meetings. Daddy was quite sporty; he was a golfer, and John was too.

Frank Tait was in his late '70s and was no doubt relieved to have a reliable and astute business partner who was several decades younger. And John also undoubtedly got off to a brilliant start with the company with the enormous box-office success of *My Fair Lady*, the main casting of which he had undertaken before leaving London. Bunty Turner, who starred as Eliza, years later recalled how considerately John had conducted her audition in London. Whereas most producers left you standing on stage while they discussed you, John 'was charming, he spoke to you and not *about* you, at least until you were no longer there.' In a long interview, he explained that he'd 'always been interested in management' and in his early years at Williamson's he enjoyed the 'many sides to management. The human element comes into it so much … this actress has to be stroked and the next one has to be slapped to do what you want … and all of the human side of things is very fascinating'. Many women may not approve his choice of words, but it does suggest that he was attuned to the personal demands of his new position.

John was of course no stranger to the musical stage with the background of his father's theatre and of his own experiences with Gladys Moncrieff in the 1940s, but *My Fair Lady* was something else. John knew from being in London in the latter 1950s what a huge success it had been there, with would-be theatre patrons waiting months for seats. It opened in Melbourne on 24 January 1959, at the very start of his time with The Firm, and, with record-breaking advance bookings, it got off to a flying start, which a sweltering summer did nothing to diminish. It was obviously going to run for well over a year in Melbourne and John directed a second company:

> It was because it was running so long in Melbourne, with people coming down from Sydney to see it. It ran in Melbourne for over a year. Sydney was getting impatient and asking 'When are we getting *My Fair Lady*?' Quite understandably you know, so we thought we'd better do it there simultaneously, and so we formed two companies. The new replacement one stayed in Melbourne, and the original one went to Sydney, so we had them running concurrently.

Considering the vast expense to J.C.W. of preparing costumes and settings for this ambitious production, it must have been a relief to John and Frank Tait that the show repeated its critical and box-office successes in the other Australian capitals, as well as in New Zealand, with gross takings of nearly $5million, in those days a huge figure.

It is widely agreed that John, unlike many actors, had a very good business head and had, in all his administrative dealings, with J.C.W. and other companies, the reputation for being a very 'honourable' man. He knew you had to be skilful in negotiating terms with artists' contracts and with management to ensure his own livelihood, and that spending on 'Rolls-Royce' productions such as *My Fair Lady* and the shows that followed had to ensure a lavish appearance on carefully contained budgets. He stayed with The Firm for eight years, and, in his first years with J.C.W., there was a string of successful imports, including *Camelot* which opened at Her Majesty's in Adelaide in November 1963 and Her ditto, Melbourne, the following February. If it did not enjoy the universal popularity of *My Fair Lady*, this somewhat languorously seductive adaptation of T.H. White's novel of Arthurian romance, *The Once and Future King*, was still a thing of beauty to behold. This was at least in part the result of its fabulous set design by John Truscott. Truscott was a young designer who worked for Melbourne's small St Martin's Theatre for producer Irene Mitchell, where he'd been doing imaginative work, notably in suggesting settings of a magnitude and lavishness beyond the confines of this theatre's small stage. British actor Paul Daneman was the nominal star, but it is Truscott whose name, in Australia at least, is the one most readily associated with *Camelot*. John felt The Firm should acknowledge this in a practical manner – and fell foul of Mitchell, of whom Truscott was a protégé. John suggested to Frank Tait that they should help the young man, that they hadn't paid him very much, and they agreed to give him £1000. When Irene Mitchell heard about it she was furious. She had given him a fare to London before he did the *Camelot* job, and she fumed, 'You've stolen my thunder. You put it in the press that he's had £1,000 when I'm giving him a fare to London!' Truscott went to work on the Hollywood movie version in 1967 and won Oscars for his production and costume design, but, despite this success, designed only one further film, *Paint Your Wagon* in 1969.

Truscott's internationally-won kudos for *Camelot* owed something to John McCallum's eye for spotting talent, and this, along with his managerial skills and willingness to take a risk, made him a real asset to Williamson's. In his years with The Firm it sponsored a series of popular productions, including a season of opera with Australian diva Joan Sutherland as the major drawcard. He was also committed to the staging of new shows, a condition of his joining the 'Firm', which he felt had relied too much on revivals. It was, as he describes it in his memoir, 'a golden period, the most successful the company had in its nearly one hundred years of existence'. This view is easily substantiated by the merest list of some of the international names that adorned The Firm's programmes during this time. Not that showcasing such celebrities was without its problems. John, decades later, recalled Sutherland's refusing to go on on opening night, because of an error in the programme, and despite the Governor's being in the audience. There was a delay of twenty minutes until an apology was arrived at, but after the show 'her language would have left a wharfie standing.'

Other big names included John Gielgud with his *Ages of Man* recital, Marcel Marceau with his transfixing display of mime, Harry Belafonte at the peak of his fame as a recording artist, US film comic Danny Kaye, Vivien Leigh, directed by Robert Helpmann in three plays, starring as Viola in *Twelfth Night*, Gracie Fields and many others. As well, J.C.W. finding it could no longer afford the high costs associated with the Borovansky Ballet, John set himself to securing the support of the Elizabethan Theatre Trust in the establishment of the Australian Ballet Company, believing such companies could no longer flourish without some form of subsidy. The newly formed company had its first performance in Her Majesty's Theatre, Melbourne, in 1962. So, drama, opera, ballet, solo performances: all of these made John's years with J.C.W. an ongoing excitement for theatregoers – and no doubt for him. I am jumping a few years here, but as his later business partner and co-producer John Frost says, 'Without doubt John had a very good business head… when you look at his track record, it speaks for itself'. Frost went on to name the hit musicals and star 'discoveries' that were part of that 'record'. And for John, 'For a while it was even more exciting than acting' – he had a knack for finding new talent and how it could be used.

What he brought to The Firm was a combination of theatrical know-how, derived from his own background and personal experience, and business acumen. As to the latter, probably for reasons to do with taxation, he had set up a company simply called 'J. and G. Pty. Ltd.', with no prizes for guessing what the initials stand for. This company then 'employed' John McCallum and there are letters extant that reveal how sharp he was in arriving at satisfactory terms and conditions. In one such letter, the 'Director' of the company writes to the Directors of J.C.W. about how 'J. and G.' is to provide the services of John Neil McCallum in return for the 'sum of £5,000 p.a. plus 2½ % of the profits of J.C. Williamson Theatres Ltd. during such term as that Company makes available to J. C. Williamson Theatres Ltd. the services of Mr. J. N. McCallum who shall be styled as Joint Managing Director with Sir Frank Tait.' John was not one to be daunted by the language of such agreements and was quick enough to discern loopholes. For instance, he added a further request for a personal payment of £500 p.a. to ensure his eligibility to participate in the Company's Provident Fund, and, as he intended to be with The Firm for a long time he added that he would like to become a shareholder in the Company. In an earlier letter to the Directors of Rangatira Pty. Ltd., the New Zealand company which had bought 51% of J.C.W. in the mid 1930s, he expressed 'some misgivings about a percentage share based on profits', lest these be depleted by the expenditure incurred in improving the theatres. It is not clear whether he has in mind here essentially New Zealand theatres, but it is worth noting how canny he could be in such matters.

There was plenty of other activity in the McCallums' life at this time. The family was settled at 2 Scotsburn Grove, a handsome modern house on three levels, in the fashionable Melbourne suburb of Toorak where John and Googie were famously hospitable to the visiting companies that came to Melbourne under the J.C.W. banner. As well as having a social life that involved first nights and all manner of charitable and other public events assiduously chronicled by the newspapers and women's journals, they were as likely to invite the entire company putting on *How to Succeed in Business Without Really Trying* to a barbecue lunch in 1963. John and, indeed, Googie could be said to have succeeded in business *with* really trying, but there was a strong element of sheer friendliness as well as shrewdness involved in the life they so energetically lived. Also, whereas the charity and other such appearances were bound to be reported, the attentions to visiting performers and companies were generally not. These were gestures of good will to people away from their usual turf. Googie loved the company of lively people and was an indefatigable host; John was perhaps a little more fatigable in this matter, but had a strong sense of responsibility to the international visitors he attracted to Australia. The actress Muriel Pavlow, who was in Australia with husband Derek Farr to star in *The Gazebo* (1959) and *Mary, Mary* (1964) for Williamson's, recalled fifty years later: 'We hadn't met them much in England but they were marvellous to us in Australia. John was really our "boss", and they made sure we found nice places to stay.'

Meanwhile the McCallum household was growing. While Joanna was enrolled at St Catherine's, Toorak, where she completed her education, Nicholas, five in 1961, attended Glamorgan, the preparatory school for Geelong Grammar School where he would later become a boarder, and the family had been completed by the arrival of Amanda on 25 July 1960. John claimed that touring New Zealand, as he and Googie had been with *Roar Like a Dove* in 1959, inevitably brought on another pregnancy, as had been the case following their early 1956 tour with *The Deep Blue Sea* and *Simon & Laura*, son Nicholas having been born in November of that year. There was some continuity of household staff – pretty Irish nanny Helen Gilligan, and housekeeper Violet Attwood, who shared a garden flat on the ground floor – but, even allowing for that, their time was more than full in these Melbourne years in the first half of the '60s.

John's position at J.C.W. involved him in a lot of travel, both interstate and overseas, including some theatre-packed weeks in New York when he'd suss out possible productions for The Firm to consider. And if the '60s may be seen as the decade when John came to the fore in the Australian performing arts, Googie was by no means playing full-time housewife. Given her often stated view that wives who followed careers outside the home were likely to be more interesting to their husbands *in* the home, it is not surprising to note that she was not only opening flower shows and the like but also maintaining her day – or rather, night – job as an actress. She had accompanied John willingly to

Australia, had backed him completely in taking up the position with J.C.W. at a time when her own star was very much in the theatrical ascendant in Britain, especially following her triumphant Beatrice at Stratford, but she never had any intention of turning into a meek homebody. As noted earlier, she did suggest that if John was co-managing a large theatre company there was surely at least a chance that there would be work for her on one or more of its stages. And she was right.

In her first year back in Australia she and John toured Australia and New Zealand in *Roar Like a Dove*, ironically a play concerned with a wife who refuses further conception after having produced six daughters. This play by English dramatist, Lesley Storm, was just the sort of well-crafted light-hearted piece that Googie, rightly, claimed Australasian audiences loved. They loved considerably less the more anguished follow-up drama, Clifford Odets' *Winter Journey*, which she had played to great acclaim opposite Michael Redgrave and Sam Wanamaker in London ten years earlier. Perhaps John was right in attributing its relative failure in Australia to the notion that 'Australians have a history of not liking backstage stories'. This certainly is, for much of its length, a downbeat affair, but maybe the fact that Australians had already seen the story in award-winning film form as *The Country Girl* in 1955 tended to make them wary of submitting themselves again to its harrowing elements of alcoholism, self-pity and domestic strife. You can have enough of those things in your own home can't you? Though the play didn't do well commercially, the Melbourne critics offered encouragement with headlines such as 'Googie Withers in Fine Performance', 'Play Magic… By An Ideal Cast' and 'This is Googie at her best'.

Much more to the public liking was the handsomely set and costumed revival of Somerset Maugham's *The Constant Wife* which opened in Melbourne in early 1961, with Googie again playing with her *Winter Journey* co-star, Clement McCallin. Perhaps the lady in the front stalls at Googie's 1962 performance as the slatternly *Woman in a Dressing Gown* was recalling her period elegance in the previous play when she whispered audibly to her neighbour, 'My, hasn't she gone off!' As to *The Constant Wife*, there was some suggestion that Maugham's 1927 play had dated, but the surface comedy of

John's parents: John McCallum Sr and Elsie Dyson McCallum.

Googie's mother Lizette and father Edgar.

John, aged 12, as Cardinal Wolsey, in *Henry VIII*, at Oatlands School, Harrogate.

Googie and Dolores del Rio in *Accused* (1936). (Barman is uncredited)

John in the 2/5 Field Regiment of the Australian Imperial Force (AIF).

Googie in the early 1940s.

Googie confronting Beatrice Lillie in *On Approval* (1944).

PSW-83

Googie in seductive murderess mode in *Pink String and Sealing Wax* (1945).

Phyllis Calvert and John in *The Root of All Evil* (1946).

Together: in *The Loves of Joanna Godden* (1947).

It Always Rains on Sunday (1947) opens at the Odeon Leicester Square.

Wedding day: St George's, Hanover Square, London, November 1947.

The three stars of *A Boy, a Girl and a Bike* (1948). Honor Blackman, right.

Actors Norman Wooland, John, Dermot Walsh and John Blythe at charity cricket match.

Googie dangerously involved with Richard Widmark in *Night and the City* (1950).

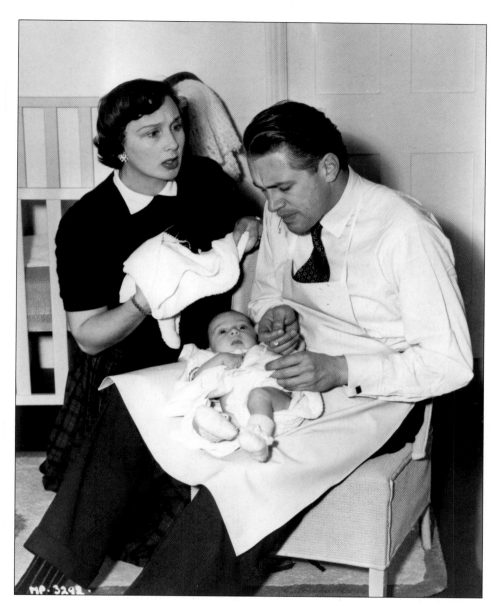

John as father to Joanna, doing his best under Googie's watchful eye (1950).

Googie as Dr Sophie Dean in *White Corridors* (1951).

J. C. Williamson Theatres Ltd. presents ★ and **GOOGIE WITHERS** **JOHN McCALLUM** ★ in **"SIMON and LAURA"**

Charles 'Bud' Tingwell, John, Letty Craydon, Googie, Collins Hilton in *Simon and Laura* (1955), Comedy Theatre, Melbourne.

J. C. Williamson
Theatres Ltd.
presents

★ THE DEEP
BLUE SEA ★

GOOGIE WITHERS
JOHN McCALLUM

John and Googie in *The Deep Blue Sea* (1955), Comedy Theatre, Melbourne.

Googie and Michael Redgrave in *Much Ado about Nothing* (1958),
Memorial Theatre, Stratford-upon-Avon.

Googie and John in *Roar Like a Dove* (1959).

GOOGIE WITHERS in
WOMAN in a DRESSING GOWN

Grant Taylor, Googie, Allen Bickford in *Woman in a Dressing Gown* (1962),
Comedy Theatre, Melbourne.

John, Googie and Ted Willis, author of *Woman in a Dressing Gown*.

Googie and Alec Guinness in *Exit the King* (1963), Royal Court Theatre, London.

Googie presents son Nicholas with school prize for under-10 long-jump at Glamorgan School, Melbourne, 1965.

Joanna, John and Googie, at John's CBE presentation ceremony (1971).

John Laws and Googie, in John McCallum's *Nickel Queen* (1971).

Googie rehearsing *The Cherry Orchard*, with Frank Thring and Fred Parslow in the background.

Googie, Joanna and John in costume for *The Circle* (1976), touring.

Googie as prison Governor Fay Boswell, in *Within These Walls* (1974–78), LWT, UK.

John, with family, friends and famous marsupial colleague, for *This Is Your Life, Australia* (1976).

John and Googie in *On Golden Pond* (1992), touring UK.

John and Googie in *Lady Windermere's Fan* (1997), Festival Theatre, Chichester.

Googie, Amanda, Joanna, Nick and John with the family dog.

Joanna, Nick and Amanda.

manners still had plenty to offer playgoers thirty-odd years later. In fact, its underlying bitterness about the constraints of marriage, especially in relation to the wife's reactions to her husband's infidelity, gave it a substance that elevated it above being merely a nice night's entertainment. It was perceptively directed by John Sumner with whom Googie would have further stage dealings; unsurprisingly, since it was so well received as 'ideal summer fare'.

Sandwiched between these two sartorially contrasted roles was Googie's Broadway debut. This was in Graham Greene's *The Complaisant Lover* which opened at the Ethel Barrymore theatre in November 1961 and which reunited her with Michael Redgrave, the Hamlet and Benedict of her 1958 time at Stratford. The Redgraves and the McCallums had been friends of long standing and would continue so. In New York, she found herself in what was always being described in the press as 'A Big Season', with the likes of film stars Bette Davis and Fredric March peddling their wares on the stage. In one such article, Googie was reported as learning 'the Twist' so as to surprise the cast at its Christmas party. This play represented the author in benignly cynical mode with Googie's character finally having her cake and eating it – that is, retaining the affections of both husband and lover.

One cast member who remembered her with great affection was Nicholas Hammond, then aged eleven, who played her son and whom she referred to offstage as her 'other' Nicky, explaining that she had a son called Nicky of roughly the same age in Australia. Years later, he realised 'what a wonderful company leader she had been as most of the crises were kept hidden from me at the time.' He recalled her coaching, while the play was still out of town, an actor who wasn't delivering quite the performance the director wanted, thereby saving the actor's place in the cast, and she was a calming influence on Michael Redgrave who was going through some personal difficulties that made him somewhat intractable at times. Hammond also related a story Googie herself told of her refusal to be bullied by the somewhat daunting producer, Irene Selznick, who came to her Boston hotel early one morning, Googie having declined to go to Selznick's office at 9am. 'Irene announced that they had a problem – Googie's figure wasn't good enough! At which Googie rose from the bed, pulled off her nightgown and stood naked before

Irene. She turned away and said "that's the back side" then turned to face her and said "that's the front side" and then with hands on hips demanded "so where's the problem?" Irene never bullied an actor again.'

Never afraid of airing her views in public forums, when she returned to Australia, she told one reporter that the play had been 'an artistic success' but claimed the public 'apparently did not see the wit of this extremely subtle play'. Furthermore, she lamented the 'sad state of affairs' on Broadway where 'theatre is too commercial'. With perhaps more self-knowledge, she spoke of her 'rather hard role... Not only is she on stage throughout, but she's an innocent thing really and I find my own sophistication constantly in danger of coming through.' Quoting these three sets of comments, all dispensed within a week in three different papers, suggests how much sought after she was as a recognisable and popular public figure, while John was getting on with life as joint managing director in the non-air-conditioned offices of J.C.W. in the height of summer. And in the following month, the magazine *Woman's Day* ran a piece headed 'Googie comes home' (she'd been away for only a little over three months but her return was an event to note), in which she asserted, 'I am completely sold on Australia as a place for bringing up children' and that "After living there for two years, I've decided Australia is the best place on God's earth'. No wonder her antipodean public took her to its heart.

What those children thought of being brought up in Australia may not be quite so unequivocally or consistently euphoric. Mandy, the youngest, trailed round with her parents on tours, attending eight different schools, whereas Joanna and Nick were in boarding schools for many years. No doubt Googie and John felt, as conscientious parents, that boarding school was a way of providing the older two with some sense of stability and continuity, but there may also have been some sense of abandonment. It was presumably no easier then than now for parents, especially the mother, to conduct a rewarding career *and* provide a domestic constant for their children. Interviews throughout these decades are full of Googie's regrets at having to leave children behind when she went on tour or overseas, which she did on three major occasions during the '60s, but there is nowhere any hint of estrangement between her (or John in his demanding administrative position which involved him in overseas travel too) and the children. There are also plenty of accounts of happy reunions when one or other of the children would fetch up for Christmas or school holidays where their parents were on tour, all of these faithfully captured by the insatiable press.

Googie's success in Ted Willis's *Woman in a Dressing Gown* recalls that comment she made when I suggested that she seemed happy to come over on screen as sensual, bold and even sluttish. 'Oh, if you're toff you can act common, but if you're common you can't do toff.' If one is being high-minded and egalitarian, it is possible to discern a hint of class snobbery in this – there is no question about which category Googie saw herself as occupying – but there may also be more than a little truth in its perception. In the play she brilliantly articulated domestic slovenliness along with the good-hearted and good-humoured attitudes that the playwright built into *Woman in a Dressing Gown*. For years after, Googie used the dingy old dressing gown of the title as a good-luck talisman, wearing it backstage as she was making-up. Willis's drama of Amy Preston, the wife whose husband falls in love with a pretty, younger (and tidier) woman began life as a television play in 1956, starring Joan Miller; it was subsequently filmed with Yvonne Mitchell as Amy in 1958; and the stage adaptation was first aired in Melbourne in 1962, followed by an extensive tour in Australia and New Zealand. While in the latter country, Googie gave an interview in which she was quoted as saying, 'It is definitely a comedy of human emotions. It is a perfect mixture of comedy and pathos combined', unlike the film 'where it was played for tragedy', which is a slight overstatement of the 1958 film's tone. One wonders if maybe she is trying to make it sound more attractive to potential audiences.

There was much talk of her taking the play to London, with co-star Grant Taylor, but nothing came of this, and the play opened in London in 1963 with Brenda Bruce as Amy. The drama behind this failure involves four correspondents and the offstage figure of Googie as the protagonist. The first of these relevant letters comes from Laurie Evans at London Artists Limited, the McCallums' London agent at the time, in which he 'very much hope[s] we are going to act for Googie when she comes here for *Woman in a*

Dressing Gown' and asking 'what sort of contract Googie wants for London', as 'Henry Sherek called me today, wanting to discuss Googie's terms for the play.' There is no letter extant setting out Googie's terms but what follows is one addressed to John at his office in Melbourne's Comedy Theatre from the London producer-impresario Henry Sherek, whose opening sentence is 'I am so staggered by what Googie is asking that it does not look as if I will be able to go on with the play at all.' He goes on to imply that, while her having been away so long may not have lessened her importance as a London draw-card, it certainly won't have increased it, and that matters such as first-class round-trip fares, and her wish for a six-month 'get-out' are impossible for the management to accept. John's reply picked up on the word 'staggered': he is not only staggered but is 'reeling about', claiming that everything Googie has done since *The Deep Blue Sea* has made a handsome profit. 'Believe me, the part in *Woman in a Dressing Gown* and the way Googie plays it are worth every penny' that she is asking. He stresses that its ultimate production in London 'has been an important part of the whole promotion of the play', that they are 'morally committed' to the UK performance and that author Ted Willis came to Australia to see Googie's opening night on that understanding. John subsequently wrote to Ted Willis, expressing some outrage at Sherek's behaviour and the hope that Willis might be able to 'dissuade Henry from his intransigence'. Well, he couldn't, but he entered the fray on Googie's side, writing to Sherek, 'Googie is, after all, a world star, and she is asking for no more than her due. From what I saw of her performance in the play, she is worth every penny she is asking.' He was willing to try to find another management to take on the play, and felt Sherek had 'behaved badly'.

Meanwhile the woman in question was completing her popular New Zealand tour with the play in question. She would certainly have been put out at Sherek's behaviour, and one would like to have seen – or, better, heard – her reactions. But outrage might possibly have been assuaged by the emergence of a better prospect's appearing in the form of Eugene Ionesco's absurdist drama, *Exit the King*, to star with Alec Guinness. Her return to England after four years was accompanied by the usual flurry of interviews, in many of which she seemed like an unofficial ambassadress for Australia.

It may be hard now to remember how significant playwrights such as Samuel Beckett and Ionesco were in their impact on theatre conventions at the end of the '50s and into the following decade. Though the notion of co-starring with Guinness must have been very attractive to Googie, she would also have been aware of the cachet involved and the broadening of her range in tackling such a play at this time. Her arrival back in England was heralded with the usual press coverage, both in England and Australia, where one paper even bothered to report that she was staying with Michael Denison and Dulcie Gray in their Regent's Park flat while first back in London to rehearse the play, then known as The Ceremonies. After a brief tour, and with its new title, *Exit the King* opened at the Edinburgh Festival, before settling to a seven-week run at London's Royal Court Theatre, home of the very innovative English Stage Company.

When Googie came back to Australia after this season, she gave a rapturous account of the way the Royal Court season played to capacity houses, with standing room only every night. This may well have been the case and Guinness's and her names, along with the trendiness of Ionesco at the time among serious theatregoers, would have been sufficient to keep the box-office happy. However, critics were by no means unanimous in their praise for the play or the production. Felix Barker and Michael Shulman, both long-time critics, found, respectively, that 'Ionesco is not an original or profound thinker' and that there was 'something uneasily dissatisfying about the play's impact', while Bernard Levin found it 'empty and cold'. In general though, there was praise for the acting of Guinness as the four hundred-year-old king who is reluctant to face the imminence of his death (as you would be after so long), and Googie as the older and more authoritative of his two Queens. However, some critics, such as Martin Esslin, who thought it 'a profound and beautiful play', felt that Eileen Atkins as the hard-pressed skivvy outshone everyone else.

Eileen Atkins, who had had such awkward accidents when playing Googie's lady-in-waiting at Stratford five years earlier, had further reason to be grateful to her now. She felt her role as the old servant should be acted by someone nearer the character's age, and had a set-to with director George

Devine on this matter when he started to make her try to walk like an old woman. Devine wanted to sack Atkins, but Guinness intervened with Devine and said he'd direct Atkins henceforth, and 'I remember Googie being on my side'. She admired Googie for her 'strong opinions and joyous energy'. She also recalled a company party at which, late at night, Googie in a burst of enthusiasm said, 'Let's dance!'. As a result the party went on till well into the small hours, even the famously difficult Guinness throwing himself into festivities. Next morning, Eileen Atkins recalls 'getting up and wondering aloud where Alec was – to his wife who said, "Oh, he's at confession". When I asked her why, she said he feared he may have said some wicked things last night.' According to Atkins, Googie was 'the one person Alec felt safe with on stage. And she got the best out of him socially – even if he did have to go to confession next day.'

Much as Googie loved the London theatre, she says, 'I cannot say how much I am looking forward to my homecoming – Melbourne is my home now – to my husband, my three children, and Australia'. Mind you, she would also say on other occasions that her roots are in England, however much she loves Australia.

When Googie returned to Australia ('my country now… it's such a young, vigorous place'), her career and John's converged, though not as co-stars. She spoke of John's hope of bringing *Exit the King* to Melbourne and said that 'there is a definite possibility that Sir Alec will bring the play to Australia next year.' This never happened, and fifty years on it seems that it would have been an improbable choice for J.C. Williamson's, certainly a dubious box-office proposition, even with star names. In the event, what The Firm did come up with for Googie was no commercial success either. In 1964, the fourth centenary of Shakespeare's birth, J.C.W. marked this occasion with a theatrical anthology entitled *The First 400 Years*, a compilation of scenes from the plays, to be directed by Raymond Westwell, who had starred memorably in Australia in 1962 in Robert Bolt's *A Man for All Seasons*. *The First 400 Years* offered Googie a chance to play Shakespearean excerpts including two from roles she'd played at Stratford – Gertrude in *Hamlet* and Beatrice from

Much Ado About Nothing – along with Cleopatra, Katherine in *Henry VIII*, Katherina in *Taming of the Shrew*, Queen Margaret in *Henry IV*, and Portia in *The Merchant of Venice*. In the *Women's Weekly*, in one of the colour spreads it so regularly devoted to her, she said, 'I haven't done a great deal of Shakespeare. Not because I haven't wanted to, nor for lack of being asked. I've always been too bogged down with film contracts… I'm finding this programme a challenge. It's frightfully good for one, changing from one role to another so quickly and dramatically.' For each of the roles she played, she had a different costume, that for Cleo with a suggestion of Queen Bess about it, and there's a great still of her with crown, flowing robe and brandishing a four-foot sword as Margaret. She claimed to be afraid of killing co-star Keith Michell as she lunged. The show started its life on tour in New South Wales and New Zealand, before playing Sydney and Melbourne. Michell was an Australian actor who had made a career in London but was perhaps not quite a big enough name in his home country to constitute an extra drawcard. Again, *The First 400 Years* maybe fell between two stools: those less familiar with the Shakespearean oeuvre may have found confusing the moving among so many plays, while those who did know the works may have thought the enterprise scrappy, perhaps preferring a full-length performance of *one* play.

ABV-2 ran a two-part television version of *400 Years* coinciding with the Sydney season at the Theatre Royal (22 June – 11 July), starting with the lighter moments in Part 1 (aired on 8 July), but neither this nor Part 2, dealing with the more dramatic excerpts, did much for the box-office, and the show played only brief seasons in the cities. In my recollection and no doubt unfairly, a little dog that featured in the bit from *Two Gentlemen of Verona* got more of the popular vote than the stars.

When Sir Frank Tait died in August 1965, John became managing director of Williamson's. Frank and three of his brothers had run Williamson's since 1920 and, as mentioned earlier, the New Zealand company Rangitira bought 51% of J.C. Williamson's Ltd in the mid '30s. A full history of the company was chronicled in *A Family of Brothers* by Lady Viola Tait, Frank's widow, in 1971. This is not the place for a history of the company, but only of John

McCallum's dealings with it. The first four or five years of his time with The Firm as joint-managing director were marked by a series of popular successes, as we have seen, and John and Frank Tait had had a very good working relationship. However, by 1964, things were not looking so optimistic for J.C.W. *The First 400 Years* hadn't been a financial hit, and in the following year, though it garnered immense critical kudos for its ambitious opera season, it in fact lost a lot of money over this venture.

Frank's love of music was gratified by this season and those close to him were grateful that he lived long enough to see it. The problem was that, whereas the programmes starring Joan Sutherland were booked out with lightning speed, the operas in which she didn't appear played to half-empty houses. In fact, Sutherland herself urged the public to attend the operas in which she was not appearing during the J.C.W. season in an item headed, 'Shame, says opera star.' This cry was taken up by the *Sunday Mirror* in a piece entitled 'Where the blame lies', accusing J.C.W. of focussing all the publicity on Sutherland and of the prices on her nights as 'exorbitant' in spite of John's having described the other lead singers (e.g., Pavarotti, Elizabeth Harwood) as being 'world class.' Whatever the reasons, The Firm lost $48,000 on the opera season, and this was on top of a further dip in profits of $52,000 in the 1965-66 financial year, partly as a result of imported musicals, *Carnival* and *Bye-Bye Birdie*, not performing up to expectations. The mounting of a production of an Australian play, *The Desire of the Moth*, was another commercial failure, in spite of starring Googie in her first Australian role, though John explicitly contradicted rumours that this was responsible for his break with the Board.

At this unpropitious time for John's taking on the reins of managing director, he was also – and ironically – in the US teeing up several shows that would prove major elements in The Firm's turnaround. But by that time, he would no longer be with J.C.W. His resignation from the CEO position was announced on 29 August 1966, and it made big news in all the Australian papers, the Melbourne evening paper, the *Herald*, scooping the pool with its front-page headline, 'J.C.W.'s chief McCallum resigns post.' At this remove in time, it is hard to pinpoint the causes that precipitated John's decision.

With characteristic concern for decent public behaviour, he was quoted as saying 'There has been some measure of disagreement. We have agreed to disagree and I am sorry. Yet our disagreement has been amicable. I have had eight years with The Firm and they have been wonderful. But there we are.' In a letter written on 1 September 1966, John sets out the bases for his resignation. He also added that, as his filmmaking commitments developed, he might need to move to Sydney to live – as he did – or go back to London – as he also did.

Over the next few days, two sources of 'disagreement' emerged most often. One had to do with the fact that the J.C.W. Theatres Ltd. Board had come increasingly to be dominated by businessmen with little feel for the theatre, and, as John allows in his letter, the parent company, J.C. Williamson's Ltd, was understandably concerned with the 'alarming drift in business resulting in heavy weekly losses'. His repeated request to be appointed a member of the Board of the parent company had been 'persistently refused'. John, as sole managing director of the Theatres company, was replaced by two serving directors: Charles Dorning, who did have some theatrical background in England and had been London manager for the last eight years, and John McFarlane (no relation to present author), who had formerly been manager of a packaging company with no experience of professional theatre, and whose appointment John regarded as 'a grave mistake'. (McFarlane himself resigned three months later.) Further, the New Zealand Board members seem primarily to have been businessmen rather than impresarios.

Now, John would have been the first to allow the importance of an element of financial shrewdness in the running of the company, but he was also enough a man of the entertainment world to realise that some insight into what the public wanted and what was worthwhile in theatre was also crucial. The business side of his approach could be seen in his wish to set up bars with liquor licences in The Firm's theatres, believing this would be an added attraction to those seeking a night out. He did not, however, favour the idea of Her Majesty's Theatre being re-named Rock City to house a pop-music programme. His eye for the sort of theatre audiences responded to could be seen in the several hit shows he lined up and which were performed after his resignation. In fact, he resigned the day after the very successful opening night of *Funny Girl*, one of the shows he'd earmarked on his last New York trip, and which proved a hit for Australian comedienne Jill Perryman.

The other recurring reason for the split appears to have been in John's aspiration for J.C.W. to venture more resolutely into film production. A long article by Patrick Tennison detailing John's work for The Firm suggests that 'He was always planning some new development. Only now [i.e., post-resignation] is it possible to reveal some he had in mind in which he found himself frustrated or, at least, received less than enthusiastic support.' To one reporter, John said that this was 'the main difference' leading to the break. The Board was not interested in pursuing the diversification into film as a major enterprise. J.C.W. had owned the stage rights to John O'Grady's *They're a Weird Mob*, but never produced it in the theatre. John had for some years been having discussions, both in Australia and abroad, about the financing of films, and began negotiations with famously maverick English director Michael Powell ('father' of Googie's film career) as early as 1961. Powell's career had foundered on the 1960 scandal of the daring psychological thriller *Peeping Tom*, now regarded as a masterwork but then critically excoriated by ladylike critics such as C.A. Lejeune who felt it should have been flushed down the toilet.

By the end of his dealings with Powell, John might well have felt that some fairly drastic treatment was in order. In the fat cuttings book that stands as a record of the efforts to get *Weird Mob* into production, there emerges a growing sense of frustration with Powell. A company called Williamson-Powell International Films Pty Ltd had been set up for the purpose of funding the production, and one of Powell's responsibilities was to interest overseas distributors, particularly the Rank Organisation in the UK, in the film. The correspondence reveals him to have been more than a little evasive in passing on information relating to this to the Australian directors of the company, including John and his lawyer friend Bob Austin. There are long handwritten letters from Powell to Austin and others urging them to trust him about this 'important' picture, and particularly about his dissatisfaction with John

O'Grady, describing him as 'belligerently provincial'. O'Grady clearly wanted the film to hew as closely as possible to the book's contours. Had he and Powell been in the same continent it is hard to believe their disagreements over the screenplay would have stopped with mere words. Powell may have been right when he claimed that 'being true to the book' isn't the same as 'a too literal translation of chunks of the book into a screenplay'. When Powell presented a screenplay by British playwright-screenwriter Roger MacDougall, O'Grady made conciliatory moves but also objected to some interpolations that he felt, probably rightly, would have been unacceptable to Australian audiences, such as gratuitous scenes showing Sir Robert Menzies opening the Sydney Opera House. In the end, the writing credit is attributed to Powell's former producer-writer Emeric Pressburger, under the name of Richard Imre. Probably unwisely, O'Grady spoke to a reporter about 'this ridiculous script', at which Powell took much offence. What they really needed was a few sharp words from Googie to sort them out, she not having hesitated when young to tick off Powell when he'd given offence! All the interminable dealings with Powell before a foot of film was shot must have had a disillusioning effect on J.C.W. who had always been less enthusiastic than John about entering into film production.

To finance the film, John not only drew on such sources as the Rank Organisation, but ended by having to mortgage his own house in Melbourne. The film proved a huge hit in Australia, though not overseas, and, as a result, it only just made a profit over-all. John was now committed to the idea of further film production and 'disagreement on the diversification of its [J.C.W.'s] activities in film' was then reported as a major reason for the parting of the ways. J.C.W. maintained its interest, at least nominally, in Williamson-Powell International Films Pty Ltd, which had produced *Weird Mob*, but it never made another film. Unhelpfully, when the film's star, the Italian comedian Walter Chiari, was arrested for alleged substance abuse and condemned by the Vatican, 'The Italian distributors quickly faded away.' The title of an article about the future of cinema in Australia – '*Weird Mob* may start a new era' – proved unduly optimistic. This was surprising, considering its commercial success here at least. Forty-odd years later, it still looks an amiable film, utterly redolent of its time and place, of an innocence when 'bloody' was as offensive as film language got. It also had a cast full of names that both recalled Australia's post-war attempts to create a local film industry (Chips Rafferty, Muriel Steinbeck) and some that would be associated with the resuscitated Australian film industry of the decades ahead, such as Ed Devereaux, John Meillon and Jeannie Drynan – and Tony Bonner who would figure substantially in John McCallum's subsequent career.

What emerges is a general sense of John's feeling constrained by the views of The Firm's Board and perhaps of being a little uncertain about where he wanted his career to go. He didn't want to become a film executive but would have favoured an executive position with, say, the Performing Arts Council or the Elizabethan Theatre Trust. Not having acted since 1959 and not having missed it, he said in interview: 'I suppose I'm less definite about my acting days being over now. But I'd be wary of tackling a large stage role, because I'm so out of training. Film work would be easier, but I've been out of them so long I'm no longer known overseas.' Despite the apparent hesitance in such a statement, John was about to embark on a period of intense – and profitable – activity. There was some vague talk about the possibility of returning to England, but this never seems to have been a seriously considered idea, and it may have derived from the news that Googie was being offered a role in a West End play.

They may well have been 'wonderful' years that John spent with The Firm, but a few hours spent with the surviving correspondence of his incumbency with J.C.W. can leave the reader astonished at the incessant demands made on his time – and, even more astonishing, the unfailing courtesy and tact with which he seems to have handled these. It is not just a matter of the serious administrative and 'housekeeping' matters that required his attention, though these were surely time-consuming enough. There is, for instance, an exchange of letters with Frank Tait re the carpeting of the restored Her Majesty's Theatre in Adelaide along with an update on the takings of The Firm's current shows, plus discussion of problems relating to the chorus and ballet ('these lower-bracket people') who are not honouring obligations. Or a letter from John re the need to move the play *Goodnight Mrs Puffin* out of the Comedy Theatre to make way for the incoming Joyce Grenfell's brilliant one-woman show. These, though, are the expected sorts of issues the joint-Managing Director might have been expected to deal with, but apart from them there is an ongoing flood of letters addressed to John at his Comedy Theatre office requesting his presence at a bewildering array of occasions. These range from a Government House garden party to a talk at Pentridge prison, with innumerable invitations to guest-speak at Rotary, the Country Women's Association annual conference, regular Royal Commonwealth Society luncheons, and personal (and in some cases almost impertinent) letters asking for assistance with jobs for relatives or friends about to fetch up in Melbourne or could he please arrange theatre seats for the writer? And one from a woman in Beaumaris, Melbourne, asking John to arrange a meeting between her and Googie for whom she is often mistaken!

What all this may suggest is that, despite John's undoubted administrative skills and his flair for handling people and potentially tricky situations with discretion and efficiency, the other side of his talents and vocation – the creative side – was not getting much of a look-in. He was after all an actor with an established reputation on stage and screen, and he was also hankering to produce and/or direct in both media and in television.

Googie did indeed go to England soon after. She had had a mixed bag of plays in Australasia in the first half of the 1960s. Audiences adored her in *The Constant Wife* and *Woman in a Dressing Gown*, and even in the lightweight and long-forgotten American comedy of modern marriage and manners, Samuel Taylor's *Beekman Place*, which, apart from noting 'the almost casually professional attractiveness of her performance', got lukewarm praise. She told one reporter that she 'has ordered three outfits and an ocelot hat for £446 from a Collins St couturier' to wear as Lady Piper in *Beekman Place*, adding that 'Choosing clothes for a play is much more difficult than buying for one's personal wardrobe' because you're 'on show', clothes mustn't crease, etc. And there were pages of colour pictures of her in the elegant costumes she wears in each of the latter's three acts in the Australian *Women's Weekly*.

Costumes notwithstanding, audiences in Invercargill, New Zealand, had been poor, but what really irked Googie was that she got a ticket for speeding while there, and even she was unable to talk her way out of it. Actually, she made things more difficult for herself by giving her stage name whereas her driving licence called her 'Mrs John McCallum', and the traffic cop then had the audacity to ask her her age, which did nothing for their developing relationship. But as to plays, Australia had been less enthusiastic about the downbeat *Winter Journey* or the compilation piece, *The First 400 Years*, and she was later very cross about the reception of her first Australian role, in *Desire of the Moth*. About the latter, she had told an interviewer that she was 'tremendously excited about playing an Australian in a play she considers has great quality.'

She always felt it would be difficult for her to play Australians, believing that 'an upper-class Australian woman is the only way I could play an Australian, the sort of woman in *Desire of the Moth*... I couldn't play a sleazy mum from a back street.' (This of course is somewhat at odds with her notion about 'posh' being able to do 'common'!) Reading the play fifty years later, one can see what would have attracted her to this play, and to the role of the apparently strong woman with a suppressed past, but it ends none too convincingly and all the situations seem to be rather artificially set up and endlessly *talked out* rather than creating a sense of natural progression. It might have worked as an all-out – and outback – melodrama, with Googie as the proud woman who, deserted by her lover, marries a stockman bribed by her father to give her child a name ... and so on, but as one reviewer remarked 'Not even Miss Withers can save the defective third act by making the wife's collapse convincing', having imbued her with 'such icy composure and moneyed imperiousness.' Though she was lauded for giving 'one of the finest performances of her career', nothing could make Sydney librarian James Brazill's play popular. Three years later, her 'eyes blaz[ing] like angry emeralds' ... 'She chops her knee with the side of her hand, karate-style. "I was crucified for it. As if I had perpetrated a terrible crime. We stood by our decision. If you feel confident in anything you should give it a go"'. Sue Nattrass, who was stage manager, recalled that relations between Googie and co-star Ed Devereaux had not been easy, but felt that Googie 'was very professional about this.' She also remembered how good Googie was about taking notes from 'a green twenty-five-year-old': she always listened carefully and took notice.

No wonder she felt like going back to England when the West End beckoned. As with her previous 1960s visit for *Exit the King*, the next play met with mixed responses. This was Bernard Shaw's *Getting Married* which opened on 19 April 1967. It attracted a good many swipes as being little more than a vehicle for an all-star cast. The *Daily Express* found the play as 'irrelevant and dated as a druid in a discotheque'; the *Daily Mail* claimed that 'Bernard Shaw defies the kiss of life' and felt 'It's a pity that Googie Withers' return to the West End is in one of Shaw's dullest roles'. However, *The Sun* set the tone for much of the reviewing when it singled out Googie as the brazen, voracious mayoress, Mrs George: 'Miss Withers blazes in the part, giving what otherwise would have been merely another safely star-studded revival.' Producer Peter Bridge took no risks with the casting of this talky, dated debate about the pros and cons of marriage, and he listed his stars alphabetically no doubt to avoid other potentially fraught possibilities. They included Ian Carmichael, Raymond Huntley, David Hutcheson, Esmond Knight, Moira Lister, Margaret Rawlings, Hugh Williams – and at the end of the roster the one who seems to have stolen the show, Googie in one of her most flamboyant parts. There were several somewhat patronising comments on the 'Australian accent' it was suggested she used to suggest the 'common' origins of Mrs George, 'representing womanhood and the working class and (I'd guess) Shaw's mother or something.' Googie must have been pleased with her reception back in England, even if critics found the play distinctly fusty and over-didactic.

Back in Australia, in the wake of John's resignation and of his future career plans, what happened was that the Toorak house was sold and the family moved decisively to Sydney. At first, they rented a house in Palm Beach for the 1966 Christmas holidays, while they pondered whether to stay in Sydney or go back to England. As John wrote: 'Our fate was decided by a kangaroo.' Meanwhile, Googie would take up the West End offer of *Getting Married*, and the two older children stayed in their Victorian boarding schools during term time. But for John and Googie, however much time they spent away from it, either on tour or working overseas, Sydney would be their 'home' for the rest of their lives.

Chapter 8

NEW DIRECTIONS

It may well have been a kangaroo that determined where the McCallum family would settle, but in fact John was not a stranger to television when he embarked on the hugely popular *Skippy* series. Both he and Googie had done television work in Britain, but his function in Australia would go beyond this. Back in 1963, John had been chosen to be host-narrator for Sydney's TCN-9 series, *The Crowded Years*, after the producers had read an article by Googie saying why she liked living in Australia. The first episode in the documentary series, aired on 7 October 1963, was called 'With Our Hands', in which he appeared with Googie and the three children. It was mainly concerned with the expansion of the Australian steel, automotive and transport industries, with John discussing the great changes that had taken place since his boyhood, with the focus especially on the period since the mid 1950s, and the second in the series, 'The Magnificent Gamble', traced the history of oil exploration in Australia. The series seems not to have met with great enthusiasm, but it was perhaps interesting enough to John to set him thinking about the possibilities of television production in Australia.

'Enthusiasm' was hardly the word for *Skippy*, which took off in such a big way. It may today look somewhat naïve in its sentiments and simplistic in its plot development but its moral values, its environmental concerns and its pacy narratives, problems usually solved by the hyper-intelligent furry heroine of the title, were pretty well exemplary. And of course it is essentially aimed at children, not at sceptical adults.

John was aware of a slump in theatre in the mid 1960s and, having failed to interest J.C. Williamson's to continue film production, in spite of the success of *They're a Weird Mob*, he proceeded to set up another company to engage in television and movie production. With his lawyer friend Bob Austin and film director Lee Robinson, he established Fauna Productions in association with the Nine Television Network. The series was to be set in Waratah National Park, so that there was always going to be the lure of mountain scenery. In their *Talking Heads* programme in 2007, Googie recalled the genesis of the series in 1966 when they were holidaying in Pittwater:

> Googie: We were sitting there with this wonderful view, with all our luggage packed to go back [to Melbourne]. And John said to me, 'What would you say if we stayed on for a bit, because I've got an idea for a series.' And I said, 'What is it?' He said, 'You see, nobody's got a kangaroo except Australia...'

> John: Lee Robinson came up with the idea of a boy and a kangaroo. It was really his idea. And we worked on that. I wanted to call it 'Hoppy'. He said, No, 'Skippy' had a better ring to it for the children. And so three or four of us put in $5,000, we made a pilot, took it around the world, sold it to quite a few countries, including England.

John credited Lee Robinson, who produced 75 episodes, with the amazing success of the series. Robinson was the 'line producer' responsible for the day-to-day working of the production. John and Bob Austin had 'executive producer' credits, and as far as John was concerned that meant 'I was in the office every day looking at next week's scripts, for the month ahead, casting, helping with casting, talking to him [Robinson] and going back about casting'. There were finally 91 episodes of *Skippy*, seen in colour and black-and-white by an estimated three million people round the world and offering unexceptional images of Australia. 'Think of the propaganda, the awareness of Australia that that will generate. It's incalculable,' John was quoted as saying at the time. Certainly, a generation of Australian children were brought up on its wholesome stories and were possibly at least as well served as their counterparts today with computer games.

It is interesting to note that episodes have been screened forty-odd years on in the early hours of the morning on the Nine network's digital channel,

Gem 90, in 2013. They are shown at hours when children might be expected to be asleep, so perhaps the target audience is those who grew up with the series. Watching ten of these episodes in rapid succession, one is struck by the skill with which each is packaged. Set in the Ranger's office in the National Park, each begins with the cast introduced in close-ups (Ed Devereaux as Ranger Matt Hammond, Ken James as older son Mark, Garry Pankhurst as the younger, Sonny, and Tony Bonner, as helicopter pilot Jerry King) with the catchy theme song, 'Skippy, the bush kangaroo', on the soundtrack. The Ranger's household is completed by Clancy (Liza Goddard), pretty enough, you'd think, to stir Mark's late teenage instincts, but nothing like sex ever seems to have been hinted at. Nor is there any sense of fraternal conflict between Mark and Sonny, except on the most benign, even facetious level. A problem is set up in the first few minutes: someone's Siamese cat has gone missing or a koala's injuries point to a cruel trapper at work or Mark wants to travel overseas but Matt thinks he's too young or there's trouble organising a surprise birthday party for Clancy. Skippy, who responds to all requests and commands with an inane clicking sound, will inevitably suss out the guilty party or the elusive solution. There are some improbable elements such as young Sonny (aged about ten) being allowed to go loose in Sydney's Luna Park, even more improbably accompanied by Skippy, but even for those of us well past the age to whom the series is addressed there is a kind of fascination in seeing how the plot pieces fall into place. Nothing is wasted; the central plotlines are clear; the family relationships are exemplary; father Matt is equally at home with simple folk as with Sir Adrian, a politician of some kind; and the villains are either obvious baddies like the animal trapper or comic figures like Mr Nimble who hides a stolen wallet in Skippy's pouch. As you would if you felt the cops were after you.

Mr Nimble is played by John Meillon and it is worth noting that, over the years of its production (1968–70), *Skippy* provided work for a huge number of Australian actors. Starting with Frank Thring who played Dr Stark, the original villain who tried to kidnap Skippy, the casts read like a Who's Who of the Australian acting profession, with such names as Edward Hepple, Jeanie Drynan, Tom Oliver, Neva Carr-Glynn, Harold Hopkins, Darlene

Johnson, Barry Crocker and dozens of others who must have been grateful to this particular McCallum enterprise. In 1969 the series spawned a feature film called *The Intruders*, subsequently sold to the British Children's Film Foundation which cut it to an hour and showed it very popularly at its Saturday matinees.

John was awarded CBE (Commander of the Order of the British Empire) in 1971 for his services to the performing arts, and, while his work with J.C.W. was obviously a major element in this, it would be wrong to underestimate the importance of *Skippy*'s contribution to performers and other artists in Australian media arts. When John was subjected to the Australian version of *This Is Your Life* in April 1976, it was only fitting that among the celebrities from the performing arts 'Skippy' should have been present. The inverted commas around her name derive from the fact (kept of course from besotted children at the time) that there were more than one marsupial called into play over the four years of production, and various sets of paws used to represent, say, piano-playing. As John recalled several decades later: 'They're very hard to train - far harder than a dog. No brains at all. Very sweet animals, but very, very difficult, and temperamental too. And ... so we had ... I'm afraid it's a bit of a giveaway, but we ended up with 35 Skippys! One was a good runner, one was a good jumper, one could get in and out of a car. That took six months of training to do that. And ... so we used different ones.'

Hugely successful as *Skippy* was, it is not surprising that John would go on to further television production, but that is to jump a few years. There were other ventures going on in the McCallum household in the later 1960s, including Googie's return to the West End stage, Joanna's aspiring towards an acting career, and John and Googie acting together again after eight years. John, of course, hadn't acted at all since *Roar Like a Dove* finished in 1959, having in the meantime done time in the most productive way with J.C.W. Then in 1968, as one journal put it, 'Relatively speaking they're together again.' After this lamely punning title, the article went on to record the couple's stage reunion on 20 March in Alan Ayckbourn's comedy of mistaken identity, of modern sexual mores and manners, and copious misunderstandings. *Relatively Speaking* won glowing reviews for the starring couple in the production at the Phillip Theatre, Sydney, with stress on how their styles seemed to complement each other. For instance, H.G. Kippax found it 'An absolute joy', praising Googie for 'carrying her massive technical armoury as lightly as thistledown' and John 'who matches her relaxation with comic acting in the same difficult convention.' Another reviewer, Norman Kessell, similarly found 'Joyous fun in errors' and praised 'the practised poise and elegance of Googie Withers and John McCallum', noting that John also produced.

Relatively Speaking was the first major success for the about-to-be prolific Ayckbourn, and it was an ideally calculated vehicle for bringing John and Googie back together on stage. It was a return to the witty, tightly constructed comedy that they'd made such a hit with in *Simon and Laura* thirteen years earlier. It may always look as if actors are having to work harder on more serious, even near-tragic material such as *The Deep Blue Sea*, but the McCallums understood the discipline of comedy and the demands this makes on the actors. They did this well enough for the production to go on to a twelve-week season in Melbourne's Princess Theatre and thence to Australia's oldest theatre, Hobart's Theatre Royal. The punning article mentioned above, while focusing mainly on the Bayview home which the McCallums had recently acquired, described how the set for *Relatively Speaking* had been designed from photos of their old house in Denham, Buckinghamshire.

Their new home was a picturesquely rambling weatherboard house, built about 1885 and overlooking Pittwater, about twenty miles to the north of downtown Sydney. All accounts suggest that they both fell for the house at first sight. Googie told a reporter that it was 'Just what [I] wanted – weatherboard, tin roof, verandah... very Australian... very different from the house we had in Toorak. The sort of house I was looking for when I first came to Australia eight years ago.' Certainly it would prove attractive enough to keep them there for over forty years, even if, towards the end Googie would claim that it was falling down round their ears. In fact, it was an irresistibly comfortable place, ideal for a busy couple in odd periods of relaxation, for holidays when Joanna and Nick were home from their Victorian boarding-schools and for Amanda to grow up in – when she wasn't travelling the world with one or both of her parents. John's later business partner and co-producer John Frost recalled that 'they always kept the house in Bayview, and every time they went to London [in the '80s and '90s], which was at least once a year, when they'd be there for four or five months, when they'd do, say, the Chichester season or a West End season during our winter, they'd ask me whether I'd look after the Bayview house. I used to move into that house every May and move out in September – I really housekept for them and looked after the dog. There was a guy who looked after the grounds, and there were two cleaners who came in twice a week. It's all pulled down now; it's a wreck', but it was undoubtedly a place they loved.

It was not only a place they loved but it was also the scene for an amazing amount of hospitality over the ensuing decades. Many years later, Joanna remembered, 'Whenever people they knew from England came to Australia, they were always welcomed for dinners and parties. Or the Americans from *How to Succeed in Business* came to spend Christmas with us. Or when Harry Belafonte walked through the door with his wife and their little boy, I'd never seen such beautiful people in my life. Or when John Mills and his wife arrived and she fell and smashed her face and they then spent the whole of Boxing Day in casualty.' And many years later, all sorts of friends, in and out of the profession, testify to the warmth of the welcome they were given there, just as they had been in their Melbourne home. This helps to explain the enduring affection and respect in which they were held: they relished good company, whether in the theatre or in the home.

By this time Joanna was finishing school where she had played the title role in Shaw's *St Joan*. In several interviews, Googie had mentioned Joanna's acting aspirations, the while suggesting that she felt it important for her to complete her schooling before heading for the stage. In an interview in 1980, Joanna said, 'My parents never pushed me into an acting career, but after I played Joan of Arc at school I decided it was the life for me.' To mark the end of her schooldays, John and Googie threw a party at Monsalvat, the former artists' colony at Eltham, on the hills to the northeast of Melbourne, and the event was recorded in what may be a page from the *Australian Women's*

Weekly, with a picture of Jo, her parents and her cousin Christopher Withers. Jo had increasingly figured in the photos of first-night attendance with one or both parents, and it was becoming plain where her future lay. She enrolled in Sydney's National Institute of Dramatic Art (NIDA) on leaving school, and on graduating in 1969 she made her professional debut in Melbourne Theatre Company's production of *Rookery Nook*, followed by a six-month contract. While valuing her parents' support for her career, she felt there were also difficulties involved in being the daughter of Googie and John. 'I've got to make my own way... you've got to prove yourself all the time.' If your parents are well-known in the profession, this may open some doors to you, but it may also impose a pressure on you to perform that would not perhaps be expected of one wholly new to the theatre.

Nick was enrolled at Glamorgan, Geelong Grammar Preparatory School, in Toorak, conveniently placed while the family was living in that Melbourne suburb. There is a carefully preserved letter from him to John with details of a cricket match his school had lost against Brighton Grammar. More cheerily, 'The electronics set you brought me is working fine'. Considering that Nick went on to work on production design in film, with all its attendant technical problems, and that he did not go on to share John's lifelong delight in cricket, this handwritten letter from the ten-year-old seems almost prescient in its emphases. However, he did win the under-ten high jump while still at Glamorgan and there is a picture of Googie presenting him with his prize! By the last years of the decade he was a boarder at Geelong Grammar's Corio campus, where he completed his schooling. Amanda, Mandy as she is known, showed no interest in a theatrical or film career, and would eventually lead a kind of life very different from those of her parents and siblings. At the present point in the story, she is about seven or eight – ideal *Skippy*-viewing age?

Following J.C.W.'s reluctance to follow up the success of *They're a Weird Mob* and with further filmmaking projects, and with 90 episodes of *Skippy* under his belt, he decided to make his own venture into film direction. The result was *Nickel Queen* (1971), on which he was also producer and co-screenwriter.

Set in Western Australia at the time of the Poseidon-led mining boom, the film got off to a roaring start in Perth. *Skippy* had spawned a feature film, *The Intruders*, in 1969, for Fauna Productions, but it was directed by Lee Robinson, with John as executive producer. With *Nickel Queen*, he was making his directorial debut, and it was a real family affair, with Googie starring and Joanna in her first film, playing appropriately enough Googie's daughter. Joanna has vivid recollections of the shoot around Kalgoorlie, which was blisteringly hot throughout, and of the brothel 'just up from the Police Station... it sported a row of red plate-glass windows where the "girls" sat and polished their nails next to neat respectable little bungalows, while they waited for trade.' She also remembered how the cast and crew came to favour a certain basic diner, and when the owners saw that their eatery was being patronised by movie people, 'candles were put on tables, which were now covered in red-and-white check tablecloths, and the menu was redesigned with French flourishes... At the re-opening, the locals were dismayed, until their usual waitress entered through the swing door, and shouted, "Hands up for soup!"'

In what was certainly at some remove from her filming past at Ealing Studios, Googie embarked on her (at least) third barmaid role, and no doubt her experiences in *Pink String and Sealing Wax* and *It Always Rains on Sunday* fed into her playing of the widowed Meg Blake who runs an outback pub in a ghost town about 400 miles from Perth, somewhere in the Kalgoorlie area. She acts on rumours of a nickel strike on nearby Spinifex Hill, stakes her claim, falls willing victim to the shyster American boss of Benson Mining Corporation who buys her shares and then makes publicity out of her wealth. She wins social status as the Nickel Queen in Perth, where she spends wildly and is taken up by pushy socialites. Naturally after she's lost everything and Benson has been exposed as a fraud, she realises it's loyal Harry (Ed Devereaux) she really fancies and heads back to a knees-up at her Mirribilli pub.

There's another plot strand involving some hippies who set up camp in Mirribilli's derelict railway station and whose shifty guru, Claude (John Laws), also has a go at taking Meg for a ride when he shaves off his beard, dons black tie and fetches up in Perth. And Joanna, as daughter Jenny, expelled from university for her part in student protests, also tracks her mother down in Perth. Oh, there's a lot going on in *Nickel Queen* and it's all quite entertaining in its predictable way. Of course the good-hearted Meg isn't going to be allowed to throw in her lot with a bunch of superficial and greedy social types, not when there's honest, rugged Harry carrying a torch for her – and daughter Jenny urging him on with 'Why aren't you with her when she needs you?' The screenplay, the work of journalist Henry C. James who wrote the original story, with input from John and Joy Cavill, makes for some lively comedy and endorses unexceptionable values.

No one is going to make great critical claims for *Nickel Queen* though it doesn't deserve the sniping verdict of one British reviewer who dismissed it as 'this antediluvian comedy of manners which hammers home its clichés with merciless bonhomie'. If this writer had turned up in Perth at the time of the film's record-breaking run there, he could easily have been lynched, for Western Australia had taken the first feature film set there to its heart. It says much for John's skills as a negotiator that, of the film's $500,000 budget, $350,000 was raised in Western Australia (the rest came from Fauna Productions), and that he was able to recruit its Premier, David Brand, and two of his ministers, Charles Court and Arthur Griffith to appear in one of the film's scenes, as well as celebrated talk-show host Laws. In an interview at the time in this connection, Lee Robinson described John McCallum as 'a real wizard, the greatest front man of all time. The sort of bloke who can get in to see a king. He's got that little extra bit of class that opens all doors. Never gets a knock-back.'

In support of this view of John's tact and persuasive powers, there was front-page coverage of John giving instructions to these political figures, and a roguish suggestion elsewhere that 'Government "stars" may have to join a union' to play their parts. Griffith, as Minister for Mines, was especially appropriate. As well, hundreds of locals were cast in bit roles or as extras, and the publicity generated was enormous – and, from a box-office point of view, invaluable. One article in a WA paper gave an entertaining account of how the extras worked all through the night on a scene set in the Parmelia

Hotel's garden restaurant: 'They knew they had to be present all through the night – from 6 p.m. till 6 a.m. – to ensure continuity for the scene. Yet they ranged from exhilarated young people about 20 to several septuagenarians'. The writer went on to say, 'When the [filmmaking] process comes to one's home town and involves people famous through stage, television and cinema itself, and familiar locations and people … the attraction is magnetic, especially with history being made [i.e., WA's first feature film]'. Headlines such as 'Glittering World Premiere for the Nickel Queen' were typical. This same paper devoted an entire page to the film, to its première with its 'high-fashion guests' and to an enthusiastic review. Another report told how 'More than 900 guests basked in the first-night lights. Guests of honour were the Governor of Western Australia, Major-General Sir Douglas Kendrew and Lady Kendrew.'

The film was an immense commercial hit in WA, where people fell upon it with all the pleasure of recognition, but it was not such a critical or a box-office success in the other states or internationally. Nevertheless, it has its place firmly enough at the start of the Australian filmmaking revival of the 1970s. Googie was unable to be present at the promotional events in Australia because she was looking after Joanna who was in England where she was making her West End debut, but both women were present when 'in a fantastic "scoop" the League of Friends of the Swanage Hospital have got the first public screening of a new Australian film starring Swanage actress Googie Withers.' Googie had of course been brought up in Swanage, where her late father, Captain Edgar Withers, lived in Ballard Estate, and her brother Col. Harry Withers and his second wife Judy now lived at Court Pound, Langton Matravers. This was not quite the Northern Hemisphere breakthrough that John may have hoped for, but there's a nicely cyclical touch about the idea of the home-town girl coming back trailing clouds of film fame.

Meanwhile, Googie and Joanna were pursuing different paths in England. As far as John and Googie were concerned, it had never been a condition that they must always be hired as a team, and over subsequent decades they would occasionally co-star but were open to other professional possibilities. Throughout the 1970s, there was plenty of evidence for this approach to their careers. For instance, while John was playing opposite Ingrid Bergman on stage in *The Constant Wife* in London in 1973, Googie was filming episodes of the television series *Within These Walls*, and, while Googie continued in the latter into the following year, John was overseeing the Australian production of his own play, *As It's Played Today*, as well as producing further TV series. Then, at the end of the decade, they would be starring together again in elegant comedy *The Kingfisher* in Melbourne.

This rapid run-through of titles and activities scarcely touches the sides of what they got up to in the '70s. Nor does it take account of what was going on in family life or the restoration of the Bayview house. Joanna, having begun her professional career with the Melbourne Theatre Company, was at age nineteen starring in its production of Brecht's *The Caucasian Chalk Circle* and the memorable Tyrone Guthrie-directed *All's Well That Ends Well* at Melbourne's Princess Theatre in October 1970. Immediately after this, she made her film debut in *Nickel Queen*, was now setting her sights on a career in Britain, and in the early '70s was seen in several high-profile television series there, including the title role in *Barbara of the House of Grebe* (1973), one of the series derived from Thomas Hardy's *Wessex Tales*. She was also appearing on the stage during these years, so her career was taking off in very promising style.

Joanna recalled that she and Googie 'flew out to the UK arriving in February 1971. On the way, we called in at New Delhi where the hotel car failed to meet us, so we took a taxi which headed off to some wasteland and demanded US$200 before proceeding. However, Googie put on a very imperious turn, threatening all kinds of punishment which led him to get us to the hotel.' Safely arrived in England, Joanna acquired as agent, Patricia Marmont, the former actress who had played Googie's understudy in *Winter Journey* twenty years earlier. Marmont very properly took her on only after she had set up a couple of auditions for her. One of these was for the role of Helena in *A Midsummer Night's Dream*, at Sheffield Playhouse. Offered this role and opting for Sheffield, she turned down the chance of making her West End debut in the long-running farce *No Sex Please We're British!*, a decision she never regretted and which did nothing to slow down her English acting career.

Googie, before making her Australian film debut in *Nickel Queen*, had done an extensive tour in Neil Simon's comedy *Plaza Suite*, which gave her the chance to play three separate roles. In this play, directed and designed by John, she co-starred with American actor Alfred Sandor, former amateur heavyweight boxer and wartime counter-intelligence agent in Germany, who was born in Budapest, but spent his youth in Germany. Googie would star with him again in *Nickel Queen*, where he played the fraudulent mining corporation boss. They had enjoyed working together in the play, so this may have explained the subsequent casting in the film. Sue Nattrass, who stage-managed *Plaza Suite*, again enjoyed working with Googie and recalled that the star took her out to lunch just before the play opened. Another of the typical anecdotes one hears about Googie as a team member.

After successful seasons in Melbourne, Hobart and Sydney, and a week in Canberra, Googie embarked on her sixth tour of New Zealand with *Plaza Suite*. She always maintained that comedy was more demanding for actors than serious drama, so she must have been quite pleased with the report in Canberra which praised her and Sandor as two people 'who know what they are doing' in what amounted to three one-acters, each of which is set in the eponymous hotel suite and which offered Googie a nice range of characters in the one play. This comparatively lightweight piece seemed to bring out the metaphors in reviewers: in Hobart, one reviewer claimed that 'it resembles a good wine with an interesting bouquet' and in New Zealand, one critical view was that 'It is the formidable acting skill of Googie Withers that makes of this airy soufflé a dish acceptable even to those who prefer the red meat of theatrical fare.' The play was directed and co-designed by John, and one journal summed up the contribution of both as follows: 'For the last decade Googie Withers has generally been considered the uncrowned Queen of the Australian stage and the three superb performances she gives in "Plaza Suite" are likely to enhance this reputation… [while] John McCallum has skilfully directed it as well as co-designing the attractive set.' Against this, and other similar accolades, the rare anti-voice querying 'Googie's rightness for Simon – and Simon's rightness for her', and suggesting that John's direction caused it to 'sag', wouldn't have made much headway.

When she and Joanna arrived in the UK, her first thoughts were to help Joanna get settled and to see her started on her career there, but it was not long before Googie was herself involved in several TV series. One of the highlights of her return to London, and one for which she was quite unprepared, occurred on 6 May 1971. The journalist Godfrey Winn, a long-time friend of the McCallums, colluded with Thames Television to get Googie to a theatre where she supposed she was about to appear in a programme about Winn. When she got on to the stage she was greeted by Eamonn Andrews holding the famous big red book and announcing, 'Googie Withers, This Is Your Life!' As the programme continued, and Googie's astonishment subsided, people from her past, including mother, Wuz, who tried to explain the name 'Googie' again, brother Harry up from Dorset, and Michael Redgrave came on to pay tribute. Or, in the case of the wonderful old character actor, Raymond Huntley, to remind her that she still owed him a penny which, as a child, she'd borrowed for a tram fare. But the real emotional peak of the evening was the emergence of John, whom she believed to be on the other side of the world, and the children: Joanna had come from Sheffield where, by lucky chance her stage performance had been cancelled for that night, and there was a tearful reunion with Nick and Amanda from Australia. She would have another forty years to go, but in 1971 'This' was indeed a resonant echo of a 'Life' already fully lived in and out of the spotlight.

Chapter 9

SMALL SCREENS AND LARGE STAGES

If anything, the 1970s were even busier for the McCallums than the previous crowded decade had been, and involved not merely flitting from one acting medium to another but also travelling regularly between two continents. For Googie and John, it could be said that television seemed to dominate in the '70s, both of them scoring spectacular successes in small-screen projects, but equally there was a good deal of successful theatre work as well. There was also the matter of getting the Bayview house in order and of keeping tabs on the lives and careers of their three children. Reading and thinking about what they achieved in their mid to late '50s, one is again and again struck by the sheer creative energy – and just *ordinary* energy – they brought to the drama of their lives at this period.

Following the pattern of divergence and convergence that always marked their careers, in the post-*Nickel Queen* period, and in television, Googie would have one of the most popular successes of her career and John would leave his mark on Australian popular culture. Back in Australia in 1972, Googie, then fifty-five, took on one of the great roles for actresses of her age: that of Mme Ranevsky in Chekhov's *The Cherry Orchard*. Others in my experience who have made their mark in the role of this flamboyant, somewhat foolish, sentimental but engaging woman include Celia Johnson (on TV), Joan Plowright and Judi Dench, and Googie's performance for the Melbourne Theatre Company's production at the Comedy Theatre holds its own among such distinguished colleagues. The production ran into unexpected difficulty before it reached the stage when her co-star, Fred Parslow, playing Lopakhin, became ill and the role had to be taken over at almost the last minute by Simon Chilvers. Chilvers, who had been playing a smaller role (Pischik) in the play, recalls that he was excited at the prospect of replacing Parslow: 'I wasn't daunted by anything in those days. I always wanted to do the part anyway. I loved the challenge of huge amounts of work and of learning and just getting it done. Lopakhin was heaven sent.' He found Googie 'wonderfully supportive. She seemed to appreciate what I'd done more than I did myself. I was just a working actor, as she was to a certain extent, and that's what you did.'

After the comparatively light-weight pieces such as *Beekman Place* and *Plaza Suite*, popular as they were, it was reassuring to see Googie attacking a major, demanding role in Australia, a sentiment echoed in an article in *The Bulletin*. This began by saying: 'One trouble which has thwarted Googie Withers' "serious" acting career in Australia has been her appearance in too many "frivolous" plays.' The author of this piece goes on to delineate her establishing of Ranevsky by the end of Act One, as 'warm and generous only in a glossy superficial way, not very bright, emotionally shallow, self-indulgent, ruthless, a silly ageing tart. And for the rest of the evening Miss Withers colours in the contradictions, ambiguities and complexities of her character.' In this detailed account of her performance, the writer commends her avoidance of pathos or nostalgia. Critics were generally full of praise, though there was the odd dissentient voice like the one who claimed she 'mugged' for sympathy.

Perhaps more interesting is the way in which her director and co-star recalled working with her. Director John Sumner remembered: 'She was just beautiful in the role, and we spent quite a bit of time in preparation. I was living in Melbourne and she was living in Sydney, and I remember on one occasion I went up and stayed with them in the house they had on the water, in Bayview. I spent some time there because we had to agree on the script, on the translation of *The Cherry Orchard*. I had the one Tyrone Guthrie had given me, as it had been done in America at the Guthrie theatre, and Googie had an older, established version. So we got together and agreed on what we would do. We altered a bit till we were both satisfied.' Sumner, who could be quite authoritarian, apparently worked well with Googie, and in his autobiography he wrote: 'The rehearsals have stayed in my mind. I can still see Googie's Ranevsky in the second act, sitting reminiscing, talking of the life around her; suddenly we realise it is her deceitful lover she is thinking about, she has heard from him in Paris, he is ill, should she go back to him? Googie would make slight adjustments to her monologue, like a painter ever so slightly touching the brush to build a canvas... At that moment of sunset, we have seen Ranevsky as a sad, undecided, thoughtless woman. But Googie has also shown that indefinable quality which goes to make a star.' One negative review, however, claimed that the direction 'instead of ensemble playing, appeared geared to Googie as its star', but the critic felt this situation was improved in the televised version.

A moment that occurred on the play's opening night in Melbourne says something about her star presence. Sumner described how her carefully planned first entrance and ensuing movements were delayed while the audience gave her protracted applause, which she could only bring to a halt by acknowledging it with a graceful nod. She entered upstage right, with entourage, and had to make her way across stage to exit down left, issuing instructions as she passed through. Again, at the end, when she and Gaev had said their sorrowful goodbye to their home, there was more applause as the audience thought this must be the end of the play. The audience clearly thought the curtain had stuck while Firs potters around, waiting for the famous off-stage sound effect of the orchard being felled. This incident is a prime example of Googie's power at this stage of her career: her audience wasn't going to let her enter or leave the stage without showing its appreciation in this, now rather old-fashioned, way. The play had brief seasons in Canberra and Sydney (attracting here a full page in the *Sunday Telegraph*, with the heading 'The plum role in a cherry orchard'), and it must have been heartening to Googie to do the kind of classic theatre that would have been more readily available in London with its hugely greater potential audiences.

Googie also remembered with pleasure the tour of country Victoria with this production. After talking to the students at one high school, 'We then did a matinee for the children, and I don't think I've ever done such an exciting matinee in my life. There were 1200 children, and they were not blinkered – they laughed and cried and cheered.' She (and John) always took seriously their responsibilities to their audiences, and touring to areas away from metropolitan theatres was one example of this.

In Simon Chilvers' view, there was nothing temperamental about her: 'She couldn't help *being* a *grande dame*, but that wasn't what she really *was*. It was the result of being in a position, doing a job, being treated in a certain way, but she didn't give herself airs and graces. She got on very well with the rest of the cast. There was no star treatment. She was just a member of the company and that's how she got on with John and with all of us.' She got on well with Frank Thring who was playing Gaev and who was, by this time, according to Googie, 'knocking back six bottles of Ben Ean [Moselle] a day, yet although he was never obviously sober he was never obviously drunk.' Relative insobriety notwithstanding, Googie must have sufficiently enjoyed working with Thring to co-star with him (and John) again at the end of the decade in William Douglas Home's *The Kingfisher*, but much bridge would be played over the waters before that.

John, meanwhile, was pursuing a small-screen career as producer, some-times director and, on a few occasions, actor on three multi-episode television series. He had always been interested in the prospect of Australia's future in television production and in ensuring its international appeal, so that it was a matter of serious gratification when he negotiated the US sale of *Barrier Reef*. Speaking on *Meet the Press*, on Channel 9 TCN, in May 1959, he had talked about how television was 'helping' the theatre in London, by showing excerpts from stage productions, and a decade later he returned elated from America with 'contracts for the sale of his TV series, *Barrier Reef*, for about $20,000, to the American NBC network' which had taken seventeen episodes, with an option for a further fifteen. Like kangaroos, the Barrier Reef had the advantage of being unique to Australia and, in television series, 'different'. It was the first Australian production sold to a major American network. This was a real breakthrough as *Skippy* had been sold on a station-by-station basis.

The series was put together by Fauna Productions (i.e., John, Lee Robinson and Bob Austin, with Sir Reginald Ansett as a partner on this project), was originally entitled 'Minus-5', and was filmed in colour entirely on location in Northern Queensland and the Barrier Reef. It is about a scientific research team which engages with environmental issues and assorted low-lifes, and its distinction lies partly at least in its underwater cinematography, as opposed to studio tanks. Anne Seddon, daughter of Frank Tait, recalled how: 'John got my first husband Oliver Streeton a job as art director on the TV series *Barrier Reef*, which John produced. We lived on a barquentine moored on the reef for three weeks. The series was a sort of science-fiction.'

John records having tracked the 'barquentine' in question to the Brisbane River and the Company bought it for $60,000, refitting it for just under a further $100,000. Shooting on location wasn't always easy, and Googie had some anxiety about John's safety when filming had to be halted because of a typhoon. The episodes do benefit from the authenticity of the setting, even when the plotting is fairly predictable, but there is also some real tension, as in the episode called 'Echoes from the Past'. In this, directed by Vienna-born British film veteran Peter Maxwell, there is indeed such tension when diving expert Jack (George Assang) is trapped on the sea floor. In 'God Bless Her', there is some naivety in the visit of the royal family but this is offset by a more serious conservationist strand.

As with all the television series on which John was producer or executive producer or screenwriter, there is a sense of clear narrative lines. These can sometimes look unduly simple in their oppositions and their outcomes by comparison with the more complex plotting of more recent comparative series but you can see why they commanded popular audiences at the time. And, sometimes, the ingenuousness of the plotting works in their favour, leaving the viewer with attention to spare for the underlying ideas. The conservationist sentiments of *Barrier Reef* offer one example of this; in *Boney*, the next series, the writing and playing of the half-Aboriginal detective lead one to reflect on the sort of liberal approach to the character and the situations in which he finds himself; and the dealings with south-east Asia and its people in some episodes of *Shannon's Mob* (1975) and in *Bailey's Bird* (1977) suggest that they have more in mind than just regular bouts of well-filmed action. John was fairly conservative politically, according to daughter Joanna, but he was also alert to broadly humane values. As well, of course, he was an adroit producer: he knew it was wise in his devising of television series to focus on aspects of Australian life which ensured a novelty factor in relation to overseas markets; and perhaps the producer's function provided an outlet for both his creative and his administrative talents.

Boney was, in terms of character and situation, a more sophisticated venture than *Shannon's Mob* and *Bailey's Bird*, but those 'aspects of Australian life' may well have included in *Boney* 'life in the outback as overseas readers hope it will be rather than what it is'. The notion of the half-caste detective, derived from Arthur Upfield's popular novels, was a reasonably challenging one for 1970s Australian television. James Laurenson, the white New Zealander who played Detective Napoleon Bonaparte, recalled his meeting in London with John and Googie at the time of the casting of the series. John was being very polite and tactful in his approach, saying, 'We do think you're absolutely right for the part with your wide cheekbones and your, ahh, nose is the, umm, right shape, ahh, and your, er, lips' and, as he began to be embarrassed, Googie took over with 'What you're trying to say, darling, is that he's got a touch of the tarbrush – come to the point'. Laurenson added, 'I must say she rather endeared herself to me.' Years later, in reference to her direct manner, he described her affectionately as 'a daughter of the Empire'! Make-up artist Peggy Carter recalled using ten or more colours on Laurenson's face, and felt her work had been successful when, made-up as Boney, he was refused service in an Alice Springs pub. Racism was of course alive and well in 1970s Australia.

One of the impressive aspects of the series, which ran to 26 episodes (1972–73), is its utter lack of patronage in the drawing of its central character. There had been speculation that Peter Finch, then at the peak of his film career, might return to star as Boney, and John certainly had him in mind, saying: 'Both in looks and in sensitivity I think Peter Finch is the ideal actor to play the role.' He had begun negotiations with Finch's London agent, but the star's other commitments got in the way. However, in Laurenson's charismatic performance, Boney is allowed a degree of intelligence, even of sophistication, that compels the viewer's attention as much as it does that of the other characters. His racial mix is no more than one aspect of the whole man, who is as knowledgeable about his black forebears as he is at home among his white contemporaries. As one commentator wrote at the time, 'I welcomed Laurenson's neutral, educated English. It is high time we corrected the impression that our hinterland is populated entirely by illiterate bush-whackers and dusky chaw-bacons. To play such a role as Boney, in which he is clearly represented on an equal social standing with his white colleagues, Mr Laurenson must not only look, but also sound authoritative. He manages to do both with considerable presence.' The characters are individuals rather than stereotypes, and, as Laurenson said of Boney, 'His arrogance has been retained. It's part of his defence... At the same time... he's very gentle, delicate, and sensitive.'

John, using the skills he was often credited with, had negotiated with Don Dunstan, South Australian premier, for co-operation with the Police Force, vehicles and other mechanical things to do with production, and he must have been pleased with the way the series was received. The *Daily Mirror* praised it for proving that 'a local drama production can make the grade if it is properly handled from the beginning...', adding that the main credit was due to John, 'the executive producer who spent more than a year planning the series'.

Viewed thirty-odd years later, it may be no world-beater, but it is un-doubtedly an efficient detective series which features good story lines, unusual background scenery, and proficient acting and direction, and photography which, as in all the series with which John was associated in the 1970s, does well by the unique scenic qualities without letting *Boney* develop into a mere series of moving postcards. Location shooting was central, but somehow *Boney*, like *Barrier Reef* before it, *uses* its setting, builds the challenges it offers into the plotting and avoids indulgent pictorialism. He directed one episode of *Boney* and acted in three, as well as one in *Barrier Reef*, but his main contribution to Australian television was as initiator of ideas that would lead to productions that, in turn, helped to give Australia some standing on the international, as well as the local, television scene. He had the ideas and the know-how to bring them to fruition, and the series he originated provided work for an amazing parade of Australian actors and other creative talents. When asked in 1983 what he considered his most significant contribution to film and television in Australia, he had no hesitation in replying: 'The penetration of international markets... *Skippy* went right across America and *Barrier Reef* on NBC.... That really was the avant-garde of Australian films and made it known that we could make films here.'

Somehow squeezed in among these multifarious activities, John also found himself locking horns with the Warringah Shire Council, Sydney. John had inherited land at Bushranger's Hill, Newport, and he decided he wanted to build a house on this property. The Council, though, wanted to preserve the land for the public. There was a lot of to-ing and fro-ing over this matter and it looked for a while as if some kind of compromise might be reached, leading to a subdivision, but this failed because John wouldn't agree with the suggestion that the hilltop area, where he wanted to build, should be preserved as a public reserve of historic significance. Locals supported the Council and John lost his battle. What is surprising is that in 1974 he could find the time and energy to pursue this matter when he was so heavily committed in professional areas, but the matter made headlines in some papers. Perhaps there was just a sliver of time between the finish of *Boney* in 1973 and the start of the *Shannon's Mob* series in 1975, but wasn't he also co-starring with Ingrid Bergman in *The Constant Wife* in London in 1973–74?

While John was being a force behind the scenes of Australian television, Googie was re-establishing herself as a household name in Britain, this time on *its* small screens. She had done several television roles in the early 1970s, some in England where she'd gone with Joanna in 1971, a couple of episodes of *Boney* in Australia in 1972–73 and she had repeated her stage role in *The Cherry Orchard* for ABC (Australian Broadcasting Commission) television in 1974. But nothing she'd done for the small screen (or perhaps even the big screen) had brought her such widespread popularity and critical plaudits as she won for her playing of prison governor Fay Boswell in *Within These Walls*.

She took the role very seriously and put herself through some serious research in preparation, including a visit to Holloway Women's Prison. With a lack of what would now be called 'political correctness', she claimed that she didn't want to play the Governor 'as a dyke in leather boots' or 'moustachioed lady with boots and a whip' and more in similar vein. Her researches had revealed that women in this position were smartly dressed and carefully coiffed and made up. Certainly that's how Fay Boswell presents. On a more important level, when she did a broadcast from Pentridge Prison, Melbourne, she was put in a cell with six men, all of whom were there for life, but found them 'charming – and very interesting'. For an actress who went on to play a prison governor, this had been her only experience of life 'inside'. Typically, she managed to charm them to the extent that they sent her flowers and a good-luck telegram on one of her Melbourne opening nights! But her visit to Holloway was an intended precursor of her role as the Governor of Stone Park in *Within These Walls*. She researched the wardrobe carefully so as to avoid the clichéd, grim figure, and did find that other real-life women prison governors took serious care of hair, make-up and clothes. She met Dr Megan Bull, who had taken over as Governor of Holloway in 1972, and found a charming and elegant woman, beautifully dressed, at odds with the common image. Googie felt it was important to look good as an influence on the inmates. While she was there, she was introduced to some of the women and found several of them prone to 'cry a tremendous amount' while some of the others were just very funny, like the woman who told of having the tattooed names of her previous boyfriends removed: 'me 'usband didn't like it so I 'ad 'em taken off'.

The authorities were pleased with the series, which attracted a viewing audience of 16,000,000 per week – and Googie herself acquired a vast army of fans and was recognised wherever she went. 'I wish you was my mum,' called out a boy she passed on a London bridge one day, and there was a taxi driver who refused to take money for a fare from 'The Guv'. Then, once when she was on a train to the country, the ticket inspector asked, 'Got 'em all locked up?' As well as these and plenty of other such incidents, there was also a bizarre letter from a woman begging Googie to forgive her and to go on writing to her. Googie had asked her to stop sending presents or she'd stop writing to this woman who writes semi-literately. The woman, who had had a very difficult upbringing, had become obsessed with Googie after seeing *Within These Walls*, and continued writing to her for several years after the series finished. A psychiatric social worker wrote to Googie: 'She has emotionally "adopted" you as a mother figure,' urging her to continue to maintain contact with the woman. Finally, Peter Dews, Artistic Director at Chichester, where Googie was currently starring, answered this letter, saying: 'It is, understandably, intolerable for an actress to be bombarded with unsought-after gifts and requests for guidance which she is neither willing nor qualified to offer.'

These instances give some idea of the influence and popularity of the series, even if the critical response didn't always match the public perception, with one paper claiming that 'what it didn't have was even a whiff of authenticity'. Today, the episodes viewed seem well written, with their interlocking strands neatly fitted. In a 1974 episode, 'One Step Forward, Two Steps Back' Fay takes 'one small step forward' in bringing a young woman, who may have strangled her child, to prison without an escort. Fay is later rebuked by the prison's board members and the episode becomes as much about Fay as about the prisoner. There is also a suggestion of a lesbian relationship between one of the staff and a prisoner. On this matter and talking of another episode, the actress Patricia Garwood recalled: 'In the episode I was in, there was a lot of dramatic confrontation. I was playing a murderess in a lesbian relationship with another inmate. It was really quite daring for a star like Googie to be involved in such an episode at that time, in the mid '70s.' One of the interesting aspects of the series, in which Googie did a two-year stretch (with no remission for good behaviour, as she said) is the continuity developed by screenwriter and actress between Fay Boswell's professional life and her private life. In the episode *For Life* (1975), for instance, there are convincing scenes of her domestic life, both in a quiet few moments as she talks with her husband over a drink, giving a sense of a comfortable marriage, and at a dinner party where there is talk about one of the women's having to give up her job if her husband takes a post away from London. A quietly feminist idea is tossed in and helps to set the episode in a social context. Whatever the less enthusiastic critics felt about the level of reality in *Within These Walls*, there seems to be no doubt of Googie's having taken her role very seriously. She came to feel that many women were unjustly locked away in prisons, and that there was a need for the treatment of prisoners to be brought up to date. 'People are sent to prison *as* a punishment, not for punishment,' said the programme's producer, and Googie concurred with his views. She won the Sun Television Award for Best Actress of 1974 for her performance in the series, and, as she was back with her family by this time, it was presented to her at the Sydney Opera House by visiting English comics, Jimmy Edwards and Eric Sykes. Her time 'inside' had significantly re-burnished her star image in Britain.

Though television may seem to have dominated either in prolificacy or profile from the late '60s to the late '70s, both John and Googie still contrived to rack up notable stage performances. While Googie's elegantly turned-out prison governor was commanding the attention of British television audiences, John was co-starring with Ingrid Bergman in John Gielgud's London production of *The Constant Wife*. He had been offered this lead just as he was on the verge of returning to Australia in March 1973, but the production was cancelled when the managing director of H.M. Tennent, the company sponsoring it, died. It was reactivated several months later, and John cabled his acceptance of the role. He was offered a salary of £300 a week against 6% of the gross takings for a run-of-the-play contract. The offer stipulated that his name would be billed under Bergman's – and that he would be paid for a first-class round-trip fare by air London–Australia.' Not a bad deal in 1973 for an actor who hadn't appeared on the UK stages for over a decade.

Googie had starred in this Somerset Maugham comedy of manners in Melbourne in 1961, when the action of the play had been back-dated from 1927 to 1910, with the wife's pretending to have had an affair. In the Gielgud production in 1973, John recorded that, in the socially changed conditions of the day, 'when the wife announced that she is really going to have an affair, the audience applauded.' Everyone, John included, seems to have relished working with Ingrid Bergman, even though her dealings with her dialogue sometimes led to suppressed hilarity among her fellow actors. Mandy McCallum recalls her famous spoonerism when she spoke of children 'snowing throwballs', and instead of saying 'Darling, just give cook her head and she'll look after you', she one night said, 'Cook will look after you, darling, just give her your head'. Despite such linguistic tangles and the suggestion that 'Bergman was thought far too nice to convince as the calculating wife', the play ran for 264 performances at the Albery Theatre. John got his share of positive reviews, including one that found him 'both bluff and remorseful in a gentle sort of way as the erring husband.'

While Googie was in *Within These Walls* and John was playing in *The Constant Wife*, Googie gave an interview about the actor's need for discipline. 'You can't afford late nights when you're working. If you're doing a film, and you have close-ups after you've been up late the night before, it shows! On this series we finish one episode on Friday night, and we start reading the next on Monday morning. I just go home and have dinner by myself – John is off to the theatre – and then I learn my lines. When John comes in, we discuss our days, then it's bed. At the weekend, John has two performances on Saturdays, so I go to a theatre. On Sundays we always try to get out into the country.' Some of Googie's quoted utterances have a somewhat top-of-the-head sound to them, but this one does suggest the practical ways in which their two careers were managed, each taking the professional opportunities that seemed most rewarding and the other adjusting to the demands these made. Sometimes, of course, that involved their being in different countries for substantial periods, and with a growing family to consider, but the fact that all five seem to come through more or less unscathed points to some careful planning.

As well as John's return to the theatre as an actor after five years (or fifteen on the London stage) as either a theatre administrator or television entrepreneur, he also starred in the Comedy Theatre's Melbourne production of his own play, *As It's Played Today* in October 1974. John invested $40,000 of his own money in this venture and talking about it at the time revealed his essentially conservative views about the theatre. 'I like to think of it as a good old-fashioned modern play. It is up-to-date in concept, is a bit risqué and has a lot of comedy. It also has a plot and a beautiful set'. There's probably a not-too-oblique swipe at the kitchen-sink approach of the preceding decades. The play is a satire on political life in Australia, set on the north-east coast and suggesting that a cynical politician could get away with quite a lot if he played his cards shrewdly enough. *As It's Played Today* had its world premiere at the Comedy on 17 October. John, as author, director and star, chose not to give away too much in advance, except to say 'I've tried to say something but certainly its intention is to entertain people'. It still reads well enough, with crisp, often witty exchanges that suggest an ear attuned to the cut and thrust of theatrical dialogue, even if its critique of the upper echelons of political life may seem muted in the light of what we've become used to since. He had written two plays previously, but this was the first to be produced, and it was backed by Fauna Productions, the company behind his television projects. The play ran for only five weeks in Melbourne, with but modest success, and there was no theatre available in Sydney at the time for a transfer. Perhaps a play with explicitly political themes was not calculated to persuade people to leave their homes in great numbers, but it attests again to the McCallum enterprise, to the willingness to accept new challenges.

Before they come together again on stage Googie followed her success in *The Cherry Orchard* with another classic revival for the Melbourne Theatre Company, this time Oscar Wilde's *An Ideal Husband* presented at Melbourne's Comedy Theatre. John Sumner, who had directed her in the Chekhov, brought to the attention of George Ogilvie the idea that Googie was interested in playing the adventuress Mrs Cheveley in the Wilde play. Ogilvie, who had greatly admired Googie since seeing her in such eminent British films as *It Always Rains on Sunday*, jumped at the chance. Forty years later, he recalled with great pleasure:

> Finally the first day of rehearsals began, with a reading and a talk I gave
> in front of a wonderful cast including my old friend Dinah Shearing and
> fellow artistes such as Dennis Olsen, Simon Chilvers and Frank Thring.
> Immediately following all this Googie gave me a hug and said what

became to me the immortal words of a true professional – someone born to act: 'Show me where to enter, darling, where to exit, where to place myself in this lovely set, surround me with these lovely actors, and I'll do the rest'.

The 'rest' of his experience of directing her in this play measured up to the expectations thus raised. Ogilvie went on to say: 'She *became* Mrs. Cheveley – immediately and without fuss of any sort, and the men around her fell in love. It was a total joy to do, with Googie becoming just one of the actors on the stage, having fun and enjoying the other actors alike.' This was a handsomely mounted and costumed production and, at the time of my writing, one of Googie's costumes as the dashing Mrs Cheveley is on display at the Melbourne Arts Centre, the work of designer Hugh Colman, recalling one's images of her deviously sashaying her way about the stage. I liked the comment made by one critic, following the play's performance at the Playhouse, Perth, who found that, after a surprisingly subdued start, Googie 'brought the scandalous Mrs Cheveley to life with an air of private amusement and unabashed enjoyment'. Another critic, who'd thought Googie's performance 'delicious', nevertheless went on to query 'Why do we subsidise with public money a play of this nature… when young Australian playwrights and young Australian players with something to say are denied subsidies?' This writer no doubt has a point, but play*goers* may not have been wholly in agreement with his sentiments, let alone Googie, who was keen for Australians to see classic plays performed.

Simon Chilvers, who played Chiltern, the eponymous ideal husband, remembered it vividly. 'For Australian audiences of the time, it was almost the ideal play, with Googie and a lot of the star players like Dennis Olsen and Frank Thring. Googie was fabulous and we were all cast as members of a great classic play, which probably nowadays isn't much done. It didn't make any particular demands on any of us: it was just a classic. The audience of the time thought it was fabulous, whereas now they'd probably think of it as a museum piece.' Chilvers also recalled a nice detail which suggests that, democratic as Googie undoubtedly was in her relations with her colleagues, she was also aware that she *was* the leader of the company and that this involved certain protocols: 'I remember after one performance we were taking a curtain call, and she looked down the line to where someone, a very well respected lady, but a bit further down the cast list, bowed or curtseyed a little earlier than Googie did. Googie looked down the line and whispered, "Take it from me". She said it in a nice but a firm way, implying "This is how it's done. Don't jump the gun."' Twenty-five years on, in London, Googie (this time with John) would appear in the play again, in a prominent supporting role – 'a bit further down the line' certainly, but it's hard to imagine either her bowing too soon or the audience's eyes not being fixed on her anyway.

After an extended period of diverging in their professional lives, across two continents, John and Googie, after their individual enterprises of the earlier 1970s, converged for two stylish entertainments in the latter half of the decade. The first of these, staged in England, was a revival of Somerset Maugham's *The Circle*, based in part on his own strained relationship with his wife Syrie, with Googie playing the 'Syrie' role and John the 'Maugham' part. They had not appeared on stage together since touring Australia in *Relatively Speaking* eight years earlier. In regard to *The Circle*, which John was also directing, the pair had years before dined several times with Maugham, then nearing the end of his life. It is a play whose action hangs on matters of married fidelity and near lapses across generations. As usual, Googie's performance garnered fulsome reviews, the *Tatler* claiming that she was both gloriously funny and touching as Lady Kitty, while John, as Kitty's former husband, 'gives a portrait of a man who covers up the emptiness of his life with geniality, good manners and discreet liaisons with young girls.' The 'geniality' and 'good manners' must have come naturally to him, and in fact John's roles, though generally less immediately eye-catching than Googie's, often repaid close attention for the subtle way he would draw on aspects of his own everyday persona.

His production of *The Circle*, began its highly successful life-span at the Chichester Festival Theatre, during which he and Googie stayed nearby at Newell's Farm House, accommodation found for them by Joanna now living in England with her husband Roger Davenport. John and Googie disliked staying in hotels and Joanna frequently found more congenial places for them to stay while acting over there. The play was very well received by critics, one of whom claimed that, 'having restored respectability to the wilting standards of Chichester, it will certainly come into the West End in autumn'. Of course it did, and when it played at the Haymarket Theatre Royal, they took a farmhouse in the village of Lower Beeding, Sussex. They found the 80-kilometre drive worth it for 'the peace, fresh air, and country walks.' And this drive would often take place after they'd entertained well-wishers backstage after the performance. After a light supper on returning home, they would be in bed by 2 am and sleep solidly until 10.30 am. After a year at Chichester and the Haymarket, the company went on a 19-week nation-wide tour that began in Brighton, went offshore as far as Canada, and fetched up in 1978 at the Ashcroft Theatre, Croydon, in the end playing over 600 performances. When the play went on tour, they appeared on stage for the first time with Joanna, who replaced Susan Hampshire as Kitty's daughter-in-law bored by a staid and luxurious life. The McCallums are hitting sixty by this time but there is no discernible sign of their slowing down. Someone interviewing Googie during the tour unwisely ventured to suggest she didn't really *need* the money, to which she got the following retort: 'What do you mean, I can't be doing it for the money? How do you know? We're working towards a comfortable old age', and, if this wasn't answer enough, Googie added: 'My favourite hobby is interior decorating… I love buying old places and doing them up. I've done up six so far.' So, of course she needed the money.

In an interview while in England at this time, Googie makes clear that while she 'adores' Australia, 'my roots are here', whereas John, always tactful, has an 'equal feeling about both countries as I have spent half my life in Britain.' A dozen years later, Googie was still telling a reporter, 'I couldn't think of anything worse than retiring'. Back in Australia, and without letting grass grow under their feet – or just putting these latter up for a change – they are acting together in Melbourne in *The Kingfisher*, which opened at the Comedy Theatre in November 1979. One newspaper celebrated the occasion with the headline 'Return of two old friends', going on to recount what they'd been up to in England. This reunited Googie with Frank Thring, her co-star from *The Cherry Orchard* and *An Ideal Husband*.

The new play was a three-hander by William Douglas Home and several reviewers suggested that it was a thin piece of outdated work, of a kind to be expected from the once-popular playwright of *The Chiltern Hundreds* and *The Reluctant Debutante*: that is, of light-hearted, well-crafted pieces of upper-class life, destined for the pleasure of middle-class audiences wishing to be entertained rather than disturbed. There is probably some truth in this. Googie plays the widow who calls on John as an old boyfriend, who is looked after by a manservant (Thring) whose feelings for his employer may be sexually ambivalent. The three players make it a stylish diversion. (The McCallums must themselves have enjoyed it as some years later, along with Gordon Jackson as the servant, they toured the play in the Middle East.) Of course Australian audiences lapped it up, paying no attention to such captious critics as the one who described the play as 'one of those pieces of frippery so beloved of ladies who play bridge and vote for the Liberal Party', going on to write of Thring's getting laughs as 'There's nothing quite like ham off the bone.' Probably the fairest summing up of the play was from the Melbourne *Age* critic who found that, though the play was 'irretrievably dated', as for the cast, 'Their acting – in a play which is far from equal to their talents – is a pleasure to watch.'

John Frost, who was stage manager on *The Kingfisher* and later became John McCallum's business partner, recalled the trouble Googie took over her hair and her costumes (all from Paris) for the play, believing these important to her and to her character. You had to treat her like a leading lady who was heading up the company, and as everyone testifies she was a good company player. Frost does however remember an occasion when she lost her temper backstage. 'This didn't happen much but she once had a frantic argument with Frank Thring backstage when *The Kingfisher* was on tour. He was complaining about going in for an understudy rehearsal, and I was trying to pull it together, and she just lost her temper with him for saying he didn't want to come in and called him a fucking amateur, and they didn't talk for about a month on the tour. But within another month they'd be friends again having a drink in the dressing room and talking about the old days. Frank was a total eccentric and pretty taxing to work with.' Frost also recalled their hospitality to the cast and crew and felt that, even if some younger actors found them a bit old-style as time went on, they felt they were in safe hands.

As far as audiences were concerned, the McCallums were back where they wanted them – that is, on the stage in a well-made play, handsomely dressed and raising a proper quota of laughs and comfortable feeling. Just in case John found himself with time on his hands, he also contrived to write the 275-page memoir entitled *Life with Googie*, which is full of agreeable recollections, gives some insight into what made theirs such a successful collaboration, and involves an all-star cast of famous names who crossed the McWithers paths at various stages.

Chapter 10

COMMUTING

Considering how much Googie feared and disliked flying, it is remarkable how much of it she engaged in. In 1961 when she and John were about to start rehearsals for *The Constant Wife*, she travelled down from Brisbane by train while John, Nick aged four and baby Amanda, along with nurse/nanny Helen Gilligan flew. But there was no easy way of getting from Melbourne or Sydney to London or New York by train, and, throughout her '60s, '70s and '80s, Googie – and John – made so many air journeys from one continent to the other that it almost seems like commuting on a grand scale. Indeed, as far back as 1985, a reporter noted of them: 'Googie and John now commute regularly between their fashionable flat in London and Australia, where they have a house overlooking the water just outside Sydney.' Actually, there wasn't just one 'fashionable flat in London'. They stayed in a range of houses, mostly outside London. As one 1990 report claimed: 'Their long-distance commuting for the last 35 years has kept their faces and personalities as well known in Britain as in Down Under,' quoting Googie as saying, as she had intimated on other occasions, 'I think of England as my home, but Australia has been very good to me.'

When they migrated permanently to Australia in late 1958, there was never any question of Googie's giving up the chance to act overseas if an attractive offer presented itself. At that time, there was a greater range of productions in which she could appear in the UK or the US than was available in Australia, and, in the 1960s, she made her presence felt in such plays as Graham Greene's *The Complaisant Lover*, Eugène Ionesco's *Exit the King* and George Bernard Shaw's *Getting Married*. There's reputable variety in a line-up like that. Meanwhile, John's position with J.C. Williamson's involved him in a good deal of international as well as interstate travel. Then, from the 1970s, they were more often than not involved in travel together. They may have been happily settled at Bayview, as all reports seem to indicate, but, well into middle age, they showed no sign of wanting to relinquish their UK ties. As well as taking up the acting challenges that came their way and the renewing of old friendships, they were canny enough to understand the importance of keeping their names before the public.

The last three decades of the twentieth century were enormously productive for them. John was involved in filmmaking and further television production; Googie scored several key roles on British TV and made a couple of appearances in Australian films; and they were on stage, most often together, in new and classic plays, smoothly adjusting from starring to character roles, without actually losing their star aura in the process.

There were several firsts for John in the 1970s. He had his first play performed (*As It's Played Today*); he directed his first film (*The Nickel Queen*); his memoir, *Life with Googie* was published; and, not a first but for the first time in fifteen years, he was back on the London stage in 1973 (*The Constant Wife*, with Ingrid Bergman) and with Googie there in 1976 in *The Circle*, which Peter Dews directed. As well, of course, he had several television series on the go during this action-packed decade. Then, at the very end of the decade (29 December 1979, to be exact) he and Googie were seen together on the Australian stage for the first time since 1968 in *The Kingfisher*, by now firmly established as Australia's leading theatrical pair.

As to *Life with Googie*, unlike many theatrical memoirs, its subject is, as the title suggests, not just – or even mainly – himself but focuses on Googie and their life together and the way that life was so influenced by her vivid personality. The book was finally published in mid 1979, though when John found time to write it is hard to discern. There is somewhere a reference to his filling in time during backstage waits while appearing *The Circle* at London's Haymarket Theatre, but, even so, to get all its information coherently together can have been no small undertaking.

The book was generally well received for its good-humoured, easy style, and it attracted plenty of publicity. It was launched at the Literary Luncheon of the National Book Council at International House, Royal Parade Melbourne; there was an eye-catching advertisement alerting buyers to the fact that John would be signing copies at the large Sydney department store, 'David Jones', on its 141st birthday; and *The Australian Women's Weekly* ran a long extract from the book. While most reviewers praised it as 'a friendly, chatty book', or as 'a chatty, disarming and gossipy, though never malicious account of the McCallum family and its show-business successes and failures', there were a few dissentient voices. The *Sydney Morning Herald* critic wrote that John 'declines to tell the public much more than it already knows' and this notion was taken up by the *Geelong Advertiser* reviewer who considered John could have given a clearer and ampler sense of his time with J.C. Williamson's, and the interference in policy and 'wrangling with people who knew little or nothing about the theatre and who made his position intolerable.'

This last matter, relating to John's suggestion of 'amicable disagreement', may well point the way in which several people who worked with him described him as an 'honourable' man. That may make his account free from bitchery but may also account for a certain blandness in the recording of what must have been a fractious state of affairs. Speaking of bitchery, there are a couple of comments from reviewers that are not immune from it. One claimed that 'what he [John] has really written is an immodest autobiography of his thirty years in show-business – complete with a plethora of name-dropping – under the ingeniously modest guise of a story about his "better half"', dismissing it (inaccurately, as it seems) as 'a McCallum ego trip.' An earlier account in the same paper wrote: 'The book is, in fact, lovingly self-indulgent towards his adored Googie and at times comes near to idolatry.' But the most interesting of these voices belongs to author and fellow-memoirist Hal Porter who concluded a rather patronising review by acknowledging that, whatever its limitations as he saw them, the book makes one 'aware of a professional displaying his and his wife's art and professional sensibilities with a certain amount of conviction and pride'.

John had been in the business of putting himself, in one form or other, before the public for too long to be much disconcerted by critical commentary. Among his papers collected after his death were many pages of new material that he was organising with a view to amending and extending *Life with Googie*, especially about Googie's early life, and my biography has drawn on the new (i.e., unpublished) information contained there. As it is, *Life with Googie* deserves to be noted, not merely for the working and personal partnership it celebrates but also for the glimpses it gives of the theatrical and filmmaking scene of the times in two continents. And it's worth noting this further string to John's bow: he could write as well as act, direct and produce, along with a flair for management and negotiation.

Chichester Festival Theatre and the West End theatre made regular appearances on the agendas of both John and Googie in the last decades of the century. There were also extensive tours of the UK, Canada and the Middle East, as well as keeping their names fresh with Australian theatregoers. All right, they were doing work they loved but, even so, the rigours of so much travelling must have made serious demands on their energies. Going back to England was of course always intended to be part of the migration project. Googie in particular welcomed the wider range of opportunities open to her there than in Australia, but she also wanted to maintain the many old friendships she had there. She was on record as enjoying her Australian friends but still missed those she'd known Back Then.

They had a special affection for the Chichester Festival Theatre, where they starred in Maugham's *The Circle* in 1976, prior to its transferring to the Theatre Royal, the majestic showplace in London's Haymarket. John wrote: 'We liked everything about Chichester – the town, the theatre, the company, the audience, and the little Elizabethan cottage we lived in at Stedham…' And Googie was back at Chichester in 1979 playing the formidable Lady Bracknell in *The Importance of Being Earnest*. This is presumably a role which any British actress of long standing and able to assume a commanding demeanour will want to try her hand at. The spectre of Dame Edith Evans seems to hang over the role, especially in the famous utterance of 'A handbag!', but it is easy enough to imagine Googie summoning up her own brand of imperiousness to meet the role's demands. (Less easy perhaps to see John subduing his usual urbane presence to those of Canon Chasuble.) As she told a reporter on the matter of playing Lady Bracknell, 'I am never intimidated… I can only do what I have to do in my own way.'

As usual, it fell to Joanna and husband Roger to look out for houses for Googie and John when they came to England. When they were doing *The Circle* at Chichester, they'd had a cottage called Newell's Farm. On the occasion of the *Earnest* season, Jo recalls:

> We found what looked perfect, a very old former coach-house out of Chichester. A TV set arrived before them, and the woman with the TV, looking for a place for the aerial, found an upright coffin in an upstairs cupboard in the master bedroom, lined with exquisite needlework. When Googie arrived later, we down below heard her screaming. We discussed with the owner about what to do – she'd gone to live in a neighbouring cottage – and she said 'Yes, I lined it myself to hedge against inflation.' She had nowhere to put it in her cottage and as I was walking back to the house I heard Mummy's authoritative voice saying, 'That coffin must be taken out now. I'm not coming to stay in this house until it is removed.' What followed was like a comedy scene from Laurel and Hardy as Daddy and Roger tried to lug it round the house in search of a hiding place.

This anecdote reveals not only Googie's very sure sense of what she wanted and what she wouldn't countenance but it – as with those other houses Jo found for them – also suggests how important a sense of the domestic was to them. They could clearly have afforded the best hotels Chichester had on offer, but they chose otherwise: a setting away from the city where they could create the feeling of a home. Further, in this sort of setting they could stage the parties for which they were fondly remembered, parties to which entire companies would be invited with a not wholly common disregard for theatrical hierarchies.

Googie was back at Chichester in 1983 to star in *Time and the Conways*, one of several plays reflecting on the concept of time by J.B. Priestley, old friend of both the McCallums. John Gale who, with Patrick Garland, had come to run the Festival Theatre in that year had very happy memories of working with Googie, and later with both her and John during the 1980s:

> They were quite theatrical, especially Googie; John was perhaps more of a business man and a producer than an actor… We loved them because they were wonderful artistes; they never threw their weight around, they were very professional, got on with their work… They were never difficult to work with; I never heard them complain about other actors or directors, whereas most actors are famous grumblers! Pros to their fingertips, they were keen for the play to be successful, didn't want to be associated with failure and were positive in their approach.

Their next joint appearance at Chichester was in Enid Bagnold's famous *The Chalk Garden*, of which the acerbic and unpredictable Kenneth Tynan remarked that it 'may well be the finest artificial comedy to have flowed from an English pen since the death of Congreve.' Tynan was never one to shy away from an extreme opinion, but in this case the play's central character, the eccentric Mrs St Maugham, was certainly magnetic enough to have attracted over the ensuing decades the likes of Edith Evans, Gladys Cooper and Sybil Thorndike. (It was at this time Googie was quoted as saying: 'The idea of retirement horrifies me: playing a part like Mrs St Maugham in *The Chalk Garden*, which both Gladys Cooper and Sybil Thorndike were still doing well into their '80s, makes you realize how long an actress can go on if she keeps her health.' No wonder Googie was drawn to it. Snobbish and autocratic, Mrs St Maugham comes into conflict with everyone in the play and the tensest tussle is between her and Miss Madrigal, the odd governess to the old woman's precocious granddaughter. Miss Madrigal had also attracted some distinguished actresses (Peggy Ashcroft, Joan Greenwood, Patricia Kennedy) and this time she was played by Dorothy Tutin, while John played the judge who knows her dark secret.

John Gale recorded a bizarre incident during the *Chalk Garden* run. 'One night a lady from the local mental hospital walked on stage while Googie and Dotty were both there, and she said, "I thought this was *Annie Get Your Gun*."

Googie took charge and said firmly, "No, my dear, this is *The Chalk Garden*", and escorted her off the stage.' Dorothy Tutin was completely thrown by it but Googie rose to the occasion, then turned to the audience, apologised for the interruption and said, 'We'll start that scene again'. Fifty years on stage had not left her bereft of resources when something untoward happened. In the event, Googie and John were pleased enough with the success of *The Chalk Garden* to do it again in 1995 at Sydney's Marion Street Theatre under John Krummel's direction.

Still at Chichester, they performed Noël Coward's *Hay Fever* the following year. This time they were directed by film and stage star Tony Britton who confessed to being in awe of the McCallums on the first day of rehearsals, because they came with 'such high and long-established reputations, and partly because it was my first job of direction' but like so many others before – and indeed after – him found them 'marvellous to direct. They both knew precisely what they wanted to do with their roles and just got on with it.' Only once did he encounter a moment's resistance from Googie when he'd suggested a minor change. She just blithely ignored this, because it didn't fit in with her idea of the part, so, probably wisely on his part, he 'just dropped it and it never became an issue.'

By this time they were both nudging seventy. This may have been a little old for the roles they were playing in *Hay Fever*, but age doesn't seem to have slowed them down. Britton said that they had checked out the best restaurants in Chichester and would pass on such information to other members of the company, and as for John, when he wasn't rehearsing, he was out practising his golf swing. Britton felt that they were very good with the rest of the company, and considerate of younger less experienced members. 'Their presence was always warm, never grand,' he summarised.

They each did one more play at Chichester, both in 1988. Googie starred in a revival of Jean Anouilh's *Ring Around the Moon*, directed by Elijah Moshinsky, the Australian-born opera director who, in John Gale's recollections, was more interested in the 'look' of the play than in the actors. She co-starred with Jose Ferrer and Michael Denison, and presumably they were experienced enough, in Gale's words, to 'just get on with it' in spite of not getting too much help from the director. He offered this as evidence of Googie's adaptability in less than ideal circumstances.

Gale also felt that Royce Ryton's *The Royal Baccarat Scandal*, John's 1988 performance, was a poor play, but it was a very big success at Chichester. 'The play was rather old-fashioned and creaky, but the public flocked to it, because it was about royalty.' It was based on Michael Havers and Edward Grayson's account of a real-life scandal about a man falsely accused, by his mistress's husband, of cheating at baccarat when Edward VII was present, and apparently the grandson of the accused man (Sir William Gordon-Cumming) came to the play. Directed by Val May, it was popular enough to transfer into the Haymarket Theatre Royal in February 1989. The writer Jeffrey Richards, who saw the play, found it 'an adroit piece of royalty/scandal drama… John McCallum as the Prince of Wales's ADC gives a bluff, soldierly performance in the C. Aubrey Smith mould', Smith being famous in mid century as purveyor of upper-class English integrity.

But, although both Googie and John had busy and successful seasons at Chichester, this by no means accounted for their professional lives during the decade. There was, for instance, also the matter of touring, and not just in England either. Actor Sir Donald Sinden had very happy memories of the tour of John Barton's production of *The School for Scandal*, which had played at two London theatres (Duke of York's and the Theatre Royal, Haymarket) in 1983 and was then chosen for the British Council's 50th anniversary tour of Europe in 1984. As well as Sinden, the company included two stellar couples: as well as the McCallums, Michael Denison and Dulcie Gray were on board. This proved an enjoyable tour but one that was not without its unscripted moments. Sinden recalled their first night in a Norwegian city (Bergen, he thought) 'where we didn't like the look of the accommodation offered, so found a lovely hotel with a waterfront view. It had begun as a warehouse and been beautifully transformed. On our first night in town, we sat around having drinks before going to bed. Then suddenly at about 3 or 4 in the morning, there was a terrifying sound of an explosion. We were all in adjacent rooms and rushed out on to the balcony to find that an enormous ferry-boat had exploded, not ten yards from the hotel.'

His other memory of the tour had to do with the other end of Europe. There is a scene in *School for Scandal* when Lady Teazle (Googie) is caught in a compromising position with her lover when her husband comes in. Donald Sinden said, 'They are behind a screen which suddenly falls over, and this moment always brought screams of laughter, or a cacophony of disapproval – except in Belgrade. The Company couldn't understand why there was no sound from the audience, but the Director of the Belgrade theatre company explained later: "So sorry, but in Yugoslavia, the scenery is always falling down!"' It is easy to imagine Googie taking this in her stride – and perhaps as seeing no more than her due when a British Council representative ordered four people to give up their seats at the Ljubljana Opera House so that Googie and company could see the performance of *Madame Butterfly*. The reactions of the evicted four have not been recorded.

In 1987 there was an extended tour of *The Kingfisher*, which they had played in Australia in the late 1970s. This was one of the theatrical touring parties organised by actor Derek Nimmo, and, joined by Gordon Jackson, the indefatigable duo took off for the Middle East, including such locations as Cyprus, Egypt, Jordan, Dubai and Yemen. Gordon Jackson's widow, actress Rona Anderson, joined the tour for its last four weeks, and her comment perhaps suggests that 'indefatigable' applied more tenaciously to Googie than to John: 'She had great energy; she never stopped and maybe sometimes wore John out a little; she had great curiosity about life. She was absolutely not the English-rose type. Some of those a bit daunted by her would make snide remarks, and I guess her sense of being "full-on" attracted its share of bitchy comment. As far as I was concerned, whenever she was a bit "high" with people, I tended to agree with her.'

There were other UK tours in the '80s and '90s, including one of *The Cherry Orchard* in 1981, with Googie repeating the role she'd first played with the Melbourne Theatre Company a decade earlier, and this time with John as brother Gaev. When this was launched at Nottingham Playhouse, a critic wrote of her performance: 'Madame Lyuba Ranevsky might sometimes be silly and histrionic, but Googie Withers counterbalances such qualities with a warm heart, a bubbly spirit and the scars of genuine suffering'. There was publicity about the search for the right dog for the play, which was toured with John Galsworthy's *The Skin Game*, filmed by Alfred Hitchcock fifty years earlier and not much seen since, and Arthur Wing Pinero's farce, *Dandy Dick*, on which the McCallums were joined by Anthony Quayle. And just in case there wasn't enough work for them in performing the classics, Ted Willis, so impressed with Googie's playing of his *Woman in a Dressing Gown* in Melbourne, had written for her and John, *Stardust*, which toured extensively in the south of England. It didn't make it into London but when it premiered at the Churchill Theatre, Bromley a reviewer wrote that it was less a comedy than 'a slow stroll down memory lane for its stars Googie Withers and John McCallum. Written specially for the couple and reuniting them with their old friend Robert Helpmann, *Stardust* deals with the problems faced by an ageing actress hopelessly bound to the past and frightened of looking to the future. It deals with her crisis … of marrying the public image to the private reality.' The writer also found that, though John's character seemed more of a bully than the ladykiller he is made out to be… nevertheless, the couple are convincing sparring partners.' Does that have a familiar ring? 'Public image' and 'private reality'?

Their final UK tour in these last years of the century was quite a daring choice for them. The play was Ernest Thompson's *On Golden Pond*, and, considering that the film had been garlanded with awards including Best Actor and Actress Oscars for Henry Fonda and Katharine Hepburn, not to speak of Best Picture, Best Screenplay, Best Supporting Actress and, indeed, Best Picture, the McCallums would be up against quite a memory bank among potential audiences. According to one report, Googie and John turned down the play ten years earlier, feeling they were too young to play Ethel and Norman Thayer. Now, in their mid '70s, they 'feel they have "grown into the part"… though the story-line of the divided family's search for reconciliation is far removed from their own happy family life.' The couple in the play are roughly the same age as the stars, and one review discerned an 'added touch of poignant authenticity by having the Thayers played by John McCallum and Googie Withers, who in reality have been married for 44 years.'

It's not beyond speculation that Googie may have been playing up this idea when she told an interviewer that she and John now planned only to act on stage together, that there was 'no point, at their time of life, in kissing one another goodbye and going off alone on a nine-month tour.' In fact, in this tour, though the houses were somewhat disappointing, both the play and the stars were warmly received by critics. On this occasion, it was John's crusty old man who was perceived as having the best lines and making the most of them.

The moving images of film and television also kept them off the streets for slabs of time in the '80s and '90s. Googie's experiences in these media were more prestigious than John's but his were the more demanding. She only had to *act* in the films; his responsibilities as producer meant he had to deal with actors and all the other personnel involved and this sometimes became very complex. The first of John's two films, which were both released in 1982, was *Attack Force Z*, in which Fauna Productions (again with Lee Robinson) and John McCallum Productions were the driving forces. John and Lee Robinson had always felt they'd like to make films in Asia. This proved to be a more dangerously fraught matter than they'd expected. They tried a couple of other projects, one of which had to be dropped because of fighting in New Guinea, and the other about dope-running in Thailand. John made a broadcast in Brisbane about this latter proposal and the studio manager received an anonymous phone call saying, 'Tell McCallum if he makes that film he's a dead man.' Unsurprisingly, this had a rather deterrent effect on the venture, John feeling they couldn't send a crew up to Chang Mai as planned.

The film that did get made, the Australian-Taiwanese co-production *Attack Force Z*, was loosely based on a World War Two attack by commandos on an island, but the rest was fiction. The cast was full of actors then making their names in Australian films – Mel Gibson, Sam Neill and John Waters. The director credited on the finished film is Tim Burstall, but the production began with Phillip Noyce directing, and this proved another source of conflict for the producers. In 1997, John recalled that all began well with Noyce but things changed when they were on location in Taiwan and Taipei. Filming conditions were very difficult; the Chinese general appointed to the production knew nothing about film; and they had to fly in their own editing machine because there wasn't one to be had in Taiwan. Finally Noyce left the film following a disagreement about a tiny role in which he claimed the man looked too urban to be a peasant, but also because he wanted a slant on the film's subject different from John and Lee Robinson's. As well, according to one report, Noyce 'was unhappy with the producers' choice for the lead actor, a second-string Hollywood star called John Phillip Law', and, on the basis of Law's lacklustre showing in the film, I think Noyce was right. John flew back to Australia and fortunately found Tim Burstall was available and the rest of the film was finished in good time. The final film, in John's view, was a bit 'gung-ho' and it didn't do well in Australia but it picked up somewhat in the US on the strength of Mel Gibson's rising fame. Viewed now, it seems like a scramble of hectic action sequences in which lots of 'Japs' get shot, and for quite a bit of the time one is uncertain about who is doing what to whom, let alone why.

The other film on which John was executive producer, *Southern Cross* (aka *The Highest Honour* in USA and UK), was also a co-production, this time between Australia and Japan. This was another war film based on the exploits of Z Special Unit during World War Two. If *Attack Force Z* was scarcely seen in Australia, *The Highest Honour*, as it now seems to be known, wasn't screened there at all. Co-directed by British director Peter Maxwell and Japanese Seiji Maruyama, it deals with an expedition by Australian soldiers to destroy ships in Singapore harbour in 1943. A later attempt to repeat this successful venture ends in the capture of the Australian force, their conviction by their Japanese captors of war crimes, and their subsequent execution in Japanese Bushido ritual, as a token of respect. (Perhaps not the sort of respect most of us would aspire to.) There are some interesting possibilities such as the growing rapport between the Australian captain and the Japanese interpreter, but in general the film straggles from one incident to another without building much impact. It was shown in a much longer version in Japan, with more emphasis on the Japanese characters, but for Australian audiences John felt 'it got bogged down with too much Japanese dialogue', which their Japanese backers insisted on, and indeed this sustained use of subtitles and interpreter does become tedious, as it did indeed in the earlier *Attack Force Z*.

John made no further films, and it is likely that the rigours of these two would be enough to discourage a producer. He was always interested in productions whose significance would be felt beyond Australian borders, even when he was making something as utterly indigenous as the *Skippy* series. However, the disappointments of *Attack Force Z* and *The Highest Honour* might have made the securities of the Chichester classics seem doubly attractive. The politics of co-production, the frictions on location and then the problems of distribution, might well have led him to abandon film production and to concentrate on the stage. They also led him to abandon plans for a third World War Two movie, *Naked Sun*, to be based on a novel by friend Ted Willis.

Googie had a very good run of character roles on both television and film. In England, she was in some very star-studded company. In *Time After Time* (1986), the first of three for the 'Screen Two' series, she shared the screen with the likes of John Gielgud, Helen Cherry and Trevor Howard. This was based on Molly Keane's novel, about a family of decaying Anglo-Irish gentry getting on each other's nerves in their run-down home. When Googie fetched up to work on this, Gielgud reminisced about how he'd wanted to have her act with him in the 1930s but couldn't countenance the idea of 'Googie' as a name. 'Well, you've got me now,' was her reported reply, as though to suggest how wrong he'd been fifty years earlier. *Time After Time*, shot in County Wicklow for the BBC, is a superlatively acted telemovie with Googie as a blinded war victim (or not, as the case proves to be), the Jewish cousin to the difficult household, whose motives for returning after many years are ambiguous, possibly vengeful. Googie, beginning to look plump and swanning around in black, with dark glasses, provides a compelling focus for bringing the family's little secrets to the surface – which is not a good place for them to be.

The other pair of roles she played in the 'Screen Two' series offered scope for her comic talents. In fact there is a certain amount of overlap between the two rather silly middle-aged women she deals with so sharply in *Hotel du Lac* (1986) and *Northanger Abbey* (1987). She's an incurably gossipy resident at the hotel in the former, with an all-but infantilised grown-up daughter. Observed by the quietly restrained novelist Edith Hope (Anna Massey), she chatters away without, apparently, a thought in her head – and is very funny indeed. She apparently based this characterisation on Barbara Cartland! In the adaptation of Jane Austen's novel, she is rather curiously billed second and above the title, whereas the novel's and film's heroine comes after it. As Mrs Allen, full of good-natured gossip and shopping plans in Regency Bath, she is again comically apt, but hers is distinctly a supporting role. Perhaps this billing has something to do with Googie's still-potent drawing power. A couple of years later, her star name would no longer be enough to guarantee a London stage season.

As she said on several occasions, 'No one ever retires in this profession', and her belief in this notion probably helps to account for her squeezing in these television roles in the interstices of an already busy theatre programme. The last of her British TV parts was for Thames Television in the appropriately titled *Ending Up*. Not only was it her final television role anywhere, but the theme of this teleplay, derived from Kingsley Amis's novel, is about geriatric lives ending up. These 'lives' are played by a hand-picked cast including Wendy Hiller, John Mills, Michael Hordern and Lionel Jeffries as well as Googie. There's comedy along the way but a practical joke causes the film to end in tragedy. One critic felt that 'If *Ending Up* had been screened on Christmas Day the case for euthanasia would have received a powerful boost.' It was described by another reviewer as 'Stunning work – especially from Googie Withers as the demented child-like Marigold.' To be singled out 'especially' among those names suggests Googie, at 72, had lost none of her capacity to rivet the viewer's attention. She played the childish Marigold who dotes on a little collection of china animals and a cat for which she asks fellow septuagenarian Adela (Hiller) to buy 'a little fishy-wishy for pussy cat. Such a treaty-weaty for her.' Inane as Marigold sounds, Googie still invests her with both the panache of her dress sense and an unexpected pathos when she talks of the husband she can scarcely remember.

Back in Australia in the telefilm *Melba* (1988), she played Lady Armstrong, mother of the diva's husband Charles Armstrong, whom, coincidentally, John had played in the largely fictionalised British film back in 1953. In view of Australia's burgeoning film industry around this time, I asked Googie why she had made only three films in Australia, with a gap of over twenty years after the first, *Nickel Queen*, in 1971. She replied firmly, 'No, there were no more I could have made. There wasn't one when I thought, "My God! I should have played that part…", because they're all intensely Australian, and I'm not an Australian and I find it very difficult to act one.' She went on to recall the failure of her attempt at an Australian play, *Desire of the Moth*, thirty-odd years earlier which had made her wary of accepting Australian roles.

In the event, she played supporting roles in two Australian films in the '90s, one of which pleased her and the other, when she saw it, decidedly didn't. The first was Michael Blakemore's *Country Life*, in which Chekhov's *Uncle Vanya* is transplanted to the Australian outback (out of Maitland, New South Wales, in very hot weather), with the disruptive visitors coming from London to upset the running of the family property, ironically called 'Canterbury'. This was an intelligent film that never had the success – or even the screenings – it deserved, but there was no persuading Googie about it. In a letter she said, 'I was persuaded to jump in the deep end with that character part – it went too far!!' '[T]hat character' was Hannah, the cook-housekeeper (old family nurse in Chekhov), who serves up mutton in a variety of unappetising guises and bosses anyone who displeases her.

Googie is actually very entertaining in the role but she found it 'a very difficult transition for an actress who always played rather glamorous parts', even in those television films of the '80s. 'It was the first time I saw myself looking one hundred and forty-eight on the screen and that threw me for a loop,' and she gave director-writer-star Blakemore a very forthright reply when he told her 'You've got to be brave'. 'I said "Screw being brave!" I don't know what they meant by "brave". I mean I've seen that play *Uncle Vanya* a hundred times and the old nurse is quite a pleasant little old woman, she's not this grotesque creature that they made me into.' Hannah doesn't at all emerge as 'grotesque', but for the first time Googie is looking seriously plump;

keeping her weight down had become increasingly a problem, especially for someone who loved her food, and her costume, with cook's apron and cap, was hardly becoming. Nevertheless, her grumpy, frumpy Hannah makes the most of those moments in which she takes command of the screen as in her starring days, and she was singled out by many reviewers, including this one from *The New York Times*: 'Several shrewdly created minor characters fill out the household. Googie Withers is especially lively and likeable as the no-nonsense housekeeper, Hannah, who sees nothing wrong with a steady diet of mutton.'

Michael Blakemore's experience of working with her on the film offers a quite different perspective. He recalled that initially it was John's persuasion that led her to accept the role, hoping that it might lead to further character parts in British or Australian films. He had great admiration for her as an actress and knew her name would 'embellish' the cast. 'She was extremely easy to direct; she was also very supportive. She was always fully prepared. I knew she was nervous, mainly about remembering her lines, but she didn't let it show', and, at this late stage of her career, had the respect of the rest of the cast. This was also borne out by the film's producer, Robin Dalton, who became a friend to Googie: 'John came up on location at weekends and they were like two teenagers in love. When we were shooting we stayed in the same hotel in Maitland, and I had the bedroom next to hers, and I tell you they were like a honeymoon couple.' This reminds one of the voluminous letters she wrote, almost daily, to John when she was in England in the 1960s, while playing at the Strand in July 1967, in *Getting Married*: 'My darling darling one' was a common opening address, and the letters were full of affection and longing to be back with him. As well, Ms Dalton recalled, 'she loved her food; she didn't care about her weight. We'd sit down to dinner and she'd have steak every night, with never a thought to her weight or health.' She seems to have enjoyed the location shooting and her dissatisfaction with the film can most probably be traced to the shock of seeing herself for the first time in an elderly character role without that touch of glamour she had always been used to. Perhaps a little less relish for the hotel food might have helped her to retain something of her traditional image.

Her last film ever was *Shine* which became an international hit with Geoffrey Rush winning an Oscar for his performance as the damaged pianist David Helfgott. Googie played the small but striking role of author Katherine Susannah Prichard, who helped raise the money to send Helfgott to England to study music. When this casting was announced, Prichard's son, Ric Throssell, expressed his disapproval, on the grounds that 'you [Googie] don't sound like an Australian woman, you sound like an English woman.' As she pointed out to him, she *was* cast and it would be more helpful to talk about his mother – how she dressed, how she behaved – and he 'gave me the most wonderful clues. He had no idea he was doing it but… there she was in front of me.' She enjoyed working with director Scott Hicks ('You felt he knew what he was doing'), and he arranged for someone to help her with an Australian accent, but though this proved satisfactory she still believed she couldn't play a full-length role as an Australian woman. And this time, unlike for her role in *Country Life*, she was immaculately coiffed and clad, with no suggestion of frump in her several brief scenes as mentor to the youthful David Helfgott (Noah Taylor). She plays these with warmth, sophistication and authority, doing justice to the real-life character of Prichard. Twenty years later, Hicks wrote: 'Googie was an absolute delight to work with. She had that calm confidence that vastly experienced actors can radiate, a certainty about their place in things. I found her very collaborative and cooperative about potentially awkward elements like wigs and so on, as well as at perfect ease with her age and that of the character – which is not always the case! I think she formed a lovely connection with Noah which made their brief scenes quite memorable.' She didn't have scenes with Geoffrey Rush but he remembered with affection the generous letter she wrote him a decade later when he had made such a hit on the Broadway stage with Ionesco's *Exit the King*: 'I played it in England 25 years ago [actually more like 45] with Alec Guinness and if I may say so I think you were better!'

In interviews around this time, the matter of retirement is often raised – by the interviewers, that is, *not* by John or Googie. When it is raised, it is emphatically dismissed, especially by Googie. 'Actors *never* retire' she asserted to one reporter. In another article, 'Googie, vibrant as ever, guides proceedings with her crisp, resonant, authoritative voice, and John sits more quietly in the background, speaking his mind when appropriate… Any hint of retirement is quashed with vigour. "Retire from what?" says Googie… You only stop acting if they don't want you any more, if you can't find your way across the stage or if you can't learn your lines.' This was 1989, when they had another thirteen years of performing ahead of them, and, sadly, remembering the lines would become a problem to Googie.

But that was still some way off. There were two more co-starring plays whose titles brought out the punster in most reporters and critics: that is, *The Cocktail Hour* and *High Spirits*. *The Cocktail Hour* saw John and Googie acting with Joanna again for the first time in over a decade. Naturally the papers ran stories with titles like 'A toast to the family that plays together' in the run-up to the play's opening in Sydney in 1989. When the season began and the critics went to work on it, their reviews had headlines such as 'Vintage partnership' or less enthusiastically, 'Vital substance missing from this light cocktail's ingredients.' *The Cocktail Hour*, by American playwright A.R. Gurney, is a comedy of manners in which family dynamics are put under strain by the return of a son who wants to clear with his parents the autobiographical piece he is writing. John plays the somewhat curmudgeonly, very conservative father; Googie is the good-natured matriarch, partial to her martinis; and Jo is the dog-obsessed daughter. The returning son is played by American actor Nicholas Hammond who, as a child, had played with Googie on Broadway in *The Complaisant Lover* and was a well-known face since playing Friedrich Von Trapp in the film of *The Sound of Music* twenty-five years earlier.

Critical response to the play was divided. Some reviewers regarded it as lightweight, but there were others who found that it 'packed a punch', being 'cool and dry, with a dash of vermouth and a twist of lemon', and there was nothing but praise for the acting. By this stage of their careers, John and Googie were seen to embody a kind of graceful professionalism, recalling a different world but still embracing the present with a vigour and tenacity that would have been admirable in actors half their age. As noted earlier, several critics remarked on the fact that they were perhaps too old for the parts they played at Chichester in *Hay Fever* in 1988, but *The Cocktail Hour* gave them the chance to play leading roles of roughly their own age.

The play toured Australia, with Elspeth Ballantyne taking over from Joanna in Melbourne when Joanna had to go home to England. Elspeth felt a little intimidated at first, coming in to a show so well-rehearsed that she almost felt choreographed, but understood that John and Googie knew what they were doing. 'I did what I realised they liked and wanted, and Nick Hammond was a good buffer for me if I had a problem.' John, who had put up 50% of the production's $100,000 budget, was keen to take the play to England. The play's director, Richard Cottrell recalled that they did the same production at the Theatre Royal Windsor, then toured it for sixteen weeks. However, he said, 'it didn't come into the West End. I knew it wouldn't because Googie and John on their own weren't enough and they needed another name, and they didn't want to recast Nicholas [Hammond], and obviously weren't going to recast Joanna. John and Googie thought and hoped it would come in, and I didn't tell them that Duncan (Welden, producer) wasn't going to bring it in because I didn't want them to lose heart and hope on what was a very long tour, but by then their name wasn't quite enough of a draw for the West End.' It went on though to a successful tour, with Googie gamely asserting that actors have a duty to take their plays to audiences rather than just expecting audiences to come to them.

Their next co-starring venture in Australia, *High Spirits*, was also a family affair. This was a sort of theatrical anthology piece devised and directed by John as a journey through his and Googie's stage careers, and the set was designed by son Nicholas. Divided into two parts, set in contrasting post-earthly destinations, it draws on such diverse sources as Shakespeare, Noël Coward, Chekhov, C.J. Dennis and Oscar Wilde, as the apparently ageless pair recall their experiences in the theatre over the preceding fifty years. One writer described the play's opening: 'After a moment or two we discover John welcoming Googie to the afterlife! They're on the light rail to paradise. "I only just scraped in," says John, "it must have been those charity concerts for

Ethiopia"'. This hints at the diverting lightness of touch the pair brought to this entertainment, spiked from time to time with reminiscences of engaging malice.

Bearing in mind that a good many of their fans were also of a certain age, they opened in Melbourne with a matinee because Googie felt that 'lots of their Melbourne fans feel more comfortable going to matinees.' There was a strong element of nostalgia about it of course as they brought back memories of plays and people, but it wasn't syrupy. The problem was that, for younger audiences, the references to 'Edith' (Evans) or others of that vintage were a bit esoteric. However, they had built up a large and loyal following since they first trod Australian boards in the 1950s and *High Spirits* was predictably well received by the intended audiences. One reviewer aptly described its charm as 'a kindly night of nostalgia', saying that 'it's a bit like sitting at the feet of two favourite elderly relatives as they turn the pages of their photograph albums.'

They toured extensively with it, with sell-out performances in Nambour, Queensland, and a further 11-town tour of that state which always had a special place in John's affections. The tour included Bundaberg, where they played in the Moncrieff Theatre, named for John's once-celebrated musical-comedy co-star of the 1940s. In another venue touched with nostalgia, the McCallums also attended an exhibition of memorabilia called 'Pull Back the Curtain – Vaudeville at the Cremorne,' at the Brisbane Performing Arts Centre where a theatre is named for John's father's famous Cremorne, source of his first interest in the theatre. As if Australian touring wasn't taxing enough, they also squeezed in (between Paramatta and Wollongong) a short season of *High Spirits* at the new theatre in Raffles Hotel, Singapore!

Still commuting, the couple divided the rest of the '90s between London and Australia. As Googie said, 'we do go where the work is and that is usually in Europe and England. Besides, you can't come back to the well too often in Australia… The trick is to get [people] to say, "Oh, how lovely, they're back."' They repeated their roles in *The Chalk Garden* at Sydney's Marion Street Theatre in 1995. Back in the previous decade, Googie had been having a little trouble with her lines and John had wanted to try it out at Marion Street before going to Chichester, but, as producer John Krummel recalled, he had to say regretfully: 'I don't have a spot for it in my season, and we left it at that. So, later I returned to Marion Street in the mid '90s, and when John approached me again with "Well, what about *The Chalk Garden* now?", I said, "You're on." And we settled on it to open the season, it was an enormous success, and John Frost [John McCallum's business partner] took it on tour. It was a mutually good idea for John [McCallum] and me because it was good for Googie to feel secure in a play she knew and it was good for us because of course she and John spelt publicity.' They may not have had the hold over the Australian public they had had when younger, but in the right play they could still pull a crowd.

In John Krummel's recollection, they were easy to direct, and the rest of the company valued the chance to work with them. In his view, 'it was a question of the rest of the company fitting in with Googie and John, because they were the stars. They were *stars*! And the rest of the cast were *actors* who were fascinated to be acting with John and Googie.' As a couple, they were complementary, Krummel felt: 'Yes. He was always the smooth operator and she was the diva and that was the way it worked. She was a sort of motor-mouth in interview. Just ask her a question and off she'd go; whereas he was more considered. He was a greater intellect than Googie, but she had the spark of a star. And she had a sharpness and perception. She knew exactly what she was up to and he was well aware of that.'

In the last years of the century, they were much preoccupied with Oscar Wilde whose plays had so thoughtfully provided roles for aging actors. In England, they'd played in Peter Hall's production of *An Ideal Husband* at the Old Vic in 1996 (with John conjuring up a wonderful array of 'hrrmphs' as Lord Caversham and Googie as haughty Lady Markby, concerned about 'the modern mania for curates') and in *Lady Windermere's Fan* in 1997. They then returned to Australia in 1997 with Hall's handsome production of *An Ideal Husband*, with Stephanie Beacham as Mrs Cheveley. David Marr, writing of this production, said: 'It's worth the journey to Pyrmont [Lyric Theatre] simply to watch Googie Withers. She has a little trick as she walks on stage that's gone in the flick of an eye but grabs our attention at once. It's a dip of the head and a twist of the mouth that says, "Sweet of you to think of applauding now but wait until I show you what I can really do." After firing Wilde's one-liners into the crowd in Act 3, it's like the bombardment of the Dardanelles all over again, with the guns of the whole British fleet thundering. Then out she sweeps, to huge applause with a little "I told you it was worth waiting for" smile.' Perhaps she had mastered this since she stopped the show in *The Cherry Orchard* all those years ago.

John Frost recalled working with John McCallum as co-producer, when the latter was also appearing in the plays. Frost felt that John never lost his business acumen, though he had been away from this side of things for some decades, even if by the late '90s he was astonished by the cost of the production of *An Ideal Husband* – and even more shocked, and pleased, at the box-office returns. Frost said:

> I could sit down with John and say, 'Here's the budget for *An Ideal Husband*, at $1,500,000', and I remember him saying, 'I cannot believe you're spending all that money on this.' He was frightened of what it cost to do a show in later years, and this wasn't surprising when, in the '90s, he'd been out of the business for a few years. He went with the flow and he understood it, but then he could hardly believe that a show like *Ideal Husband* made nearly $2m, whereas in the old days it might make a half- or quarter-million. He was surprised at the very large figures involved in later productions. He was acting in *Ideal Husband*, but he also had 50% invested in it, and co-produced with me. I did all the day-to-day management, the running of it, but he was the co-producer, we'd have meetings and we'd talk about advertising, and I found him very sharp. You couldn't have put one over him. He never lost his acumen in these matters, and even up to the days when he was dying in hospital he'd always talk about shows and producing and the cost of things.

Frost, more perhaps than any of their colleagues in the last decades of their lives, had an acute understanding of how they worked as a team. He recognised that Googie would go off on a tangent at times and John would bring her back to something approaching reality. When they were floating the idea of a starry *Chalk Garden* in the early '90s, Googie would protest that *they* were stars, so why would you need Joan Collins? Insisting that she would have to have top billing, because 'my public expects it,' John's reply was: 'Googie, your public are dead!' He was used to exercising gentle control of her whenever she got a bit grand, Frost observed.

Sandwiched in between the Wildean ventures was a strange one that sent them back to England, Bristol to be exact, in 2000 to do a play called *A Busy Day*. This oddity of romance, comedy and intrigue, written by diarist and novelist Fanny Burney in 1800, had waited two hundred years for its first production in Bristol. John and Googie had become friends with Stephanie Beacham during the Australian tour of *An Ideal Husband*, and Beacham, visiting her daughter, happened to be in Bristol on the opening night. It became clear that Googie was not well, was also having trouble with her lines, and, when it looked as if the play was going to transfer to London, John asked Beacham to take over Googie's role. As she pointed out in her memoir, the Regency English was hard to learn at short – or any – notice 'and I was taking over from an 84-year-old. I was taking over [from] Googie: a wonderful, big, elderly woman.' A reporter writing about the play's imminent opening at the Bristol Old Vic, with a cast headed by the McCallums, wrote (under the very original headline, 'Age shall not wither her') of them as a 'most exciting husband-and-wife double-act.' By the time it reached the West End, at London's Lyric Theatre, it was well enough received as a 'constantly engaging and sharply observant study of snobbery and the English class system' and John's performance described as 'delightful'. Googie no doubt felt the disappointment at, for the first time in over sixty years, having to withdraw from a production because of ill-health.

We know her views on retirement but the time was coming – she was after all well into her '80s – when she would have to think seriously about what she'd so often and so strenuously opposed. But not *quite* yet.

Chapter 11

WINDING UP

On 26 February 2002, Googie (then nearly 85) and John (nearly 84) began what proved to be their last theatrical season. This was Peter Hall's revival of Oscar Wilde's *Lady Windermere's Fan* at the Haymarket Theatre Royal where they had enjoyed some of their biggest theatrical successes. John and business partner John Frost were co-producers, with an agreement that, in return for their investment, they would receive between them 25% of 60% of the profits. Appropriately, much of the critical attention was focussed on the starring mother-and-daughter duo, Vanessa Redgrave and Joely Richardson, playing indeed mother and daughter, but Googie and John, as the loquacious Duchess of Berwick and her blustery brother Lord Augustus Lorton, received their share of plaudits too. John Frost felt that they were both wonderful in it and actually stole the reviews. 'No one knew it was their last play; I don't think *they* knew.'

As David Yelland, playing Lord Windermere, recalled:

> Peter Hall knew them terribly well and was delighted to get them to do it I know. Peter was also very adept at just giving everyone as much direction as he felt they needed. And with John and Googie it was mostly a matter of providing them with a good position on stage for them to do their stuff. He wouldn't have dreamt of giving them detailed direction because they knew a great deal more about playing Oscar Wilde than he – or most other people – did. They were certainly not high-handed; they would *take* direction, but I don't think they needed a great deal.

Wilde had been good to the pair in their last decades, offering plum parts that enabled them to make their mark even with limited onstage time. Most of John's dialogue requires the suggestion of an exclamation mark at the end of each utterance, as he expostulates about families for instance, with 'Demmed nuisance, relations!' or about Mrs Erlynne, 'She's deuced clever, too!' Googie must have enjoyed her pronouncements about Australia to antipodean Mr Hopper: '... dear Agatha [witless daughter] and I are so much interested in Australia. It must be so pretty with all the dear little kangaroos flying about. Agatha has found it on the map. What a curious shape it is! Just like a large packing case.'

As in this, their final play, John and Googie enjoyed acting together, like playing tennis with someone whose game you knew very well, as they once said. There were suggestions from time to time that, in their earlier days, love scenes with other actors might have had an edge over those with one's wife or husband. Googie may well have raised an eyebrow when John admitted that it was pleasant to kiss Ingrid Bergman twice nightly when they were co-starring in *The Constant Wife*. *Lady Windermere* was a well-chosen swansong. It was a play they'd done before, and not long ago, so that it was familiar territory; as brother and sister they had some entertaining sparring at each other's expense; and on another level they were very long-time friends of the Redgrave family. John, and John Frost, wanted to bring the production to Australia, but Vanessa Redgrave was unable to come. A *name* was needed and John canvassed other suggestions. One was the luminous Helen McCrory, but at that stage she wasn't well enough known in Australia, and eventually the project was dropped.

They may have stopped appearing on stage and screen but they never seemed to be out of the public eye for very long. There were still lengthy interviews, even if the trend of daily newspapers was away from the sort of reporting that had once charted every move of the McCallum family, and the gossip magazines focused on youth, preferably of a certain notoriety. Among other talk-fests, in June 2003, Googie did a very long session for the Sydney Film Festival, with interviewer Claude Gonzales taking her through everything from the colourful story leading up to her Karachi birth, her 1930s career as a sassy blonde in British films and so on, all the way up to her role in *Shine*. And both Googie and John were the subject of a very long interview at their Bayview home on 5 June 2008, much of this shedding light on John's dealings with J.C. Williamson's, about which he was a little more forthcoming than he had been at the time of the split. As well, there was the joint conversation on the ABC's *Talking Heads* programme in 2007 when, encouraged by presenter Peter Thompson, they trawled enjoyably through the familiar territory yet again. In this, there was the choice anecdote about a moment of domestic furore which led to Googie's biting him: 'He was lying on the bed and we were arguing, and I was getting so angry with him, and he happened to have bare legs because it was a hot day... And I bit him on the thigh very hard! And blood poured out and he had to have a stitch or two. It was terribly funny, actually. I laughed my head off.' To which John's good-natured reply was, 'Well, you expect an actress to have temperament.'

In hindsight, how do their careers emerge? Both had been honoured for their work in the obvious ways: Googie had been the first non-Australian to be awarded Honorary Officer of the Order of Australia in 1981. The Governor-General flew to Adelaide, where she was perfoming, to invest her with this distinction because she couldn't get to Canberra for the ceremony. Then, in 2001 she was appointed CBE (Commander of the British Empire). This seemed a long overdue honour and many believed that, if she'd stayed in England, she would undoubtedly have been made a Dame. The title would have suited her: 'Dame Googie' has a certain ring to it, and she would have had the 'manner' to carry it off with aplomb. John was awarded the same two honours as Googie's but they came to him in the reverse order. He was appointed CBE in 1971 and made an Officer (as Australian, his was not Honorary) of the Order of Australia in 1992. In all four instances, the awards were given for their services to the performing arts. But awards such as these, thoroughly deserved as they were, or John's stint as President of the Australian Film Council in 1971–72, are just the outward and visible signs of the respect in which their contributions to the entertainment arts were held.

Less easy to pin down, though, certainly to those around in the crucial decades, no less palpable, was the almost 'royal' status they acquired in Australia. Many people involved in Australian theatre would agree that they gave a real lift to the local theatrical scene from the time of their first visit in 1955 with the popular success of *Simon and Laura* and the even greater cultural cachet attaching to *The Deep Blue Sea*. While there may have been some prevailing sense of overseas visitors' being flown in to take roles that locals could just as easily have filmed, this kind of criticism never seemed to afflict the McCallums. Possibly John's own Australian roots helped to deflect it, but Googie's serious film and theatre reputation in England meant that she wasn't one of those imports seeking to prop up an ailing career in the colonies. When they came to live here at the end of 1958, she was still in demand for work in the US and Britain, while John adapted himself to filling several really influential roles here.

In assessing their career achievement, there is one obvious distinction to be made. Googie was without doubt one of the most commanding actresses of her generation. She stood out from most of her British contemporaries in the heyday of Britain's wartime and post-war cinema, purveying a kind of boldness that made her a force to contend with. In the 1950s, in both Australia and Britain she was staking similar claims for stage work in a series of contrasting and demanding roles – from Beatrice in *Much Ado About Nothing* at Stratford to her memorably heart-breaking Hester Collyer in *The Deep Blue Sea* in both countries – and would continue to do so for the next forty-odd years. Even as a *Woman in a Dressing Gown*, she could rivet the attention of audiences, and she had the sort of stage presence that stood her in good stead when star parts gave way in later decades to supporting roles. She could slide up and down the social scale convincingly and without losing any of her capacity to command the scene.

John's career – and his legacy – is more wide-ranging. When they returned to Australia in 1955, 'They were a big deal and when you look at the newsreel footage the stress is on John bringing his movie-star wife back to Australia,' John Frost recalled. He had established himself in England as a vigorous and handsome leading man across a range of film genres, several of them co-starring with Googie, but when they came back to live in Australia he had set his sights on other possibilities. He helped guide one of the world's biggest theatrical firms through a highly prosperous run of hits, beginning with *My*

Fair Lady, and he found the managerial role he had with J.C. Williamson's stimulating, but it also presented him with other challenges. He directed the second company of the hit musical and then took The Firm into film production with *They're a Weird Mob*.

As it happened, his departure from J.C.W. proved very much in the interests of Australian television where his production of *Skippy* helped the local industry to leap into international consciousness and popularity. But even television production wasn't quite enough to absorb the creative energies that he felt increasingly were being stifled by the end of his time at J.C.W. After several more TV series, he ventured into film production with a couple of demanding shoots in Australian-Asian co-productions. These – *Attack Force Z* and *The Highest Honour* – probably failed to live up to his expectations, but they are indicative of his enterprising approach to the various media. Away from acting for over ten years in the 1960s and early '70s, he returned to it with unabated enthusiasm from the mid '70s, often co-starring with Googie as they commuted between continents. But even as late as the 1990s, he was still interested in the management side of the theatrical profession and co-produced the Wilde plays.

Googie was the more vivid presence, as actresses of a certain demeanour are likely to be, but it can be argued that John exerted a more extensive influence on the Australian performing arts scene. Frost believes that 'John was not recognised enough for his contribution to the Australian arts – the Australian Ballet, the Elizabethan Theatre Trust, etc. He contributed to a lot of places people are not aware of, with his knowledge and his sitting on boards, particularly with the formation of the Australian Ballet, and television production.' Actors are out there for everyone to see, but a lot of serious work no doubt goes on behind the scenes in providing the showcases for performers, and much of John's skill was exercised in this way. They did quite a number of plays and films together, but they also maintained separate identities: Googie's by acting with other players, John's by taking on a range of non-acting ventures.

Three other names have been winding their way through this book and these names belong to Joanna, Nicholas and Amanda McCallum. In the extraordinary prolificacy of the Withers-McCallum partnership, among the most impressive achievements is that of raising a family of three children who went on to have productive lives in the fields of their choice, stayed friends with each other and with parents who, however much in the public eye, always seemed to value family above all. The three McCallum children have all spoken frankly about their lives, aware of the advantages that come with famous parents but also realistic about the sorts of difficulties they dealt with as well. One family member and long-time friend, Claire Baistow, recalled of the McCallums:

> They were very supportive parents... of Joanna and Nick in their professions and Mandy going off to do different things. They've all been very successful in their own ways, and they're all great company. Googie was always telling you about what they were all up to. ... she and John were in constant contact with their children, always knew what they were doing.

This sense of a family that was often physically widely separated but somehow always in contact pervades much of the talking and writing about the McCallums.

Joanna always maintained that she'd had every encouragement to pursue an acting career but that she was never pushed into it. When she was born in 1950, John and Googie's film careers were at their peak, and, as a result, Googie said in a much later interview: 'Firms were falling over themselves giving us things for the new arrival. Cots, prams, flowers, oh, everything you could think of.' Joanna was in the spotlight from the start and one reporter described how the six-year-old Joanna entered the room where he'd been interviewing her parents and 'took centre stage immediately, and I realised she was determined to hold it... she draped herself in a big chair and looked up at me in impudent imitation of her mother.'

At St Catherine's School, Melbourne, where she became a boarder, she starred in and as *St Joan*. Googie was sitting anxiously at supper in the Adelphi Hotel, London, after appearing in a play nearby, and awaiting John's phone call after his seeing Joanna's performance as Joan. He reported, 'She can do it… She can, you know. It was a marvellous young St Joan: you don't often see a 17-year-old play it like that.' And Googie added, 'It is one of my greatest regrets that I missed it.' One of the negative aspects of having parents whose profession took them to different corners of the globe must have been just this kind of disappointment at not having them *there* on such crucial occasions. Though Joanna did once say 'When my mother came to school functions, I was slightly embarrassed because she was famous and would always look amazing. And as well as being glamorous, she is a very emotional and warm woman.' Googie was not one of those mothers who could just fade into the background on these special days at school, not because she sought the limelight but because there was inevitably a star aura about her, whether on or off theatrical duty. As well, while other students' parents might burst with pride at school performances, Joanna's were apt to be critical, as when John once told her she was using her hands too much.

So, there were no doubt pros and cons in having parents in the public eye. About being hailed as 'the daughter of…', Jo once said: 'It's inevitable, I suppose, but I'll be furious if they're still saying it when I'm 40. No, make that 27.' It is probably easy for outsiders to think an aspiring actor's path may be smoothed as a result of famous forebears. It could also be a challenge, as Joanna found, to establish herself on her own credentials, to show her own abilities so that no one could suppose she was having an unearned easy ride. The one occasion on which John put her to work was as the student activist in *Nickel Queen*; she played Googie's daughter in *Last Year's Confetti*, an ITV 'Saturday Night Theatre' entry in 1972; she appeared in one episode of Googie's long-running TV success, *Within These Walls* in 1974; in 1978, she was cast, without parental intervention, as their daughter-in-law in Somerset Maugham's *The Circle*, when the play went on tour; and nearly twenty years later in Melbourne she joined both parents again in A.R. Gurney's play *The Cocktail Hour*. These widely separated performances look rather sparse in Joanna's ever-growing resumé. They enjoyed the experiences of acting together, but Joanna was committed to making her own way.

When she finished her two years at NIDA, she was almost immediately taken on by the Melbourne Theatre Company. Its chief administrator/ director John Sumner had seen her graduation performance as Elizabeth Proctor in *The Crucible* and offered her a range of roles including 'Grushka' in *Caucasian Chalk Circle*. She spent a year with the MTC, working with such notables of the period as Frank Thring, who became a close friend and to whom she was kind when this can't always have been easy. For instance, he gave her his opinion of her first performance, 'You were dreadful', but she forgave him because he amused her. She also had the challenge of having to simulate sex on stage in the MTC's production of John Whiting's play, *The Devils*, in which she and co-star Fred Parslow are seen making love before the altar at the back of the stage. Joanna wrote about this: 'Fairly decorously choreographed and barely visible, I was nevertheless topless and the minute the scene started the audience to a man suddenly turned to look at my parents who were sitting in the stalls!'

Joanna grew to nearly six feet, tall for an actress in a profession in which leading men generally didn't want to have to look up to their opposite numbers. However, she made her height work for her and told an interviewer in 1970 that 'she isn't letting it worry her. "It did when I was younger… But I even wear high heels now. I can see better!"' Her parents had been concerned for her rapidly increasing altitude when she was a schoolgirl, but Googie later remembered their deciding against the proposed treatment and said, 'She carries it [her height] beautifully, even wears very high heels and looks her father in the eye: he's six feet two!'

Certainly her height often gave her a commanding presence on stage or screen, but it never turned her into a stereotypically *grande dame* actress. A quick look at her long and immensely varied credits would dispel any such notion. From her arrival in London in 1971, she was in demand for stage and television. She made her West End debut opposite Tom Courtenay in *Charley's Aunt*, had seasons at the Crucible Theatre, Sheffield (1972), leading roles at the Young Vic Theatre (1975–76) and the Bristol Old Vic. There was a whole string of potent roles ranging from Helena in *A Midsummer Night's Dream* (described by respected critic J.C. Trewin as 'simply the best Helena

I have known in a long experience') to Lady Macbeth (1974) and Nora in Ibsen's *A Doll's House* (1982). This latter suggests her willingness to take on daring assignments, in a role more usually played by smaller actresses. The range of opportunities on television was similarly eclectic, including miniseries such as *Testament of Youth* (1979) as well as one-offs such as *The Franchise Affair* (1988). This is not the place for a detailed account of her career; it is enough to say that, in classic and new works, it has gone on unabated to the present.

Once settled in London, she never really lived in Australia again, but she and her family would enjoy holidays at Bayview. A friend, Rosie Caws, recalled that she and Jo shared a flat in Sheffield when they were both appearing at the Crucible Theatre in 1973 and then decided to do so when they returned to London. They fetched up at 24 Earl's Terrace, Kensington, and Rosie had happy memories of the senior McCallums visiting. 'John and Googie were such good fun. When she walked into a restaurant she commanded attention. And she loved restaurant-dining, dressing up and going out. She had huge energy, and she was a very attractive woman. At a party we gave at our flat, one of our friends made a massive pass at her in the early '70s! She was, though, very dependent on John and was much quieter when he was away.'

Joanna married actor/writer Roger Davenport in Chelsea in 1978. They'd met at the Bristol Old Vic while both appearing in a play called *The Golden Pathway Annual*. Roger's background included grandfather Arthur Davenport, a popular lyricist, and grandmother Muriel George and her second husband Ernest Butcher, two fondly remembered character players from British films of the '40s and '50s. Roger has vivid memories of his first meeting with Googie: from a seated position, she not so much offered her hand as 'proffered' it, with a majestic flourish! Warm-hearted as she undoubtedly was, Googie could nevertheless present such an image. Jo said that whenever they went shopping together she always felt like a lackey as Googie swept her way through the stores, and this tallies with the various reminiscences of her children and friends, though it doesn't seemed to have alienated any of them. Jo and Roger, who have two children, Alexandra (herself married in 2014) and Harry, have stayed in the domestic comfort they established in Chiswick shortly after their marriage, both continuing to find satisfaction in their chosen careers.

Nicholas's experience of boarding-school life was less wholly to his liking than that of his sisters. Having been born in London in 1956, he came to Australia as a toddler, but does still visualise clearly the house they bought in Scotsburn Grove, in the Melbourne suburb of Toorak in 1959. In 2013, he wrote:

> In my mind, I can still walk through the rooms. The house had three levels – the playroom at garage level, drawing room, telly room, kitchen, etc on the first, and the bedrooms on the second. There was an elegant stairway where Mum would make her entrance to the cocktail parties they held – Dad already hosting at the bar – and it was somewhat terrific to spy from behind the banisters. The parties were always noisy affairs. The great parties and dinners are among my main recollections in Toorak and certainly at Bayview. There was a large back garden, with cumquat and crab-apple trees and passion-fruit vines. The tram stop was just a block away on Toorak Road from which I would catch the tram to Glamorgan School from the age of six – until eight when I began boarding.'

Boarding later at the Corio campus of Geelong Grammar School gave him a sense of independence that he finds invaluable today, even though he claims that he never much enjoyed the school, and 'utterly despised Timbertop and the crew that ran it. I was making a film there when the headmaster intervened, caned me for daring to turn Timbertop into a reform school, and wrote to my parents suggesting I have psychiatric treatment!' The film in question was a project developed during a regular weekly period set aside for students to develop their own interests, and Nick and his friends set out to make a film about the least attractive aspects of a school from which pupils sought to escape. No doubt some of their insights came from their time at Timbertop but it was never intended to rubbish the school.

However, that year apart, the school 'did have all the space and freedoms I needed' and he was there, a secondary-school boarder, for seven years, and did his best to conceal the fact of having famous parents. In a 1987 interview, Googie expressed the view that, though both daughters were 'happy as bees' at their boarding schools, 'our son Nick wasn't. He felt quite wrongly that by sending him away to school we were getting him out of the way... I said to him: "Do people know who your parents are?" and he said: "I make sure they don't"'. This was probably not easy on that day when Googie presented him with his 'under-10 high jump and long jump' prize!

In reply to my asking when he first realised his parents were famous, he wrote:

> I began to realise [this] from an early age when at restaurants or in the street strangers would approach and say what fans they were and ask for autographs. Then I began to watch their older films as they were shown late night on TV and looking through their scrapbooks. And with the opening night parties and the flow of acting guests that arrived at the house, it all made sense by the time I was 7 or 8. When watching Mum on stage I was struck by the applause she would receive on her entrance and this stayed with me.

These perceptions must have been substantially reinforced when, along with John and younger sister Amanda, he turned up on the TV stage in London to surprise Googie on the occasion of *This Is Your Life* in 1971. Not everyone's mother – or father for that matter, as John's *Life* was similarly showcased some time later – can command such a spotlight.

He played Hamlet at his school when he was eleven and his father recalled him reading a comic in the wings when waiting to go on stage. However, despite this auspicious start and a follow-up small role in Tim Burstall's 1969 film, *2000 Weeks*, plus seeing as many as three films a day during holidays, acting was not where his career would eventually lie. Directly after leaving school he worked for the summer season of 1975 at the Chichester Festival theatre, scene of several engagements for John and Googie. At Chichester, he had some acting experience in plays including *Cyrano de*

Bergerac and *Othello* (with Topol as the Moor), and was also employed as assistant stage manager and set-building assistant during the season presided over by Australian theatre director Keith Michell. He trained at the London Academy for Music and Dramatic Art (LAMDA) and, on graduating from here, worked at the BBC for six months as assistant floor manager on various productions.

On return to Australia, he found his way into television. The taste for filmmaking had been fanned by his incessant movie-going as a schoolboy on holidays – and, also during holidays, by visiting film sets with John. He'd been on locations for *Nickel Queen* in Perth, *Skippy* in Sydney, and *Boney* in Alice Springs, and these gave him an insight into the excitement of telling stories with film. Back in Australia, after writing applications to all the major television stations, he landed a job designated 'Stand By Props' in the Art Department with Grundy Production's *Bellamy*, a 1981 crime series. This is the real start of his now over-thirty-year career as Art Director or Production Designer on many feature films and television series. He has been often nominated for awards for his production design, including his work on such diverse features as the very funny Gold Coast crime comedy, *Gettin' Square* (2002) and the domestic drama *The Black Balloon* (2007), both of which testify to his capacity for creating a convincing setting for diverse genres of film. So did the miniseries, *Answered by Fire* (2005), for which he spent a week in Dili, exploring and taking photographs to ensure the set was true to the relevant East Timor landscape.

In 1995 he married Louise Thompson, an Englishwoman who'd come to Australia at sixteen. She later worked as the London sales representative for an eyewear designer and also did some work in Nick's production office in Australia. Married for sixteen years, they had two children, Casper and Abigail, bringing John and Googie's grandchild yield up to six. At the time of this writing, he is moving into film direction – and dealing with all the intricate negotiations that this can involve, especially if it involves several countries. The film at issue is *The Stone Forest*, an Australian-Chinese co-production, for which Nick has written the screenplay and is co-directing.

Amanda (Mandy) was born at Melbourne's Mercy Hospital in 1960, and this event, along with her christening at St John's Church, Toorak, was widely noted by the Australian press. Mandy, like Nick, has strong memories of the Toorak house and walking to school with her much bigger sister, ten years older than she. Unlike the other two, she had a much more itinerant childhood and education. She first went to England with Googie in 1967, when Googie was starring in *Getting Married*. Mandy doesn't remember much about this except how much she hated going to school there. She'd left a very free Australian school, and was put into a school off London's Sloane Square called Garden House, that was extremely strict and disciplined, and instead of rewarding you with gold stars they gave you black blobs. Mandy recalled: 'I was there for a year with her and don't have many happy memories of that time, mainly because of the school and I think I gave Mum a very hard time because I refused to go to the school unless she took me.' Mum told me later she was the only "Mrs" at the school – the other mothers were all "Lady" or "Duchess"! Actually, one doesn't see Googie being in the least cowed by this, but she may well have found the early morning risings a trial.

Apart from this early school experience, Mandy seems to have adjusted more or less happily to the other schools she attended. By the time she was in secondary school, her parents had moved to Bayview and she found living there idyllic. As well, she enjoyed boarding at Ascham School, a school for girls in Edgecliff, an eastern suburb of Sydney, and felt that this changed the course of her life. She loved animals – Googie and John always had dogs about the house – and as a teenager she became mad about horses. At Ascham, she made friends with lots of country girls to whose properties she would often go in the holidays. One of these girls years later became her sister-in-law:

> She was a good buddy at school, and I used to go home to her country place at Scone, in northern New South Wales, and her parents were a bit like my "second parents". So when Mum and Dad were away, I'd often go back to the Archibald family place. I didn't actually meet my husband-to-be for some time because he'd left school well before I started going there. It wasn't until I came back from overseas when I was twenty that I met him. And how fortunate, because we fell in love

and got married. So I really married into the family that was always my surrogate family.

What all three children seem to have had in common is that, despite their parents often being on tour, they felt secure in the arrangements that had been made for them, in terms of schools or household help. Jo recalled her nanny, Helen, as being a fixture in her early life, and they remained friends long after she had left; Nick remembered a volatile housekeeper called Violet, who did the cooking at the Toorak house; and Mandy's chief memory was of nanny Helen, and housekeeper Mrs Attwood who lived with the family at Bayview from about 1968 until Mandy married in August 1983, and was always there in the holidays. For Mandy, Bayview was her 'rock', whereas Jo and Nick's continuity largely derived from their boarding-schools. She grew up feeling closer to her father who was around more often than Googie whose tours were longer than John's interstate trips. He was the sort of father who would get up early to take her riding at Smoky Dawson's ranch at Ingleside, north of Sydney, whereas when Googie came home she needed the respite which wouldn't have fitted easily with the 5 a.m. rising.

Mandy's recollection is that her parents' fame only dawned on her when she was in high school. Here she became aware that hers weren't the regular sort of parents and that there was some whispering about 'Do you know who her parents are?' She was cross when John came to tell her that they were going to England to surprise Googie on *This Is Your Life* in 1971: she didn't want to go because she was due to run in the 100-metre sprint at school. In the event, she did enjoy herself, especially with the bonus of Disneyland on the way. Her Australian schooling finished when John and Googie went to England in late 1976 in preparation for a season of Somerset Maugham's *The Circle*. Mandy briefly attended a local school at Horsham, Sussex, near where her parents had rented a farmhouse from which they would commute to London. Her education was then 'finished' at a school in Switzerland which taught only French – and skiing. At this school she became very attracted to her ski instructor, was asked to leave when word got out, and went to London where Googie and John expected her to join them in going to Australia for Christmas, but instead went back to live with the instructor in Switzerland.

What is impressive is that her parents took this well, only urging her not to *marry* the man, who was eleven years older than she.

Mandy decided on the basis of taking a drama subject at her Horsham school that acting was not for her. Her real interest was in working with animals, and when she came back to Australia in 1979, the interlude with the ski instructor having ended, she studied Equine Management at Glen Ormiston Agricultural College in south-western Victoria for a couple of years. She went back to the Archibald property to help with the horse sales, met Sandy Archibald, her husband-to-be, married in 1983, had two children and settled on their property, 'Fernleigh', near Ellerston, in northern New South Wales. In 1995, she was written up in *The Land* as demonstrating at the Sydney Royal Show Sheep and Wool Showcase: 'A mother of two, Mandy, of "Fernleigh", has developed a line of practical machine washable jumpers and cardigans for adults and children sold under the label, Fernleigh Yarns,' which became well known as an innovative company. She'd researched the matter carefully and maintained production for fifteen years. In making a success of it, she had exercised her own creative impulses in her own individual way. These impulses also found outlet in the role of president of the Murrurundi Arts Council, supervising, among other activities, photography exhibitions and a biennial opera season, and in doing radio talks on the history of the area. One local newspaper report summarised her as 'A woman of passion, creativity and that zest that gets things done.'

Googie's innumerable interviews, in whichever country, were firm about one thing: there was no better place than Australia for bringing up children, she asserted again and again. She knew that, as a mother whose profession often took her away from home for long periods, she would come under some critical scrutiny from more conventionally situated housewives. And she was ready for this. For her, 'the secret lay in being a very efficient organiser "… I worked out schedules with the nurse and housekeeper so that I could even say months ahead what they [the children] would be having to eat on a particular day. What is even more important, the children knew they would never come home to an empty house; there was always someone who cared there. And they knew that their father or I was always at the end of the telephone and ready to return at a moment's notice.'" It can't have been quite as clear-cut as this suggests, and there must have been difficulties not easily settled by phone or live-in staff, but these matters were always uppermost in Googie's mind. While she was touring New Zealand in the late '60s, she told one reporter how, 'I keep my thumb on the domestic situation. Certainly I miss the children more than they miss me'.

While these three major productions were getting established in the '70s, and while John and Googie seem to have been in a state of almost constant professional activity, together and separately, they were also settling in for the long haul at the house in Bayview. Googie, as many accounts attest, loved redecorating houses, only barely constrained by thrift, and the National Trust of Australia wrote an enthusiastic account of her Bayview renovations: 'Admittedly the waterfront location was a stunning one but the house, a clutter of small and pokey rooms, would have daunted many people.' What the McCallums established for their offspring in its elegant, commodious comfort was a life-style that offered both reassurance and glimpses of a glittering world beyond. Or on one occasion bringing the glittering world of filmmaking actually into the home, when Bayview was used as one of the locations for Michael Pate's 1979 film *Tim* starring Hollywood leading lady Piper Laurie – and handsome young Mel Gibson just getting started.

Actor David Yelland, who appeared with Googie and John twice, summed up:

> They were great family people. Living to that great age and keeping the family together must often have been logistically difficult. I think the success of the three children is an indication of the warmth and generosity of them in general. Fundamentally they were just very close and they had their priorities right.

Their rambling, ultra-comfortable Bayview home continued to be the scene of ongoing hospitality for family, friends and visiting celebrities alike. Their children had grown up with a procession of famous names being hospitably received there. Over the years they had seen, among others, Rex Harrison, Twiggy, Harry Belafonte, Vivien Leigh and John Mills. And apart from the celebrity roll-call, there were numerous visitors from England, old friends (like actress/agent Patricia Marmont) or friends of friends who had been passed on to the McCallums, and who were always assured of a friendly welcome, good fare and a good time.

But it is the family's responses to the home and its occupants, whether as parents, grandparents or parents-in-law, that are most important. Given that John and Googie's careers so often led them to be away from home, and often, too, in different directions, the kind of closeness that characterises the family looks like a major achievement, and the Bayview house was its rallying point for several decades. Nick, whose wedding took place there, remembered that, 'After Toorak, Bayview was very tropical – mozzie coils, mosquito nets, sea-grass matting, waterfront, banana trees. This house was magic.' And for Mandy, 'I always knew it was there and the dog was there. It was the anchor I could always come home to if things got tough. In my parents' later years, their periods of respite were more frequent, so we – my family and me – saw them a lot, and my children were lucky to have Bayview and my parents as their home away-from-home.'

Time can certainly bathe memories in a nostalgic glow, but there is such consistency of pleasure and affection in the recollection of the three younger McCallums that it is hard to be sceptical about them. Especially when there are the further tributes of grandchildren, who say things like this: 'Some of my fondest memories are of times spent around the dinner table with my grandparents and family at Bayview, as they were always wonderfully entertaining and convivial evenings... Muti [Googie] loved food. We always ate well whenever we stayed … Grandpa enjoyed food too, but he was always just as happy to have sausages and mashed potato.' This recollection of Gus Archibald, Mandy's son, is supported by his sister Emma's memories: 'Seemingly never-ending summers were spent in the pool and on the mud flats, copious amounts of food and countless glasses raised from one dinner party to the next. Most happy memories of Muti and Grandpa revolve around food, with Muti ordering the grandest thing on the menu, and Grandpa being satisfied with the simplest dish. Summers at Bayview seemed to be a never-ending stream of food, guests and toasts. Lots of grand gestures, smells of perfume, and laughing.'

These family images of parents and grandparents conjure up the personal aspect of this long-lasting pair. Even in the matter of food, their distinctness is maintained, but, whatever their differences (and sometimes 'differences' would be too gentle a word), they seem to have been united in the need to provide a steady family context for at least the two generations after them. In personal terms, their 62-year marriage might be seen as their major achievement, particularly in the theatrical context where the longevity of such unions was not often the order of the day. Googie was once asked for the secret of a happy marriage and from the top of her head, a populous region indeed, she replied, 'Separate bathrooms', before going on to deal with matters such as sense of humour and having professional interests in common. They were never one of those married pairs who claimed not to discuss these interests at home. John, questioned along the same lines, on numerous occasions echoed the fabled wisdom about marrying actresses: they are usually beautiful, talented and they go on tour. Both echoed Dame Sybil Thorndike's account of how each return, after a separate tour, was like a little honeymoon, the romance of the marriage kept fresh. Well, it's a point of view.

When I asked Joanna if her parents ever disagreed about much, she was emphatic. 'Disagree!' she exclaimed, as she went on to describe how there would be 'the odd big blow-ups and Mummy would be quite histrionic while my father would be quite quiet and continue watching the golf or the cricket. Then, about an hour later after she'd flounced out, she'd come back and say I'm terribly sorry.' What is interesting is that Googie 'never let fly in professional circumstances. She was a team member; she was a trouper; she never pulled rank.' There is widespread agreement that she was a good 'company member' and Jo remembered a piece of advice her mother had given her: 'When I was once asked to do something I felt wrong for the part: "Darling just nod your head, then completely ignore it!"' (recalling how Googie had reacted to a suggestion from director Tony Britton at Chichester.) On political and religious matters, John was probably the more thoughtful, whereas Googie was more apt to be beguiled by their theatrical aspects. And as John said in the *Talking Heads* interview: 'You know, marriage has to have a bit of turbulence. It would be very dull if it didn't. And Googie's not easy to live with. She's very bossy. And we have a lot of rows, but … we get over them pretty quickly.' Mind you, Googie can be seen sitting next to him as he makes these pronouncements and retaliated with 'Well, you're worse. You go into a silence.' Volatility no doubt helped explain why dullness never became an issue.

One of Joanna's clearest memories of their disagreements had to do with cars. John used to pull motorcars to bits and put them together. He loved cars, especially old ones, but Jo recalls he had the very irritating habit of getting all the family in the car to go off somewhere, then remembering he needed to dash inside for something, leaving the family to get cross while he was inside for fifteen or twenty minutes. Googie, on the other hand, was not always an easy passenger. The children in the back seat would hear the recurring 'John!' followed by a complaint or command: 'John, there's a draught at my feet. Please fix it. Could you please get rid of it', and so on. Finally after some sort of tiff, these 90-year-olds driving off somewhat precariously, 'We got to the lunch place, they made their orders and we were sitting there in silence when Googie in a plaintive voice said, "John, I don't think you love me any more". He replied, "Googie, darling, of course I love you, I've always loved you. If I didn't, I would have murdered you years ago."' Such an anecdote may well sum up a good deal about what accounted for a remarkable 62-year marriage: their differences were as important to the success of the union as the professional interests they obviously shared.

Joanna's daughter, Alex Davenport, wrote eloquently of her grandparents and the place they had in her life. 'They loved their work and the people they worked with. They adored their family and wanted to be a part of each and everyone's lives. This is what kept them vibrant in their late years. They continued to have curiosity also and very much liked meeting new people and being out and about – even when lack of mobility would make it difficult.' On an everyday basis, she recalled the pleasures of staying with them and had a vivid memory of breakfast with her grandparents in their later years, with 'the smell of charred toast, an infinite number of pills in ever increasing plastic containers, freshly squeezed orange juice, muesli topped with bran and every type of marmalade and preserve out and on the table with the newspapers. Whether in London, Bosham, Swanage or Bayview this never altered.' Grandson Gus Archibald fondly remembers 'Muti's proud demeanour – whether going to the cinema, a restaurant or walking into a room full of people, she always seemed to carry herself as though on stage. She was a kind and endearing grandmother, always wanting to know what was happening in our lives,' while 'Grandpa was an excellent storyteller. He was a master of holding an audience at the dinner table with an interesting anecdote or some witty repartee.' Gus's sister Emma confirmed this: 'Grandpa was known for his jokes and stories at mealtimes. He would always hold an audience captive, even if we'd heard the story several times before. It was comforting to hear him speak jovially, especially when he laughed', while Muti was 'An incredibly strong-willed woman, with firm (and of course, always correct) opinions.' Well, so she was, but some of these were expressions of genuine liberality of attitude, as in her detestation of anti-Semitism as she met it in the US, or of apartheid in South Africa. So, strong will sometimes showed up well. And fifty years earlier, she acknowledged that John 'has a seriousness that I lack.' There could be moments of self-awareness that emerged from the more usual outgoing liveliness. John's seriousness, too, was balanced by a humour that is glimpsed when he claimed that if a show he'd sponsored 'is not a success I will jump off a Yarra Bridge tied to a 100-lb sinker – I will have to.'

In canvassing as wide a range of opinion as possible, I have been confronted with a remarkable consensus about this professional and personal partnership. People would speak frankly, but again and again the outcome of such discussions was how much others had liked working with them or how well they complemented each other or what good troupers they were and so on. There was little sense of serious contention and none at all of scandal.

The last of my more formal meetings with them (formal in the sense that they knew writing about them was to follow) took place in May 2009, by which time they had moved from the Bayview house to an apartment not too far from it. This time I was writing a piece about their joint careers for the Melbourne-based journal *Meanjin*. The day before I was due to fly up from Melbourne to meet them for talk and lunch, John rang to say he was sorry he wouldn't be there as he had to go to court to do battle with actor Tony Bonner over *Skippy* payments, but that Googie would nevertheless be there, so do come. In the event, after half an hour's talk with Googie, John rang to say the case had been thrown out of court and he'd be home very shortly. According to the legal secretary involved, Cheryl Gagliano, 'They'd signed the agreements in 1966, assigning all their rights back to Fauna. But the case had to be defended because, if Tony Bonner had won, then all the other actors would have had a go as well.' It was also suggested that John had tried to talk Bonner out of the court action because the legalities were all in place and he would lose his case. Philip Austin, the son of John's lawyer and business partner, confirmed this, and said, 'I was at the court when Bonner was suing John. It was thrown out of court very briskly. The contracts were fair and reasonable, they looked after Bonner; they paid him very well, a lot more than they would normally get paid in those days. But Fauna took complete control and actors didn't get any residuals from it… It was all very distressing to John, because he was one of the most honourable men you'd ever meet… the judge said to Bonner, "I've read the contract. I've heard what you said. And go away." John was awarded costs but didn't pursue them and Bonner never paid them.'

So, after this short-lived courtroom drama, John joined us and this was the last time I saw them. The new apartment was perfectly pleasant, if a little cluttered because Googie had said she was willing to leave Bayview, which she claimed was 'falling down round our ears', only on the understanding that she wouldn't be throwing anything out. This included books, for which she'd had shelves built down the passageway, so that it was almost necessary to walk sideways, and one moved around carefully so as not to disturb small tables lying in wait for the clumsy. A few weeks later John, now formally diagnosed with terminal cancer, phoned asking if I'd write an obituary for the Melbourne and Sydney papers as he wanted it written by 'someone who knows what I've done.' At the Melbourne *Age* office, someone said, 'Why don't you do one for Googie as well?', though I didn't pass this on to Googie, believing discretion to be the better part of valour here.

Reading one's way through the staggering amount that was written about them during sixty and more years, and listening to all the recollections of those who worked with them and knew them in all kinds of situations, they *do* seem remarkable. Googie was obviously more outspoken, could make outrageous pronouncements, could be – as several people, including her children have noted – imperious, but none of this seems to have detracted from the infectious delight and interest in other people, from a genuinely good-natured, outgoing gregariousness. John was always more considered in what he said, more given to weighing matters before pronouncing, but was also astute in his professional ventures and a witty raconteur. He could be a tough negotiator, but as everyone agrees was entirely open in his dealings.

John died on 3 February 2010 after several months in hospital where he was treated for leukaemia and was apparently lucid till the end. His obituaries all highlighted his triumph with *Skippy*. Life became lonely for Googie. She enjoyed talking on the phone, and I remember in one conversation putting forward my scholarly theory that whoever invented people should have done more research first so that we all lived till 120 with nothing wrong with us. Her reply was: 'Oh no, my dear. The great thing would have been to have all these terrible things happen to us when we were young and strong, so that we could have shaken them off and the rest would have been plain sailing.' It seemed to sum up so much about her attitude to life. As did another occasion, after John's death, on which she said some friends of his were coming to visit and bringing lunch with them. To my wet reply, 'You'll enjoy that Googie', she quickly replied, 'No I won't! I want them to take me *out* to lunch and then to a movie.' She was barely 94 at this point, so naturally she wanted to be out and about.

Annam Road neighbour, Liz Goodman, felt Googie coped well with John's illness and death, maintaining a 'stiff upper lip', and sitting unblinking at the wake for John at the Bayview Yacht Racing Association rooms. Ms Goodman admired her courage as she had relished her zest and vitality. Another neighbour, Doreen Telfer, remembered her as being delighted with company, and, when anyone from the Annam Road apartments would pop in, Googie would always urge them to stay for conversation and a glass of champagne. After John died, she had during the week a live-in carer who would be replaced by another at weekends. There were some minor problems with the onset of dementia, including some memory-loss, and Googie finally had to move into a nursing home where she died after only a short time there, on 15 July 2011. At first she resisted this move, then, when she went into the lounge of the Avalon nursing home, she found she had a whole new audience. Despite failing health, her star aura stayed with her to the end.

Their deaths were marked with fitting memorials (one at a favourite restaurant) in Sydney and in London at a crowded memorial service for Googie at St Paul's, the Actors' Church, Covent Garden, with tributes from family and colleagues, including affectionate recollections from Vanessa Redgrave. This was apt because, though Googie had so thoroughly adjusted to life in Australia and despite her European heritage, she still thought of herself as primarily British. London: that's where she became famous, creating unforgettable images of sensual authority in British cinema and on British stages. A final gesture to Britain: Joanna scattered some of her ashes from the Dorset coast where she had lived as a girl.

It is hard to think of a contemporary couple who have given rise to quite such media coverage for over half a century as John and Googie did (maybe Brangelina will eventually?). Perhaps those celebrities whose faces adorn the covers of journals to be found at supermarket check-outs could give them a run for their money, but what was amazing in their case was the coverage they received in the respectable (more or less) daily press, in Australia, New Zealand and the UK (sometimes in the US, too), as well as in more specialised journals. Nowadays it seems that only sports personalities behaving badly get that sort of attention. Back then there was an avid readership for accounts of their domestic lives as well as for when they were on the job. They clearly understood that being constantly in the public eye was important for people in their profession. What may seem even stranger today is that the incessant reporting of their doings never seemed to unearth any scandal. Robust disagreement from time to time, but hardly the sort of thing that would make the cover of today's *New Idea* or *Hello!*

But what also strikes me on reading the voluminous cuttings that charted their lives when they were household names, in Australia at least and prior to that in the UK, is the sheer fleetingness of celebrity. Like them, so many who worked with them have now gone from the scene and it is sometimes shocking to be confronted with the sheer brevity of the collective memory. Apart from the interest inherent in what they did, it may be worth recording here what was once remarkable, as a reminder of what *can* be done – and, indeed, what can *be*.

BIBLIOGRAPHY AND NOTES

References

Barr, Charles *Ealing Studios* (Second edition), London: Studio Vista, 1993.

Drazin, Charles *The Finest Years: British Cinema of the 1940s*, London: André Deutsch, 1998.

Fisher, John *George Formby*, London: Woburn-Futura, 1975.

Fitzpatrick, Peter *The Two Frank Thrings*, Clayton: Monash University Publishing, 2012.

McCallum, Joanna Boxes of her parents' personal papers.

McCallum, John *Life with Googie*, London: Heinemann, 1979.

McCallum, John Notes for unpublished update of 1979 memoir.

McFarlane, Brian (ed) *Sixty Voices*, London: British Film Institute, 1992.

McFarlane, Brian *An Autobiography of British Cinema*, London: Methuen/British Film Institute, 1997.

McFarlane, Brian (ed) *The Encyclopedia of British Film*, 4th edition, London: Manchester University Press, 2013.

McFarlane, Brian, Mayer, Geoff and Bertrand, Ina *The Oxford Companion to Australian Film*, Melbourne: Oxford University Press, 1999.

Ogilvie, George *Simple Gifts: A Life in the Theatre*, Strawberry Hills, NSW: Currency House, 2006.

Performing Arts Collection, Melbourne Arts Centre (40 boxes of papers)

Powell, Michael *A Life in Movies*, London: Heinemann, 1986.

Strachan, Alan *Michael Redgrave: Secret Dreams*, London: Weidenfeld & Nicolson, 2005.

Sumner, John *Recollections at Play: A Life in Australian Theatre*, Melbourne: Melbourne University Press, 1993.

Withers, Googie 'Acting for Stage and Screen', in *The Penguin Film Review*, London and New York: Penguin Books, 1947.

Abbreviations used in notes (to avoid undue repetition)

Titles

NB Definite article preceding newspapers and journals is omitted in the notes (e.g., *The Sun* is listed as *Sun*).

Australian Women's Weekly – AWW
Autobiography of British Cinema – ABC
Life with Googie – LWG
Oxford Companion to Australian Film – OCAF
McCallum, John Notes for unpublished update of 1979 memoir – JM's notes
Monthly Film Bulletin – MFB
National Library Oral History Project – NLOHP
Performing Arts Collection, Arts Centre Melbourne - PACACM
Sydney Morning Herald – SMH
Talking Heads interview – TH

People, as referred to in notes:

John McCallum – JM
Googie Withers – GW
Amanda McCallum Archibald – AMA
Joanna McCallum – Joanna
John Frost – JF
Nicholas McCallum – NM

Chapter notes

The purpose of these notes is to enable readers to trace sources where they wish and to avoid spraying the text with small numbers to indicate foot- or end-notes. The numbers in the left margin below are the page numbers.

Introduction

xi   'criminality', 'Hell's road and good intentions', *Age*, Melbourne, 11 January 2013.

     'happy together', interview with AMA, November 2013.

xiii   'of a life', 'Not knowing: the art of the biography', *The Author*, Spring 2014.

Chapter 1

1   'crazy child', *Picture Show*, 5 September 1936.

     'Vizzers', *Daily Dispatch*, 23 May 1964.

2   'despite her name', *ABC*, p. 608.

     'I'll not change', *Telegraph*, Sydney, 30 July 1955.

3   'stage experience', Max Breen, 6 February 1937.

     'learn to dance', 'A Woman Must Play Many Roles', *Woman*, 5 December 1955.

4   'Gandhi', interview in Hollywood May 1946, in JM's notes.

5   'beatings on our bottoms', Frances Brierley, 'Hometown', *Times Magazine*, 25 January 1997.

     'school reports', held by Joanna.

     'Elocution Festival', Leamington Open & Competitive Music Festival Scoresheet (undated), held by Joanna.

     'Holy Family' school reports, held by Joanna.

     'very good dancer', interview with author, Melbourne 1990.

     'her father', ibid.

6   'Madame Lehmiski!' http://beyondthetrenches.blogspot.co.uk/2012/03/lehmiski-babes.html.

7   'Lola Anderson', author interview, London, May 2013.

     'picture in the papers', unsourced cutting in PACACM.

     'Bradley', interview with Bill Stephens, 1993, for NLOHP.

8   'damaged her left arm', 'Golden Couple', interview by Michael Gartside in *Classic Images*, October 2003, p. 71.

'return to the stage', *Times*, 5 June 1935.

9   'Hammond style', *Sunday Graphic*, 23 May 1937.

'her present one', *Sphere*, 29 May 1937.

10   'Schack', Monja Danischewsky, *White Russian, Red Face*. London, 1966.

11   'my preference', interview with author, 1990.

'all-embracing vamp', *Cinema*, 3 January 1935.

'when she started', *West London Observer Series*, 4 October 1935

12   'servant girl', *Film Pictorial*, 23 May 1936

13   'absolutely ludicrous', interview with author, 1990.

'unpleasant man', Brian McFarlane, 'The director who knew too much', *Sunday Age*, 24 April 1994.

14   'friend for life', 'Golden Couple', *Classic Images*, October 2003, p. 69.

15   'about three seconds', quoted in http://www.georgeformby.co.uk/ladies/withers/biog.htm

16   'she could do it', Powell, *A Life in Movies*. London: Heinemann, 1986, p. 391.

17   'his accent', GW, interviewed at Sydney Film Festival, June 2003.

'adored each other', 'I made it clear I did not fall for furs or diamonds', *Daily Mail*, 11 June 1996.

'kind to me', *A Prince among Stones*. London: Bloomsbury, 2013, p.6.

'inbuilt conceit', in JM's notes.

18   'living in Paris', 'A New Amanda for *Private Lives*', *Tatler* 12 December 1945.

'women in uniform', GW, interviewed at Sydney Film Festival, June 2003.

19   'Antwerp', on ABC television, Australia, 8 October 2007. Numbers killed vary from 700 to 900 to 1200 in accounts of the incident.

'war has changed her', report by Ealing publicist, Monja Danischewsky.

20   'Dr Goebbels', letter held by Joanna.

22   'provocative remarks', in *The Penguin Film Review 1947*, pp. 36–40.

'bring it down for film', in JM's notes..

23   'well-being', 'My favourite role', in F. Maurice Speed, *Film Review 1949*).

'brought the love story out more', *The Noël Coward Diaries*, Da Capo Press, 1982, p. 44

24   'brunette', 'My Favourite Role', *Film Review 1949*.

'Shepherd's Market', email from Joanna, 10 May 2013.

Chapter 2

26   'sound-film screening', see http://www.austlit.edu.au/run?ex=ShowAgent&agentId
      for a history of the Cremorne Theatre.

      'stage career', letter from N. Freeman, 7 December 1936.

      'talkie theatres', undated handwritten script for talk by John McCallum Sr after
      time in 'the old country'.

      'gorgeous raiment', 'Johnny M'Callum's Wardrobe', *The Patriot* (undated cutting in
      PACACM.

27   'wonderful old couple', JM's notes.

28   'Oatlands School', *Huddersfield Weekly Examiner*, 25November1947.

      'boarders' A booklet entitled *Oatlands Infant School: A Centenary Celebration* makes
      no such reference, and conversation with Ms Sue Sowden at the school in April
      2013 confirms this.

      'weeks at Easter', letter dated 16 April 1928, held by Joanna.

29   'theatreland', *Harrogate Advertiser*, 19 July 1930.

      'golf card', 'Away they go', unsigned article about Australians in Britain, *Photoplay*, 1946.

      'honourable and trustworthy', on CEGS letterhead, 4 August 1936. His Senior
      Public Certificate from the University of Brisbane recorded these results: B in
      English, C in Latin, A in Modern History and B in Economics. 31 January 1936.

30   'read the lesson'. The School, from the mid 1920s, was praised for its increased
      attention to Biblical stories and their practical applications. Religious instruction
      appears to have been important to the syllabus during John's time there. (cf.
      Oatlands Infant School: A Centenary Celebration, p.20)

      'playing Horatio', *Telegraph*, 14 September 1936.

      'professional work', letter from RADA secretary, 19 April 1938.

31   'a most lovely Portia', letter, 10 July 2004.

      'training at RADA', in conversation with author, *OCAF*, p. 296.

      'Zanuck' Letter from McCallum Sr to Zanuck, 17 June 1938.

      'a part in London', letter from Zanuck secretary, 21 June 1938.

32   'typically scholastic', *Tonbridge Free Press*, 12 January 1939.

      '*Gaslight*', all three quoted remarks in undated cuttings held in PACACM.

      'about his acting', cutting, 6 January 1939, in PACACM.

33   'tradition of the family', unsourced cutting, in PACACM.

34   'gave a hoot', unpublished diaries, Donald Friend Collection, National Library of
      Australia, Canberra, MS 5959.

'Antonio', JM to Ian Britain, Friend's biographer, 12 May 2008

'tropical downpour', in 'Away They Go', *Photoplay*, undated cutting in PACACM.

'beautiful speaking, '*Land*, 23 January 1948

35 'splendidly vulgar', *LWG*, p. 128.

37 'his contract', letter sent from mother's home in Bower Street, Manly, 25 May 1945.

'20 weeks', letter from Managing Director, J.C.W., 24 December 1944.

'old anopheles', from JM's notes.

38 'over her crutch', ibid.

39 'the big part', unsourced cutting in PACACM.

'Film Lead', *News, Adelaide*, 5 July 1946.

'Star Film role', Clem Cleveson, *Sun* (Melbourne), undated cutting.

'New English Film', unsourced cutting, in PACACM.

40 'his eye', *Home Notes*, 11 July 1947.

41 'terrible film', interview with Brian Johnston, Sydney, 2008.

42 'second-rate story', undated cuttings, in PACACM.

'rustic lover role', *Today's Cinema*, 7 February 1947.

'this sequence', *Illustrated*, 8 June 1946, photographed by Peter Waugh.

'in all directions', unsourced cutting, in PACACM.

Chapter 3

43 'bottom of the stairs', interview with author, 1998.

'Hollywood contracts', *Daily Telegraph*, Sydney, 30 July 1956.

44 'you beaut', *Daily Telegraph*, Sydney, 8 December 1955.

45 'a good look at her', *LWG*, p. 6

'Googie Boogie Withers', *Kent Messenger*, 7 September, 1946.

'living in the most beautiful house', interview with author, March 1990.

46 'merry as grigs', phone conversation with author, March 2013.

'village fancy dress competition', *Daily Mail*, 23 May, year obscured on cutting, in PACACM.

'Turns to Drama', unsourced cutting, in PACACM.

47 'daffodils in the churchyard', letter to the Sheila Kaye-Smith Society, 12 April, 1946.

'responsibility for the story', ibid.

49 'Blackface', *Sunday Times*, 15 June 1947.

'a Kentish man', *Evening Standard*, 13 June 1947.

'notable music', *Tatler*, 25 June, 1947.

'practically nil', *Observer*, 15 June, 1947.

50 'John is unmarried!', *Coventry Evening Telegraph*, 11 July 1947.

'young character actresses', *Tribune*, 13 June 1947.

'Royal Garden Party', Elspeth Grant, *Daily Graphic*, 13 June 1947.

'a long way', *What's On*, 13 July 1947.

'another star', *Picturegoer*, 10 May, 1947.

52 'sexual element in his films', *Independent*, 3 July 1999.

53 'before the "cut" came', 'Outlawed Scenes at Ealing Necessitate Special U.S. Shots', *Cinema*, 26 March 1947.

'hardworking farce', *Punch*, 25 June 1947.

'awful risks', *ABC*, p. 610.

54 'Don't sock her in the jaw', *East End Advertiser*, 12 January 1948.

'happy couple', unsourced cutting, in PACACM.

'our married life', recalled in interview with Brian Johnston, 2008.

'a lot in common', *Sydney Sun*, 10 April 1947.

56 'many they'd worked with', invitation and guest list held by Joanna. *Tatler*, 11 February 1948.

'for the wedding', *Sydney Sun*, 25 November 1947.

'life-long friends', phone interview with Doreen Hawkins, May 2013.

57 'flat in Portland Place', Joyce Lambert, *Woman*, 19 January 1948.

'film about a spiv', *Observer*, 30 November 1947.

58 'bombs were falling', *Palmers Green Gazette*, undated piece headed: 'A film people are talking about.'

'1948 film poll', *Film Review*, 10 April 1948.

Chapter 4

59 'warm-hearted and affectionate', 6 December 1951.

'a fool or a liar', *Daily Express*, 31 July 1954.

60 'in the same business', *Yorkshire Evening Post*, 26 June 1950.

'a good change', *Daily Dispatch*, 10 April 1948.

'a cascade of comedy', *Daily Mirror*, 9 April 1948.

61 'innocent fun', *Daily Graphic*, 9 April 1948.

'favourite role', F. Maurice Speed, *Film Review Annual* 1949.

'more than £12,000', *Evening Standard*, 24 January 1949.

'tucking-in', *Thames Valley Times*, 19 January 1949.

'withers unwrung', *Sun Chronicle*, 6 February 1949.

62 'trapped in a lift', *Kensington News*, 20 August 1948.

'without a hat', *Illustrated*, 2 April 1949.

'became friends', interview with author, London 2013.

'Bakery Industries Ball', *Bakers' Record*, 4 November 1948.

'National Committee', *Liberal News*, 5 November 1948.

'personal appearance', *Yorkshire Evening Post*, 2 August 1948.

63 'Britain's New Male Star', *Movie Magazine*, Autumn, 1948.

'not half as amusing', *Sunday Chronicle*, 30 May 1948.

'mildewed sporting farce', *News Chronicle*, undated cutting, in PACACM.

'chap you'd like to be', *Sound*, June 1948.

'pleasantly wayward', *Star*, undated cutting, in PACACM.

64 'seasoned racer', *Cinema Studio*, 8 June 1949.

65 'cloudy day', *Yorkshire Evening News*, 29 May 1949.

'Yorkshire Dales', interview with author, Melbourne 1989.

'unhappily overplayed', P.H. *MFB*, November 1950, p. 170.

'point I started from', 'Jean Kent' in *ABC*, p. 341.

66 'their wedding days', unsourced cutting, November 1947, in PACACM.

'Arctic expedition', *Thames Valley Times*, 17 December 1952.

67 'when the singing stops', *Daily Worker*, 29 August 1953.

'Dilys Powell', *Sunday Times*, 25 January 1953.

'strength and affection', *Daily Express*, 23 January 1953.

68 'interesting heroes', *East End News*, 3 December 1948.

'London Stage Play', *Sydney Sun*, 9 December 1948.

'a few months to live', *Television Weekly*, 16 April, 1949.

69 'put on an apron', *WEEKEND*, 29 September- 1 October, 1950.

70 'conflict between them', Googie at Sydney Film Festival, June 2003.

'threw me terribly', interview with author, London 2013.

71 'in oilskins', *Daily Express*, 7 June 1952.

'so desperately', *Daily Telegraph*, 2 January 1953.

'passion that drives Hester', conversations with author, UK, 1989, 2013.

'most moving piece of acting', *Daily Express*, 18 January 1954.

72 'Actress of the year' *TV Mirror*, 20 November 1954.

'sacrifice my home', *Daily Sketch*, 19 January 1954.

73 'the house', *Woman's Weekly*, 21 August 1954.

'shed his priggishness', *Times*, 22 April 1954.

74 'with a bad filling', *Manchester Evening Chronicle*, 28 April 1953.

'teaches absolute control', *Yorkshire Evening News*, 6 May 1953.

'more restful periods', phone interview with Hon. Frances Russell, London 2013.

75 'quality of atmosphere', P.H. *MFB*, April-May 1950, p.59.

'cuddle his head', *ABC*, p. 612.

76 'loved being in the film', interview with author, Melbourne 1989.

'Maybe in Hollywood', letter from Dassin to 'Darling Googie', 30 January 1950.

'I was a surgeon', interview with author, Melbourne 1989.

77 'to become doctors', 'Googie Withers and John McCallum', interview by Michael Gartside in *Classic Images*, 1998, p. 73.

'director Pat Jackson', *LWG*, p. 86.

'strong-meat', *Variety*, 27 June 1951.

'films of this country', *MFB*, October 1951, p. 295.

'I hate it now', *AB C*, p.610.

78 'terrible stuff', *ABC*, p. 611.

'actors you act against', *ABC*, p. 611.

'had this in his hand', interview with author, Melbourne 1989.

'popular audiences', *Today's Cinema*, 18 March 1954.

'elevated moral tone', *The Daily Recorder*, 19 March 1954.

Variety, 31 March 1954.

'moderate scope', unnsourced cutting in PACACM.

79 'shifting props', *Evening News*, 10 November 1953.

'small and unsmart', *Daily Express*, 13 February 1953.

80 'classical actor', Interview with Bill Stephens, Oral History Project, National Library, Canberra, March 1993.

Chapter 5

81 'plum West End role', programme notes for *Simon and Laura* at Her Majesty's Theatre, Perth.

82 'running out of steam', *A BC*, p. 612.

'contract artistes', *L WG*, p. 108.

'widely reported', all 31 December 1954.

83 'like a pasha', *Telegraph*, 8 December 1955.

84 Both verses in papers held by Joanna.

'their mother', phone interview with Mrs Nan Austin, formerly Mrs Ian McCallum, November 2013.

'skiting about', *Woman's Day and Home*, 24 January 1955.

85 'before their departure', *Sunday Telegraph*, 13 January 1955.

'passion for hats', *Daily Mirror*, 6 January 1955.

'cooking and antiques', *Sunday Telegraph*, 9 January 1955.

'husband to be boss', *Sun*, 7 January 1955.

'saying goodnight', *Women's Weekly*, 23 May 1955.

'Sights of Sydney', *Pix*, 22 October 1955.

'returning to England', *Adam & Eve*, 1 April 1954.

'West End stars', *AM*, 5 July 1955.

'domestic brawling', interview with author, Sydney 2009.

86 'supposed suffocation', *Sun*, undated cutting, late 1954, in PACACM.

'challenging plays', *Herald*, Melbourne, 4 November 1954.

'good publicity', *Listener-In*, 8 January 1955.

87 'her birthday', unsourced early 1950s cutting, in PACACM.

88 'their capabilities', *Courier-Mail*, Brisbane, 26 December 1955.

'a leading lady', *Sydney Telegraph*, 26 December 1955.

'rather than the actor', interview for Oral History Project of National Library, Canberra, 26 March 1993.

'emotional strain', *Age*, 16 May 1955.

'opportunist to the life', *Listener-In*, 21–27 May 1955.

'Freddie is impeccable', *Truth*, 9 October 1955.

89 'both amateur and professional', *Stock and Land*, 11 May 1955.

'Randwick Race Course', newspaper cuttings held in PACACM.

'a very good actress', interview with author, Melbourne, February 2013.

'poolside refresher', *Listener-In*, 12–18 November 1955.

90 'friend of understudy', Joanna's words, but confirmed by Dame Eileen Atkins, Rona Anderson and others who worked with them.

91 'lack of polish', *Daily Worker*, 30 June 1956.

'hope a sequel', *Evening News*, 29 June 1956.

'Lord Mayor', *Telegraph*, 23 December 1955.

'mud crabs', *Courier-Mail*, 24 December 1955.

92 'humanity', *Telegraph*, 10 January 1956.

'duplicated here', *New Zealand Herald*, 1 February 1956.

'happiness with life', unsourced cutting, PACACM.

'in bed with a book', *New Zealand Women's Weekly*, 26 January 1956.

93 'parking tickets', *Oomaru Mail*, 18 April 1956.

'loyalty and support', *Truth*, 15 January 1956.

'impact of television', *Times*, Palmerston North, 9 March 1956; reply 12 March 1956.

'happiest company', *Auckland Star*, 1 February 1956.

'two boxer dogs', *Femina*, February 1956.

94 'world audience', *Truth*, 15 January 1956.

'wait till later', *New Zealand Herald*, 11 February 1956.

'Kilkenny cats', *New Zealand Herald*, 1 February 1956.

'superlative entertainment', *Times*, Palmerston North, 7 March 1956.

'Rattigan play', *Sun*, Christchurch, 6 April 1956.

'sympathy with him', *Auckland Star*, 14 February 1956.

95 'proscenium arch', *LWG*, p. 147.

Chapter 6

96   'to have a boy', *Evening News*, 15 August 1956.

'sort of husband', *Woman's World*, 13 October 1956, p. 4.

'shy of publicity', *Woman's World*, 13 October 1956.

98   'friendly Philistines', unsourced cutting, in PACACM.

'praise for Australia', *Sunday Telegraph*, 28 May 1956.

99   'Inland Revenue', *LWG*, p. 157.

100 'so normal!', conversation with author, UK, 2013.

101 'easy to work with', conversation with author, July11, 2013.

'to feel guilty', personal papers held by Joanna.

102 'profoundly moving', personal diaries.

'opera production', Strachan, p. 333.

Interview with author, London 1913.

103 'memorable performance, *LWG*, p. 166.

'best ever', quoted in letter from Vanessa Redgrave to Joanna, 25 July 2012.

'Stratford station', Jean Fox to author, 2013.

'with her lines', ibid.

104 'managerial job, letter, 26 June 1956, held by Joanna.

'Skakespearian parts', letter,19 December 1957, held by Joanna.

'London office', ibid.

105 'established', *Daily Express*, London, 9 May 1958.

'never come again', in Godfrey Winn, 'When a wife has to decide', *Daily Express*, 10 May 1958.

'shocked my friends', *Manchester Evening News*, 2 October 1963.

'some misgiving', Alan Trengove, 'And THEY said it wouldn't last!', *Sun*, 5 July 1966.

'luckier ones', in Winn, 10 May 1958.

Chapter 7

107 'Melbourne or Sydney', 'A Look Around', *Australian Theatre Year 1959-60*, Sydney, p.9.

108 'largest management, *Stage and Television Today*, 19 July 1962.

'Isla Baring', telephone interview with author, London, 2013.

109 'spoke *to* you', unsourced cutting, PACACM.

'very fascinating','Return to the Footlights', long, unsourced interview with JM, PACACM.

'running concurrently', interview with author, Bayview, May 2009.

110 'honourable', word used by several associated with him, including Roland Rocchiccioli and Phillip Austin in conversation with author, 2013.

'fare to London', conversation with JM, Sydney 2009.

111 'a golden period', *LWG*, p. 178.

'wharfie standing', interview with Brian Johnston, Bayview, 2008.

'track record', interview with JF, Melbourne, September 2013.

112 'Joint Managing Director', Letter from 'Director' of J. and G. Pty. Ltd. to 'The Directors', J.C.W., 11 May 1960.

'shareholder', ibid.

'based on profits', letter from JM to 'The Directors, Rangatira Pty. Ltd.', 6 April 1960.

113 'nice places to stay', telephone interview with Muriel Pavlow, June 2013.

114 'backstage stories', *LWG*, p. 111.

'Googie at her best', *Age*, *Herald*, *Sun*, Melbourne, all 15 November 1960.

115 'ideal summer fare', *Sun*, 30 January 1961.

'Christmas party, Earl Wilson, 'Talk Station, CA', 29 December 1961.

116 'bullied an actor', email from Nicholas Hammond, September 2013.

'subtle play', *Age*, 9 February 1962.

'too commercial', *Herald*, Melbourne, 8 February 1962.

'coming through', *Sun*, Melbourne, 3 February 1962.

'on God's earth', *Woman's Day*, 12 March 1962.

117 'do toff', interview with author, March 1990.

'played for tragedy', unsourced cutting from NZ paper, PACACM.

118 'terms for the play', letter from Laurence Evans, London Artists Limited, 14 March 1963.

'Henry Sherek', letter from Sherek, 6 April 1963.

'that understanding', letter from JM to Sherek, 16 April 1963.

'intransigence', letter from JM to Ted Willis, 16 April 1963.

'worth every penny', letter from Willis to Sherek, 23 April 1963.

'unofficial ambassadress', *Sunday Telegraph*, UK, undated cutting, PACACM.

119 '*The Ceremonies*', *Age*, 1 June 1963.

'empty and cold', in *Evening News*, *Evening Standard* and *Daily Mail*, all 13 September 1963.

'hard-pressed skivvy', Martin Esslin, *Plays and Players*, November 1963, p. 163.

120 'confession next day', interview with Dame Eileen Atkins, June 2013.

'my homecoming', *Herald*, 11 September 1963.

'vigorous place', *Sun*, Melbourne, 8 January 1959.

'Australia next year', *Sydney Morning Herald*, 14 November 1963.

121 'quickly and dramatically', *Australian Women's Weekly*, 17 June 1964.

122 'opera star', *Sydney Morning Herald*, 23 July 1965.

'blame lies', *Sunday Mirror*, 25 July 1965.

'break with the board', Patrick Tennison, 'McCallum', *The Australian*, 12 November 1966.

123 'there we are', *Herald*, Melbourne, 29 August 1965.

'weekly losses', letter to Chairman of Directors, J.C. Williamson Theatres Ltd., 1 September 1966.

'persistently refused', ibid.

124 'frustrated', Tennison, 12 November 1966.

'leading to the break', *SMH*, 30 August 1966.

'cuttings book', in PACACM.

125 'ridiculous script', *Sydney Telegraph*, 17 June 1963.

'faded away', *Veteran*, No. 130, Spring 2011.

126 'known overseas', ibid.

'honouring obligations', exchange of letters, August-September 1962.

127 'professional attractiveness', unsourced cutting, PACACM.

'clothes mustn't crease', *Herald* 27 April 1965.

'elegant costumes', *Women's Weekly*, 26 May 1965.

128 'great quality', Pat Weetman, *New Idea*, 26 March 1966, p. 14.

'back street', unsourced cutting, PACACM.

'moneyed imperiousness', *Daily Telegraph*, Sydney, 18 April 1966.

'give it a go', unsourced cutting, PACACM.

129 'very professional', interview with author August 2014.

'star-studded revival', all 20 April 1967.

'representing womanhood', D.A.N. Jones, *New Statesman*, 28 April 1967.

'a kangaroo', *LWG*, p. 231.

Chapter 8

131 'oil exploration', unsourced cutting, dated 19 October 1963, PACACM.

132 'including England', *TH*, interview conducted by Peter Thompson, screened on ABC1, 8 October 2007.

'about casting', interview with author, Sydney, May 2009.

'It's incalculable', *SMH*, 20 March 1968.

134 'different ones', *TH* interview.

'together again', *Woman's Day*, 15 February 1968.

135 'difficult convention', unsourced cutting, PACACM.

'eight years ago', 'Claudia's Mid-week Corner', undated, *Herald*.

136 'place they loved', interview with author, Melbourne, September 2013.

'Boxing Day in Casualty', conversation in London, June 2013.

'the life for me', 'Granny Googie takes a back seat', *Daily Express*, 26 February 1980.

137 'Christopher Withers', unsourced cutting, PACACM.

'prove yourself', *New Idea*, 24 January 1970.

'working fine', letter from NM to JM, 5 March 1967.

'with his prize', unsourced cutting, PACACM.

138 'Hands up for soup!', email from Joanna, October 2013.

139 'merciless bonhomie', Tom Milne, *MFB*, February 1973, p. 32.

'knock-back', John Sorell, *Herald*, Melbourne, 10 June 1971.

'political figures', *Daily News*, WA, 26 November 1970.

'play their parts', *Weekend News*, 14 November 1970.

140 'several septuagenarians', Caroline Plummer, 'They worked all night, gaily', unsourced cutting but clearly from a Western Australian paper, PACACM.

'World Première', *Daily News*, Perth, 2 April 1971.

'guests of honour', *Australian Exhibitor*, 15 April 1971.

'Swanage actress', *Swanage Times*, 27 May 1971.

141 'all kinds of punishment', conversation with author, October 2013.

142 'out to lunch', interview with author, August 2014.

'interesting bouquet', unsourced cutting, PACACM.

'theatrical fare', *New Zealand Herald*, 26 February 1970.

'attractive set', R.S., *Stage and Television Today*, 20 November 1969.

143 'rare anti- voice', Ray Taylor, *Australian*, undated cutting, PACACM.

Chapter 9

145 'heaven-sent', phone interview with author, January 2013.

'"frivolous" plays', Brian Hoad, *Bulletin*, 31 March 1973, p. 83.

'for sympathy', Leonard Glickfield, *On Stage*, undated cutting, PACACM.

'both satisfied', interview with author, Melbourne, January 2013.

146 'make a star', Sumner, *Reflections at Play*, Melbourne, 1993, p. 234.

'televised version', Ray Stanley, *Theatre Australia*, November 1972.

'graceful nod', interview with author, January 2013.

'plum role', *Sunday Telegraph*, 18 March 1973.

147 'cried and cheered', *Mercury*, Hobart, 29 March 1990.

'all of us', interview with author, January 2013.

'never obviously drunk', Fitzpatrick, *The Two Frank Thrings*, 2012, p. 467.

'stage productions', reported in *Daily Telegraph*, 1 June 1959.

'further fifteen', unsourced cutting, PACACM .

148 'science fiction', phone interview with author, London, June 2013.

'$100,000', *LWG*, p.239.

149 'conservative politically', conversation with author, London, June 2103.

'in the outback', F.C. Kennedy, *TV Times*, 2 September 1972.

'endeared herself', 'Boney, by a Nose', *TV Times*, 2 September 1972, p. 12.

'daughter of the Empire', phone conversation with author, May 2013.

'Alice Springs pub', phone interview with Peggy Carter, 25 February 2014.

'ideal actor', 'Will Peter come home?', unsourced Sydney newspaper cutting, PACACM.

150 'considerable presence', *Australian*, undated cutting, PACACM.

'delicate and sensitive', *TV Times*, 2 September 1972.

'planning the series', *Daily Mirror*, 1 September, 1972.

151 'make films here', 'John McCallum – multi-media man', *Encore*, Feburary 1983.

152 'leather boots', *Bulletin*, undated cutting, PACACM.

'a whip', unsourced cutting, PACACM.

'very interesting', article by Simon Lee, *TV Times*, 3 January 1974.

'tattooed names', *TV Times*, 3 January 1974.

'locked up', interview with Brian Johnson, Bayview, 2008.

153 'semi-literately', letter held by Joanna, 17 December (no year given).

'mother figure', letter from a Dr Dale, 6 September 1979.

'qualified to offer', letter from Peter Dew, 13 September 1979.

'whiff of authenticity', Richard Last, *Daily Express*, 5 January 1974.

'mid '70s', interview with author, London, 2013.

'no remission', *Weekly News*, 23 February 1974.

154 'not *for* punishment', 'It's a better life now for girls in jail', *Sun*, 4 January 1974.

'air London-Australia', from International Famous Agency, 8 March 1973.

'audience applauded', *LWG*, p. 196.

155 'snowing throwballs', interview with author, November 2013.

Life With Googie, p.249.

'calculating wife', Jonathan Croall, *John Gielgud: Matinee Idol to Movie Star*, London, 2011, p. 549.

'erring husband', Jane Sullivan, *Evening Argus*, Brighton, 28 August 1973.

'into the country', *Woman's Weekly* London, 1974 (undated), interview with Margaret Montgomerie.

156 'beautiful set', *TV Week*, 9 November 1974.

157 'I'll do the rest', email from Ogilvie, 15 February 2013.

'unabashed enjoyment', *West Australian*, 10 February 1973.

'denied subsidies', David Thorpe, unsourced cutting, PACACM.

'museum piece', phone interview with author, 24 January 2013.

158 'young girls', *Tatler*, December 1976.

159 'in autumn', *Spectator*, 31 July 1976.

'until 10.30 am', Sheila Scotter, 'A super-star hostess', *AWW*, 5 May 1977.

'buying old places', Avril Deane, *Journal*, 14 June 1978.

'life in Britain', John Phillips, 'More than a foot in two worlds', *Australian,* undated cutting, PACACM.

'retiring', *Daily Telegraph*, 9 July 1991.

160 'ham off the bone', Peter Coster, 'In Black and White', unsourced cutting, MPAC.

'pleasure to watch', Leonard Radic, *The Age*, 1 December 1978.

161 'to work with', interview with author.

Chapter 10

162 'outside Sydney', Michael Dawes, *Sun*, 3 January 1985.

'very good to me', *Argus,* Brighton, 25 August 1990.

164 'long extract', *Australian Women's Weekly*, 6 June 1979.

'chatty book', *East Anglian Times*, 7 July 1979.

'successes and failures', *Newcastle Morning Herald*, 7 July 1979.

'already knows', *Sydney Morning Herald*, 13 October 1979.

'position intolerable', *Geelong Advertiser*, 31 July 1979.

'ego trip', Alex Kennedy, *Adelaide Advertiser*, 4 August 1979.

'idolatry', *Adelaide Advertiser*, 1 June 1979.

'conviction and pride', Hal Porter, *Australian Book Review*, September 1979.

165 'at Stedham', *LWG*, p. 264.

166 'my own way', *Post*, 8 September 1989.

'hiding place', interview with Joanna, London, May 2013.

167 'their approach', interview with John Gale, London, May 2013.

'death of Congreve', Tynan, 'Glorious Sunset', *Observer*, 15 April 1956.

'her health', Sheridan Morley, 'The family way of acting', *The Times*, 17 June 1986.

'bizarre incident', interview with Gale.

168 'got on with it', interview with Britton, London, May 2013.

'*never* grand', ibid.

'Moshinsky', interview with Gale.

169 'about royalty', ibid.

'soldierly performance', letter to author, June 2013.

'terrifying sound', interview with Sir Donald Sinden, London, April 2013.

170 'falling down', ibid.

'agree with her', interview with Rona Anderson, London, June 2013.

'genuine suffering', Emrys Bryson, unsourced cutting, PACACM.

171 'private reality', Louise Chase, unsourced cutting, PACACM.

'family life', Anne Patch, *Women*, 14 July 1992.

'44 years', *Mid Sussex Times*, 12 June 1992.

172 'nine-month tour', *Evening Chronicle Bath*, 18 August 1992.

'a dead man', JM, interview, *OCAF*, OUP Melbourne, 1999, p. 300.

173 'John Phillip Law', David Stratton, *The Avocado Plantation*, Macmillan, Sydney, 1990, p. 43.

'rising fame', ibid.

'*Highest Honour*', title of DVD version available in Australia, from Umbrella Entertainment.

'Japanese dialogue', JM, interview, *OCAF*, p. 301.

175 'Barbara Cartland', information from Joanna, December 2013.

'powerful boost', John Naughton, *Observer* 7 January 1990.

'child-like Marigold', *Daily Mirror* 6 January 1990.

176 'difficult to act one', 'GW, interview, *OCAF*, OUP Melbourne, 1999, p. 544.

'went *too far!*', letter to author, 1 May 1995.

'grotesque creature', GW, *OCAF*, p. 544.

177 'diet of mutton', Caryn James, 'Another Take on "Uncle Vanya"', *New York Times*, 28 July 1995.

'rest of the cast', interview with Michael Blakemore, London, 1 May 2014.

'honeymoon couple', telephone interview with Robin Dalton, London, 2 May 2014.

'back with him', personal letters held by Joanna.

'weight or health', interview with Robin Dalton.

178 'English woman', GW, *OCAF*, p. 544.

'in front of me', ibid.

'what he was doing', GW, Sydney Film Festival, June 2003.

'quite memorable', email to author, 14 August 2014.

'you were better!', letter from GW to Geoffrey Rush, 2007.

179 'learn your lines', Jo Litson, 'A toast to the family that plays together', *Australian* 3 October 1989.

'plays together', ibid.

'vintage partnership', Carolyn O'Donnell, *Herald*, 23 November 1989.

'cocktail's ingredients', *SMH*, Bob Evans, undated cutting, PACACM.

'twist of lemon', Jenny Brown, *Daily Telegraph* 10 October 1989.

180 'a problem', phone interview with Elspeth Ballantyne, February 2014.

'West End', phone interview with Richard Cottrell, January 2014.

181 'for Ethiopia', Chris Boyd, *Melbourne Times* 9 October 1991.

'going to matinees', *Sun-Herald*, 3 October 1991.

'photograph albums', Pamela Payne, *SMH*, 12 February 1993.

'The Cremorne', *Sunday Sun*, 11 November 1991.

'they're back!', 'Friends forever,' unsourced cutting, PACACM.

182 'spelt publicity', phone interview with John Krummel, January 2014.

'aware of that', ibid.

183 'out she sweeps', *SMH*, 8 January 1998.

'the cost of things', interview with JF, Melbourne, September 2013.

184 'gentle control', ibid.

'elderly woman', Stephanie Beacham, *Many Lives*, Hay House, London 2011.

'double-act', *Daily Telegraph* 1 April, 2000.

'class system', unsourced cutting, PACACM.

Chapter 11

185 'the profits', letter from Nigel Everett, Haymarket Theatre, London, 22 November 2001.

'*they* knew', interview with author, September 2013.

'a great deal', phone interview with author, 25 March 2014.

186 'project was dropped', phone conversation with JM, 2003.

'role in *Shine*' GW, Sydney Film Festival, 2003.

187 'the split', interview with JM and GW, Bayview, Sydney, 5 June 2008 (interviewer's name not given).

'to have temperament', *TH*, ABC1, 8 October 2007.

188 'back to Australia', interview with JF, Melbourne, September 2013.

189 'television production', ibid.

190 'what they were doing', phone interview with author, December 2013.

'her mother', 'I'll not change my name for anyone', *Daily Telegraph*, 30 July 1956.

191 'warm woman', 'Mum's the glamorous star but I'm just a wallflower', *Daily Mail*, 20 January 1997.

'make that 27', 'The McCallum Girl', *Australian*, 16 May 1970.

192 'amused her', quoted in *The Two Frank Thrings*, p. 445.

'in the stalls', email from Joanna, 2013.

'see better', *New Idea*, 24 January 1970.

'six feet two', *Sunday Times*, 27 July 1986.

193 'long experience', *The Lady*, 20 June 1974, at Sheffield Playhouse.

'he was away', conversation with author, UK, June 2013.

194 'began boarding', email from NM, December 2013.

'psychiatric treatment', ibid.

195 'sure they don't', 'Googie's greatest loves', *Daily Mail*, 12 April 1983.

'stayed with me', email from NM, December 2013.

197 'Duchess!', interview with author, Sydney, November 2013.

198 'surrogate family', ibid.

199 'Fernleigh Yarns', 'Mandy's Royal one long wash,' *Land*, 4 May, 1995.

'gets things done', 'A love for Murrurundi', *Scone Advocate*, 5 December 2013.

200 'moment's notice', 'Lotus life is not for Googie,' *South Wales Argus*, 26 April, 1978.

'they miss me', unsourced cutting, PACACM.

'daunted many people', National Trust of Australia (NSW), *Newsletter*, No. 157.

'priorities right', phone interview with David Yelland, 25 March 2014.

201 'was magic', email from NM, December 2013.

'away-from-home', interview with author, 16 November 2013.

'mashed potato', email from Gus Archibald, 9 February 2014.

202 'and laughing', email from Emma Archibald, 31 January 2014.

'terribly sorry', conversation with Joanna, London, May 2013.

203 'at Chichester', interview with Tony Britton, England, April 2014.

'pretty quickly', *TH*, ABC1, 8 October 2007.

'into a silence', ibid.

204 'never altered', email from Alex Davenport, 10 May 2014.

'correct) opinions', emails from Gus and Emma Archibald, 2014.

'showed up well', 'Googie at Noosa Court', 1969, unsourced cutting, PACACM.

'that I lack', *Courier-Mail*, 20 June 1963.

'I will have to', *Sydney Telegraph*, date obscured, 1963.

205 'rights back to Fauna', phone interview with author, 30 January 2014.

'never paid them', phone interview with author, 28 January 2014.

207 'glass of champagne', phone interview with author, 30 August 2014.

'new audience', phone interview with Liz Goodman, February 2014.

INDEX